COPING WITH
CHILDREN'S TEMPERAMENT

COPING WITH CHILDREN'S TEMPERAMENT

A GUIDE FOR PROFESSIONALS

WILLIAM B. CAREY
SEAN C. MCDEVITT

BasicBooks
A Subsidiary of Perseus Books, L.L.C.

Table 3.1 is reprinted from Chess, S., & Thomas, A. (1992). Dynamics of individual behavioral development. In M. D. Levine, W. B. Carey, & A. C. Crocker (eds.), *Developmental-behavioral pediatrics* (pp. 84–94). 2nd ed. Philadelphia: Saunders. Reprinted with permission.

Figure 8.1 is reprinted from Carey, W. B. (1989). Temperament and its role in developmental-behavioral diagnosis. In M. I. Gottlieb & J. E. Williams (eds.), *Developmental-behavioral disorders* (vol. 2, pp. 49–65). New York: Plenum. Reprinted with permission.

Library of Congress Cataloging-in-Publication Data
Carey, William B.
    Coping with children's temperament : a guide for professionals /
William B. Carey, Sean C. McDevitt.
        p.   cm.
    Includes bibliographical references and index.
    ISBN 0–465–01432–1
    1. Temperament in children.   2. Child development.   I. McDevitt,
S. C. (Sean Conway), 1949–   .   II. Title.
RJ47.5.C38   1995
155.4—dc20   95-8624
                                                                CIP

98 ❖/HC 9 8 7 6 5 4 3 2

CONTENTS

2916

123930

Foreword

Stella Chess and Alexander Thomas

T HIS IS A SPLENDID BOOK.
In the past few decades, there has been a valuable expansion of information on the theory and practice of normal and deviant psychological development. Over these years, William B. Carey and Sean C. McDevitt have contributed important temperament studies to this process. Now they have written this unique book, a systematic and comprehensive guide that clarifies for health professionals and educators the dimensions of children's temperaments and illuminates their significance for behavioral problems and other childhood dysfunctions. This book carries the authority of the authors' substantial research and clinical experience, their mastery of the voluminous professional literature, and their talents as educators and writers.

During the 1960s, Dr. Carey became acquainted with our exposition of a systematic temperamental categorical system and its theoretical and practical implications. He recognized that applications of this theory would enhance the effectiveness of clinical pediatric services. As he began to apply our system to the behavioral concerns of the parents of his patients, he quickly realized that a lengthy research tool could not be employed unchanged in a busy pediatric office. A man of action, he set himself to the task of building practical protocols for his own use and for others. In 1968 he devised a simplified infant temperament questionnaire that required only about 20 minutes for the parent to rate and about 10 minutes for the pediatrician or office assistant to score. He initially chose items by referring to our publications and consulting with our staff.

This first practical instrument filled a need for a growing group of researchers and clinicians, but it soon became clear that it needed to be made more psychometrically precise and that other questionnaires for other age groups would be helpful. In 1974 Dr. McDevitt and Dr. Carey began their long collaboration, the former bringing to the partnership his knowledge of test design and statistical method in addition to his clinical skills as a psychologist. Together they revised the original infant scale and with other colleagues during the 1970s and 1980s developed four new ones for the first four months of life, toddlers, the three- to seven-year range, and middle childhood.

Over the last 20 years, Drs. Carey and McDevitt have continued their harmonious partnership, building an impressive roster of clinical and research reports. They have initiated and been key participants in many conferences in which advances in the temperament field were examined and clarified. One such conference, organized by Dr. Carey, brought an international, interdisciplinary professional group to the Rockefeller Foundation's Conference Center on the shores of Lake Como in Italy for a five-day meeting in May 1988. Its proceedings have been made available in published form (Carey & McDevitt, 1989).

After 31 years in general pediatrics practice, Dr. Carey is now clinical professor of pediatrics at the University of Pennsylvania and in charge of teaching and supervising in the behavioral pediatrics section at the Children's Hospital of Philadelphia. He has co-edited two editions of a comprehensive textbook, *Developmental-Behavioral Pediatrics*, published in 1983 and 1992. Since 1976 Dr. McDevitt has worked as a child psychologist with patients, some in residential settings, who have a wide range of clinical problems. For the last four years he has been in private practice in Phoenix and Scottsdale, Arizona.

In chapter 1, the authors emphasize the need for reorienting our professional thinking and practice. In chapters 2 and 3, they pose some fundamental queries: what do we know about temperament, and what can we do with the information we have? The subsequent chapters retain that format, carrying the reader forward in a lively and orderly manner. Each chapter begins with two case studies that illustrate different temperamental styles, each requiring its own brand of appropriate parenting to ensure a positive outcome rather than a problem. These vivid and crisp stories spring from the authors' clinical experience and kick off the chapter's discussion of specific issues. Each chapter then presents a critical review of the research bearing on the specific area under discussion and concludes with clinical applications of these research findings. Having laid the groundwork for an understanding of the phenomenon of temperament, the authors consider in sequence the stages of development: newborn, infant and toddler, middle childhood, and on through adolescence. Various areas of function are also considered: physical health, development, behavioral adjustment, and school performance.

This strategy makes the book truly a guide for both health care and educational professionals. The authors decided to limit the research presentation to studies with practical clinical relevance, omitting such areas as the neurochemical and physiological bases of temperament characteristics. Their literature reviews are scholarly and comprehensive, as well as concise and lucid. The clinical advice for each issue is authoritative but flexible and free of jargon. Furthermore, Drs. Carey and McDevitt have made it clear that, while the focus of the book is the role of temperament in children's development, it is but one of a group of pertinent factors; they also describe the interplay of the various elements involved in the goodness or poorness of fit between the child and the environment.

Of special note is their extensive critical review of the popular but confused syndrome of attention deficit hyperactivity disorder (ADHD). This is the most cogent discussion of ADHD that has yet appeared in the literature.

Throughout the book the authors' language sparkles with short, pertinent, epigrammatic comments. On the vexing question of the relative place in child behavior research of qualitative clinical reports and quantitative analysis of data, they affirm that "the proper study of childhood is the child, not the computer printout."

In the final summary chapter, the authors identify a number of unfinished tasks, indicating those areas in which more information and further skills are needed before our knowledge of temperament can be applied more fully to real children in real families and real-life situations.

Perhaps this book's greatest achievement is that, besides being an authoritative guide, it makes good reading. The skillfully rendered and sometimes humorous case studies are sure to remind readers of their own children or children they have known professionally—live and believable.

PREFACE

THIS BOOK IS ABOUT CHILDREN'S temperament characteristics: the behavioral style patterns or dispositions that influence how children interact with the people, events, and objects in their environments. We summarize our current thinking and beliefs about children's temperament based on the growing body of scientific research in the field, especially in the last decade, and on our collective 60 years of clinical experience with children and their families. Coupled with a literature review are practical suggestions on how to use temperament information in general and in a variety of specific clinical and educational settings.

We firmly believe that conflicts between temperament and environment occupy much of the considerable ground between normal behavior (and misbehavior) and major childhood psychopathology. This ground includes many mild to moderately severe clinical concerns that do not meet the criteria for any diagnoses in the latest edition of the *Diagnostic and Statistical Manual of Mental Disorders* (*DSM-IV*). The purpose of presenting this review is to educate professionals who work with children about the existence and importance of dispositional characteristics in practical settings, including the pediatric office, school, clinic, playground, and day care center. The intended audience includes pediatricians, psychiatrists, family physicians, psychologists, nurses, social workers, preschool and elementary school teachers, day care directors, child development specialists, special education teachers, and others who need to understand behavioral individuality and its implications for child care. Our book should be of interest to these professionals whether in training or established in their work. The more often they discern the difference between temperamental traits and behavioral dysfunction, the less frequently children will be mislabeled and treated inappropriately.

Although the book is not designed for parents, undoubtedly some will discover that there is useful information and advice to be found here. Since so many of the guides for parents fail even to mention that children have temperaments, some fathers and mothers may wish to supplement their knowledge of children by making use of the material collected here. They are certainly welcome to do so.

Our basic premise is that infants and children bring patterns of behavior and disposition to every situation in their lives and that this fact affects how they respond to the objective features of their environments. We assume that the reader understands that certain youngsters present challenges to their caregivers because of their temperamental status, and that it is important to children that the professional be aware of his or her options in responding appropriately. By describing our efforts as coping with children's temperament, we mean to convey that temperament characteristics are normal and should not be treated as if they were part of a disease or dysfunction, even though they may appear in a setting where the professional is expected to make a "diagnosis." Likewise, we express the view that individuality should not only be tolerated but encouraged, even though doing so may be less efficient or require more effort than promoting conformity.

The value of encouraging awareness of individuality is twofold: the professional can learn to understand and adapt to children in challenging situations in his or her daily work, and the children and their parents can be assisted in dealing with difficult or potentially adverse consequences of conflict. Both of these objectives are important to us.

Readers should be aware of some areas that we do not cover. The focus of this book is on normal temperament differences and their consequences. Therefore, we do not deal in any detail with other sorts of individual differences: with general intelligence or specific cognitive skills, such as facility in foreign languages; with talents such as music or athletics; or with differences induced by varying environmental forces, such as family, social class, and culture. Important as these variations are, they are tangential to the focus of this book and are discussed only in passing. Nor is this book a review of theoretical issues in the temperament field, such as factor structures.

We have avoided a how-to or cookbook approach, since we presume that our readers, professionals trained in their own areas of expertise, will know how to incorporate the ideas in this book into their daily routines.

Much of what we express about the management of conflicts between temperament and the environment is based on informed opinion and professional experience, not on well-documented research evidence. Often a practitioner must exercise professional judgment with a particular child or situation that presents no clearly drawn map directing him or her toward the desired goal. After all, that is why we call it "practice." Every professional is faced with too many variables and unknowns to be able to guarantee an outcome. Similarly, while much of the needed research in temperament has yet to be done, our clinical knowledge enables us to make educated guesses about what will happen in many situations. We have tried to point out in the text where our observations are based on our "educated" opinions or speculations rather than on more broadly established views or techniques.

A glance at the table of contents will inform the reader of the overall plan to be followed. We begin with a general description of the phenomenon of temperament: what it is, where it comes from, what happens to it over time, how it matters to children and their caretakers, and how in general to assess and manage it. From there we proceed through eight specific situations in the life of the developing child: the newborn period, parental care of the infant and toddler, day care out of the home, physical health care, development and social adjustment problems, middle childhood and school problems, adolescence, and various crises and social stresses. In each chapter, we first present a summary of what we know from research that has a practical bearing on child care. The second part of each chapter presents a program of suggestions from us and others as to how temperament-related issues are best handled. We pay attention primarily to the differences that matter most for children and their caretakers rather than to those that are merely of research interest.

The organization of the book according to age periods makes clear our conviction that the influence of temperament shifts over the course of development. The issues in infancy are quite different from those in middle childhood. The age periods selected are rather arbitrary, since temperament is not neatly separated into stages. Researchers and clinicians generally divide their samples by age, and much of what we know is based on research with somewhat narrow age ranges.

Numerous case studies help to clarify the points and establish their clinical importance. We hope that these concrete examples will clarify the issues and make them more realistic than would abstract discussions of generalities. These stories are all drawn from our clinical experience, but the names and circumstances have been changed to protect the anonymity of our patients.

We would like to acknowledge the valuable help we received from several colleagues at different stages in the preparation of this work. Omissions, errors, or other shortcomings are, of course, entirely our fault and not theirs. In preparing the outline for the book, we received constructive suggestions from Catherine J. Andersen, M.Ed., James R. Cameron, Ph.D., Stella Chess, M.D., Bill Smith, M.S., and Alexander Thomas, M.D. Later Barbara Medoff-Cooper, Ph.D., F.A.A.N., provided a critical review of the chapter on the newborn period. Susan Aronson, M.D., performed a similar consultative role with the chapter on child care outside the home. We mention Kate Andersen again because it was she who originally urged us to prepare this book and who then reviewed the entire manuscript from the expert point of view of a parent and the founder of a support group for parents with temperamentally challenging children.

Finally, we thank our wives, Suzi McDevitt and Ann Carey, for their patience, support, and other help while this work interrupted our daily lives.

COPING WITH
CHILDREN'S TEMPERAMENT

Reorienting Professionals to the New Understanding of Temperament Differences in Children

W E HAVE MADE great strides in our knowledge and appreciation of temperament differences in the last 30 years, but clinical and educational thinking and practice remain largely unchanged. The following example illustrates this lack of awareness in medical circles about the normal variations in children's activity.

Two-year-old Johnny was a lively little fellow. He was vigorous in his mother's womb and continued to be active as an infant and toddler. He played exuberantly. His mother found him hard to dress and diaper. He moved about in his crib at night and during his naps. His mother, a small, quiet person, reported that she was exhausted from managing him. She complained to the pediatrician and asked whether Johnny might be "hyperactive." The doctor was impressed with the way Johnny explored every part of the examining room and advised the family to consult a neurologist to help decide whether a diagnosis of hyperactivity was indicated or whether Johnny was being overstimulated by his mother. The neurologist said that he could not rule out hyperactivity at that time.

Observers were struck by the amount of physical motion Johnny exhibited but failed either to consider that this might have been a variation of normal or to obtain a more complete view of the child. He was a very pleasant, sociable child, and one who could apply himself for expected periods of time at tasks and play. He was a normal, highly energetic child who was in danger of receiving a pathological label and medication with methylphenidate (Ritalin) by professional people who did not understand temperament differences.

Similarly, the experience of shy Sally at nursery school exemplifies how normal initial withdrawal from novelty can be mistaken for immaturity.

Sally was a four-year-old girl who had always been rather shy. This quality had not bothered her parents, who had no other children and were of a similar disposition. Sally's mother left her job when Sally was born. When she turned four, her parents registered her for nursery school. Sally said that she wanted to go, but on arrival she cried and begged to be taken home. The next day she was just as upset. The nursery school teacher advised Sally's mother that her child was too "immature" for nursery school and suggested that they wait another 6 to 12 months to enroll her.

However, Sally was not immature. She was just shy. The nursery school teacher did not know about innate behavioral predispositions, but she did remember that her college professor had said that shyness is always attributable to insufficient parental nurturing. Sally was in danger of being deprived of a valuable experience in socialization because the teacher had misinterpreted normal behavior.

Why do these misunderstandings occur, and what can be done to improve the quality of care for such children?

OUR CHANGED UNDERSTANDING OF INDIVIDUAL DIFFERENCES

After the field of child development was established as a science about 100 years ago, it was soon dominated by environmentalism, the view that individual differences in behavior can be explained by variations in past experiences. The belief in hereditary contributions to behavior, or constitutionalism, which had begun in ancient Greece and persisted in various forms up until 100 years ago, was rejected as primitive and unenlightened thinking. To explain why one child is bold or flexible and another sensitive or attentive, one had only to inspect the child's present and previous life circumstances. If this search did not readily uncover overt causal events, one could proceed to a more comprehensive investigation of the mother's private thoughts and unconscious feelings. To many in the first half of this century, it seemed that the mysteries of the human mind and its complexities had been revealed beyond any question. Furthermore, it was clear to those of this conviction that blame for childhood behavior problems could always be placed on a child's parents and that treatment was to be aimed primarily at correcting parental errors and the damage they had caused.

Environmentalism appears to have reached its peak in the 1950s. Yet as the scientific study of childhood matured in the postwar era, it became increasingly evident that one could not explain all normal and abnormal individual differences in terms of prior experiences. Children with adverse family experiences often turn out to be healthy, normal individuals. Others with apparently normal caretaking develop unsatisfactory or abnormal adjustments. Something else had to be contributing to these diverse outcomes. Contrary to what prevailing theory had been teaching, there was increasing reason to believe that the parent-child interaction is what matters and that the child contributes as much to his or her behavioral outcome as the environment does. Normal temperament differences may modify children's transactions with the environment and lead to clinical problems by predisposing them to abrasive and stressful relationships with their caretakers. Some children may also have neurological malfunctions such as reading disabilities, which are likely to result in performance problems in almost any educational setting (Kohnstamm, 1989; Thomas, 1981).

The current thinking in the behavioral sciences recognizes that problems in children's behavioral, emotional, or functional status arise from three main sources (Levine, Carey, & Crocker, 1992):

1. Noxious environments continue to be responsible for a substantial proportion of the malfunctions in children. Abundant evidence confirms the harmful effects of family dysfunction, neighborhood violence, natural disasters, and poor schools.

2. Intrinsic problems in the child explain a number of disorders previously thought to be environmentally induced, including learning disabilities, autism, and possibly a number of other conditions, such as obesity. Whatever the nature and strength of the intrinsic components of these disorders, they are likely to be expressed in a wide range of circumstances.

3. A "poor fit," that is, an incompatible interaction between the child's normal temperament variations and the values and expectations of the caretakers, is a phenomenon newly recognized at the scientific level, although it has been depicted for centuries by leading literary observers, such as Dante (see chapter 12). When the fit is poor, the interaction of a normal individual and a normal environment can generate friction and stress because the two are not compatible; a clinical problem may result. An active child like Johnny, although completely normal, may be burdensome to his retiring mother, and her efforts to restrain him may make him rebellious.

Of course, these three factors may also operate in combination, such as when a child has a difficult temperament, a reading disability, and a dysfunctional family.

Problems or concerns such as those presented by Johnny and Sally can now be viewed from a new perspective and should no longer be simply blamed on parental inadequacies or on physical disorders or other faults in the child. Explanations that account for temperament differences are often more appropriate, and they require different management.

WHY DO THESE MISINTERPRETATIONS PERSIST?

Despite abundant support for the existence and clinical importance of temperament differences in children, the phenomenon is not well understood by the general public or by child health and education professionals. In our experience in pediatrics and clinical psychology, misinterpretation, as in the examples of the normally active Johnny and the normally shy Sally, is more typical than exceptional.

The reader can perform a simple experiment to verify that information about children's temperament differences is not widely disseminated. In the section on child care in a general bookstore, go through the indexes of a dozen books and see how often the word *temperament* appears. Then do the same in a medical bookstore with texts on pediatrics, child psychiatry, and clinical psychology. Unless the situation has changed abruptly since this book went to press, you will not find the word even mentioned in about half of these two kinds of books. When the word does appear, the discussion of temperament is usually no longer than a paragraph or two.

Varying degrees of recognition of temperament are evident in the official mental health diagnostic manuals. The fourth edition of the *Diagnostic and Statistical Manual of Mental Disorders* (*DSM-IV*) (APA, 1994), being largely an adult-oriented codification of pathology, does not consider it at all. On the other hand, the *Diagnostic and Statistical Manual for Primary Care—Child and Adolescent Version* (*DSM-PC*) (AAP, forthcoming), an interdisciplinary effort with a developmental orientation, is expected to make appropriate mention of temperament when it is published in 1995 or 1996. The *Diagnostic Classification of Mental Health and Developmental Disorders of Infancy and Early Childhood* (*Diagnostic Classification: 0–3*) (Wieder, 1994), although making only passing explicit reference to temperament, appears to have included it as abnormal behavior in one of their primary diagnostic categories, "regulatory disorders." For example, Type 1, or hypersensitive regulatory disorder, seems to consist of either difficult or slow-to-warm-up temperament along with other characteristics such as low sensory threshold. This overlap is confusing.

How can it be that in our modern scientific age so few of the experts have absorbed and disseminated this valuable information? Several explanations come to mind. In the first place, novelty in science tends to be distrusted (Carey, 1993). Many of the writers of professional textbooks and advice manuals for parents were educated in the old environmentalist model of child development, and the notion of inborn temperament may seem to them too new and untrustworthy. The modern scientific study of temperament has been prominent only in the last quarter-century, but the basic concept has been around for at least 2,500 years and was merely thrust aside temporarily by the environmentalists in the early twentieth century (Thomas, 1981).

Another reason for the meager acceptance of temperament and its clinical importance is probably the state of mind referred to as the "medical model." Although not uniformly defined, the term commonly refers to the view that a condition is either normal or abnormal and that an abnormality comes only from another abnormality. Adherents of the medical model have difficulty accepting the possibility that a normal child and a normal environment can interact pathologically. The medical model maintains that a clinical problem has to arise from a preexisting problem, such as pathogenic bacteria, brain damage, or parental dysfunction.

It seems likely that this sort of reasoning is responsible for the widespread assumption that almost any inattentiveness in a school-age child must be due to a cerebral malfunction called attention deficit hyperactivity disorder and cannot simply be a normal temperament variation that does not fit well in the particular school situation. Here is an example of a major area of temperament-environment mismatch being routinely ascribed to pathology in the child. There are theoretical arguments that encourage this approach (see chapter 9), but one must also acknowledge that current economic forces drive physicians to make pathological diagnoses in order to have their professional time compensated by health insurance plans.

A third possible cause of the slow acceptance of the concept of temperament is that it requires a more complex model of child development. Instead of simply looking to the environment to find explanations for a problem in a child (and sometimes to an underlying disorder in the child) and blaming the parents for what has gone wrong, the clinician, educator, or researcher must bear in mind a more intricate set of factors and make a broader differential diagnosis. Everyone craves simple explanations for life's perplexing problems, as has been admirably accomplished in the physical sciences, such as physics. Unfortunately, biology and psychology are not as reducible to basic unifying principles.

Simple theories in the life sciences do not usually stand up to the multitude of complexities and contradictions these disciplines study. Human psychology is not as predictable as planetary motions but often presents a confusing and unpredictable pageant of diverse interacting forces. Our wish to see things in uncomplicated terms should not lead us to ignore a more elaborate model that seems to be based on the way things really are. Furthermore, as long as there remains convincing evidence that reality is rather complex, we should not yield too readily to the insistence of some researchers of temperament (Prior, 1992) that the complexities of temperament itself should be simplified and reduced to as few variables as possible. The recognition of human diversity should not leave us feeling bewildered and burdened but should rather be a source of stimulation and challenge.

Finally, we must remember that our psychosocial thinking is influenced by our politics. In our nation of immigrants, we still cling in varying degrees to the "self-evident" truth celebrated in our Declaration of Independence that "all men are created equal." For some people, any hint of interest in biological contributions to behavior may be interpreted as covert fascism. Perhaps Richard Restak (1991) is right that "we, as a society, have decided that information about temperament, however interesting it sounds, is potentially too divisive and controversial to be tolerated."

Why does it matter that the concept of temperament has been poorly understood and utilized in the last 30 years? Several important consequences stand out. Since knowledge of this significant aspect of child behavior improves diagnostic accuracy and therapeutic effectiveness, the lack of this information has resulted in conceptual and diagnostic errors, decreased skill in management, and less satisfaction in the professional and parental care of children. It is time that we do better.

PREVIOUS BOOKS ON TEMPERAMENT

Books addressed to professionals on the practical application of temperament concepts have not been numerous. Most deserving of mention is *Temperament in Clinical Practice* (1986) by Stella Chess and Alexander Thomas, the first volume of its kind of which we are aware. Three years later we published a summary of an international conference, *Clinical and Educational Applications of Temperament Research* (Carey & McDevitt, 1989). Both of these books contain much valuable scholarly material but do not include a program of simple steps for practical applications. Last year we edited a Festschrift for Chess and Thomas entitled *Prevention and Early Intervention: Individual Differences as Risk Factors for the Mental Health of Children* (Carey & McDevitt, 1994), which does have several chapters with practical suggestions.

Books for parents have been a little more numerous. Chess, Thomas, and Birch opened the field with their early work *Your Child Is a Person* (1965), which was written while they were still collecting data from their New York Longitudinal Study (NYLS). Another valuable early book was T. Berry Brazelton's *Infants and Mothers: Differences in Development* (1969). A later work by Chess and Thomas, *Know Your Child* (1987), was enriched by the findings of that research and also dealt with a broad variety of other issues, such as cognitive development and maternal employment.

Other books offering advice to parents about temperament differences have begun to appear in recent years. Perhaps the best known is *The Difficult Child* (1985/1989) by Stanley Turecki and Leslie Tonner. Many parents have found this book helpful in understanding perplexing behavior in their children. A comparable book by Mary Sheedy Kurcinka, *Raising Your Spirited Child* (1991), which describes temperamental adversity in greater detail and with a different label, has also found a large and grateful audience among parents. Less well known manuals of advice include James Dobson's *The Strong-willed Child* (1978) and Linda Budd's *Living with the Active Alert Child* (1993).

Finally, some books for parents refer to temperament as an aspect of a specific clinical problem. The importance of individual differences in the crying behavior of young infants is discussed by William Sears in *The Fussy Baby* (1987) and William Sammons in *The Self-calmed Baby* (1989). Also, bookstore shelves are crowded with publications on the problem of attention deficit hyperactivity disorder, which may in reality be attributable to temperament differences. Some actually discuss a possible relationship (Goldstein & Goldstein, 1992). Several books, such as *Healthy Sleep Habits, Happy Child* (1987) by Marc Weissbluth, suggest ways of overcoming sleep problems, which may be related to temperament. This list is not complete.

Thus, it seems fair to say that no book is available at present that fully informs child health, education, and care professionals about the full extent of research on temperament differences and makes specific suggestions about applying that information for the benefit of children. Some readers may be surprised to discover how much pertinent research is available but not widely circulated.

The aim of this book is to present a review of the pertinent technical information in the professional journals and books, coupled with practical suggestions on how to use that information in general and in a variety of specific clinical and educational settings. We offer a more complete summary of the clinical research findings than was available in the two books for professionals published in the 1980s, and we have assembled and organized several subsequent years' worth of practical experience with efforts at prevention and intervention.

CHAPTER 2

The Nature and Practical Relevance of Temperament: What Do We Know?

Normal individual differences are real, not imaginary, as some critics have proposed. They can have an extensive impact on children and their parents and other caretakers. The following case study portrays how a pattern of difficult temperament, a vexing but normal inborn variation, may be misinterpreted as something wrong with an infant.

The Browns were a busy young couple, both successful in business. Their first child, Jimmy, fulfilled their dreams of what a baby should be. Pleasant, flexible, and predictable, he had a smiling, friendly manner during feedings, procedures like nail cutting, and even colds. The Browns decided that they should have a little girl just like their son to complete their family. Their new baby, Jennifer, did turn out to be a girl, but not an exact replica of Jimmy. At four months, she was smiling but was more likely to frown. She vigorously protested any change in routine and there was very little pattern to her expressions of physical needs. Mr. and Mrs. Brown were perplexed. They could not understand how the same two normal, healthy people could produce such a different baby. They were plagued with troublesome doubts. Was the baby's brain damaged by the cesarean section? Were they given the wrong baby in the nursery? Was little Jennifer allergic to the formula?

No. These parents had a temperamentally difficult baby, and nobody had helped them to recognize this reality, the inborn nature of their baby's behavior, and the expected outcome.

An infant's temperament can have a great impact on the parents and other caretakers. The case of baby Ralph demonstrates how it can jeopardize the parents' marital adjustment.

The Joneses were a happily married couple who put off having their first child until they had completed their studies. They looked forward eagerly to establishing their family by having one or two children. They spent hours during the pregnancy discussing their fantasies of the happy activities they would share. After a moderate labor and an uneventful delivery, little Ralph was born. His parents and the relatives were ecstatic. However, not long after going home they realized that taking care of Ralph was not going to be quite as they had imagined it. Because he cried so much, Mrs. Jones concluded that her breast milk was not good enough and changed to formula feedings. The switch did not help, and the fussy, irregular feeding pattern continued. Both parents found it hard to soothe the baby and spent hours every day holding and rocking him. Mr. Jones gradually withdrew from participating in the baby's care and let the burden fall entirely on his wife. He found excuses to work late at the office in order to avoid unpleasant confrontations with his wife over how best to handle the baby. He moved into the guest room to try to get more sleep at night. When asked by friends how things were going, they bravely reported that Ralph was healthy and growing well, but privately they acknowledged that this baby was putting a severe strain on their marital relationship.

In this chapter, we review the current state of our knowledge about the nature of temperament differences and where they come from, then describe in general terms the extent of their impact on children, their parents, and other caretakers. We shall revisit Jennifer and Ralph at the beginning of the next chapter.

THE REALITY OF TEMPERAMENT

In view of the recent doubts in some circles about the existence of the innate behavioral style tendencies or temperament and the continued description of temperament as more of a "construct" or a "perception," it is essential to begin this discussion with an affirmation of the reality of temperament.

Although there was no scientific basis in ancient and medieval times for the humoral or constitutionalist theory of temperament (described in the next section), people had no doubt that behavioral differences existed. When the opposing environmentalist theory became dominant in the first part of the twentieth century, it was promoted primarily by the behaviorists and psychoanalysts. Their assumption that all behavioral differences are attributable to variations in experience also lacked a firm scientific basis. Environmental causation was often inferred because no organic physical explanation was available, as in the case of enuresis, or bed-wetting. By the middle third of this century, the notion of inborn temperament differences was considered old-fashioned and even harmful, despite the support it received from eminent researchers such as Ivan Pavlov and Arnold Gesell. As the interactional or transactional model of developmental theory emerged in the last 30 years, the view of the complex relationships and interactions between individual and environmental characteristics became more balanced. Temperament has once again become a respectable concept, and its reality and clinical importance are now backed up by scientifically collected data. However, acceptance of the concept is far from complete. Temperament is still described by some as a "perception" (Bates, 1980, 1989), that is, an inescapable mixture of parental and child data. Furthermore, an abundance of evidence indicates that many health professionals report acquaintance with the concept but ignore it in their diagnostic procedures and therapeutic plans.

TEMPERAMENT IS BEHAVIORAL STYLE

The word *temperament* is derived from the Latin verb *temperare*, "to mix." That must have seemed an appropriate term in ancient times, when the particular mixture of the four humors (blood, black bile, yellow bile, and phlegm) in a person was thought to determine both temperament and physical health. Although there is no universal agreement on a definition at this time, the general usage in accord with the view of Thomas and Chess (1977), is that temperament refers to an individual's behavioral style—the characteristic way he or she experiences and reacts to the environment. Thomas and Chess explain it as the "how" of behavior as contrasted with the "what" (abilities or developmental level) and the "why" (motivations and behavioral adjustment). This conceptual and empirical separation of temperament and cognitive function has been demonstrated at various times in childhood, including infancy (Plomin et al., 1990, 1993) and the elementary school years (Keogh, 1986; Martin, 1989a, 1989b).

The term "infant temperament" is often used, as if the two words were inseparable. This usage betrays the erroneous view that temperament is something that can be observed only in infants, before the environment has reordered the child's personality, and that temperament becomes radically changed, insignificant, or even disappears as the child grows older. Since the available evidence indicates that temperament continues throughout life, sometimes changing but typically stabilizing with time, placing the adjective "infant" before the word "temperament" should be done only with caution. It follows that a child's temperament is his or her temperament *at the time*. At all times temperament is formed by a mixture of elements and is probably never "pure." If the temperament changes, the new style is just as much the true style as was the previous one.

An example should clarify the differences between temperament and other aspects of a child's personality. A five-year-old child who has learned how to tie his shoes is displaying a normal developmental achievement for his age, and if he also wants to do it, he is making appropriate progress in the self-care component of behavioral adjustment. But children with different temperaments perform this task in a variety of ways. Active, persistent, and negative Bert may do it rapidly, with a frown on his face. Inactive, positive Betty may perform it slowly, singing merrily all the while. Active, unadaptable, nonpersistent Mike may delay doing it until he has run around the house for a while. Distractible Lucy may tie her shoes partway, become diverted by the fascination of passing cars, but eventually return to the job. The same developmental level and motivation may be expressed in a multitude of styles.

Dimensions of Temperament
The best-known conceptualization of temperament was developed by Thomas, Chess, Birch, Hertzig, and Korn (1963) in their New York Longitudinal Study (NYLS). The NYLS view is the only one in current use that is based on clinical observations of children, and the only one that has been tested widely in clinical and educational settings. The nine characteristics (also referred to as dimensions or categories) consist of:

1. Activity: The amount of physical motion during sleep, eating, play, dressing, bathing, and so forth

2. Rhythmicity: The regularity of physiologic functions, such as hunger, sleep, and elimination

3. Approach/withdrawal: The nature of initial responses to new stimuli—people, situations, places, foods, toys, procedures

4. Adaptability: The ease or difficulty with which reactions to stimuli can be modified in a desired way

5. Intensity: The energy level of responses, regardless of quality or direction

6. Mood: The amount of pleasant and friendly or unpleasant and unfriendly behavior in various situations

7. Persistence/attention span: The length of time particular activities are pursued by the child, with or without obstacles

8. Distractibility: The effectiveness of extraneous environmental stimuli in interfering with ongoing behaviors

9. Sensory threshold: The amount of stimulation, such as sounds or

light, necessary to evoke discernable responses in the child (adapted from Thomas & Chess, 1977)

These characteristics were originally abstracted from a series of interviews with 10 parents, verified by comparisons with observers' reports, and refined as the main longitudinal study of 133 children from 1956 on.

On the basis of factor analysis and clinical observations, the NYLS group distinguished three major clusters of the nine characteristics:

1. The difficult child, who is irregular, low in approach (withdrawing from novelty), slow to adapt, and intense, displaying much negative mood (about 10% of the study population)

2. The easy child, who is regular, approaching, adaptable, mild, and predominantly positive in mood (about 40% of the total group)

3. The slow-to-warm-up or shy child, who is typically withdrawing in novel situations, slow to adapt, and low in activity and intensity, displaying much negative mood (about 5–15% of the study group, depending on the interpretation of the criteria).

The remaining 40% of children combine these qualities and have been referred to as intermediate (Carey, 1970).

Other groupings of these nine characteristics have been found to be useful, such as sociability or flexibility, consisting of approach, adaptability, and mood (Keogh, 1986; Martin, 1989a), and task orientation, encompassing persistence/attention span, distractibility, and activity (Keogh, 1986). Other possibilities include low stimulus tolerance (low sensory threshold) and disorganized style (low in predictability and persistence).

Some academic psychologists have proposed either that the nine NYLS dimensions are too numerous and should be reduced in the name of "parsimony" or that they are not the correct ones. Rather than returning to direct observations of the behavior of children, these critics have preferred to take the shortcut of entering the 100 or so items from some of our temperament questionnaires into item factor analyses to see whether the computer can rearrange them into tidier packages. Since these questionnaire items were selected on the basis of their demonstrated ability to measure certain clinically verified behavioral qualities and do not represent the universe of child behaviors, new insights about the components of temperament rarely result from this exercise. Deductions from material already collected are seldom as valid as what can be discovered inductively by returning to direct observations of nature. The proper study of childhood is the child, not the computer printout. The computer's rearranged dimensions may satisfy the urge of the researcher for data reduction, but none of these computer-derived dimensions has been verified clinically or found to be more closely related to clinical problems (Prior, 1992; McClowry, Hegvik, & Teglasi, 1993). Our understanding and care of children will not be well served by a proliferation of new dimensions of uncertain meaning or clinical utility.

The simple appeal of these descriptive labels of "difficult," "easy," and "slow-to-warm-up" resulted in their rapid and extensive use by professionals and others. Unfortunately, it led to a variety of misuses as well. For some researchers, it seemed that temperament data were good for nothing more than dividing children into these two or three groups. Others have even expressed the complex phenomenon of temperament in a single numerical score somehow based on the degree of difficulty. For some clinicians, the terms have become pejorative labels. Also, the discrepancies between these definitions of temperamental difficulty and others in popular usage by nonprofessionals have generated confusion.

A newer and more neutral term was needed; it appeared in the form of "temperament risk factors," conceived as "any temperament characteristic predisposing a child to a poor fit (incompatible relationship) with his or her environment, to excessive interactional stress and conflict with the caretakers, and to secondary clinical problems in the child's physical health, development, and behavior. These factors are usually perceived as hard to manage but may not be. The outcome depends on the strength and durability of the characteristics and the environmental stresses and supports," and the outcome criteria being used (Carey, 1986). Temperament assets or protective factors would be any characteristics that promote a good fit in certain circumstances and are conducive to a child's physical, developmental, and behavioral health.

Examples of temperament risk factors are:

1. The difficult child: Low in rhythmicity, approach, and adaptability; high in intensity; negative in mood

2. The slow-to-warm-up child: Low in approach, adaptability, intensity, and activity; negative in mood

These two temperament clusters were originally shown by Thomas, Chess, and Birch (1968) to predispose 2- to 10-year-old children to social behavior problems in an urban middle- and upper-middle-class population. Other examples of temperament risk factors are:

1. Low task orientation: Low persistence/attention span, high distractibility, and high activity

2. Low flexibility: Low approach and adaptability, negative mood

3. High reactivity: Low sensory threshold, high intensity, and negative mood

These three clusters were found to be significant factors in school performance (see chapter 9).

In summary, almost any temperament characteristic, or group of them, can become a source of friction between caretaker and child, depending on the circumstances, and no temperament cluster is universally a source of distress or invariably acceptable.

Goodness of Fit

Contained in the definition of temperament risk factors is Chess and Thomas's (1992) essential concept of goodness of fit. Goodness of fit

> results when the properties of the environment and its expectations and demands are in accord with the organism's own capacities, motivations and style of behavior. When this *consonance* between organism and environment is present, optimal development in a progressive direction is possible. "Poorness of fit" involves discrepancies and *dissonances* between environmental opportunities and demands and the capacities and characteristics of the organism so that distorted development and maladaptive functioning occur. (Chess & Thomas 1992)

The practical significance of a child's temperament, therefore, resides in how it may or may not fit with the values and expectations of the caretakers. The fit improves when the caretakers achieve a better understanding and tolerance of the child's temperament and make reasonable concessions to it in order to reduce interactional stress.

One might conclude that any temperament can be comfortably accommodated simply by situating the child in the right environmental circumstances. However, there are limits. Easy children are likely to fit into a broad range of environments, but more difficult children have narrower limits. Some characteristics, such as low adaptability and negative mood, are undoubtedly welcomed in fewer settings. Similarly, some environments, such as elementary schools, may not be flexible enough to provide stress-free circumstances for all sorts of children. Therefore, a variety of elements must be considered in evaluating the impact of temperament risk factors on the goodness or poorness of fit: the temperament itself, the other characteristics of the child, the environment, and the outcome (Carey, 1990).

1. *The strength and duration of the temperament characteristics.* Negative and unadaptable children are not all equally so, and inattentive children do not have the same degree of this behavior. The stronger, the more pervasive, and the less modifiable the characteristic, the greater are the chances that the child's temperament will be incompatible with any setting, and the more likely it is that the child will be subjected to clinical appraisal whether there is maladjustment or not (see table 2.1).

2. *The other characteristics of the child.* The age of the child makes a difference: inattentiveness is not the problem in toddlers that it becomes in

schoolchildren. The child's gender matters: Shyness is often better tolerated in girls than in boys in our culture. The child's intelligence is important too: An inattentive bright child may have less trouble keeping up with schoolwork than the equally inattentive but less well endowed child. Other temperament characteristics may increase or lessen the impact of the risk factor. For instance, the highly active child who is also adaptable may be able to lower his activity level when it really matters to him.

3. *The environment.* The environment cannot rightly be conceptualized as a single force in the interaction ("the family") since it is made up of numerous components. The "developmental niche" can broadly be divided into three subsystems: (a) the immediate physical and social structure in which the child lives and such elements as the family configuration, the climate, and the housing arrangement; (b) the larger culture or customs of child care and child rearing provided and promoted by the community, such as whether certain behaviors are rewarded or discouraged; and (c) the individual psychology of the caretakers and their beliefs, values, and practices of affection, stimulation, and organization (Super & Harkness, 1994). An example of the importance of this cross-cultural perspective can be found in the report of Savita Malhotra (1989) that in rural India the NYLS configuration of difficult temperament has less meaning because there is so little daily change and so much greater flexibility in the culture of the caretakers.

4. *The outcome.* Whether a temperament characteristic is a risk factor and the fit is good or bad depends to some degree on the outcome being considered. For the outcome of behavior problems in middle-class urban America, the difficult child cluster would be a risk factor; for survival in a situation of widespread starvation, as in East Africa, the same temperament could be an asset (deVries, 1984). Diverse educational requirements and teacher preferences for performance make different characteristics more congenial or more disruptive in the classroom (Pullis, 1989).

Temperament should not be thought of only in terms of risk factors. There are also temperament assets—any characteristics that promote a good fit in certain circumstances and are conducive to physical, developmental, and behavioral health. Emmy Werner and Ruth Smith (1982) provided a convincing illustration in their longitudinal study in Kauai of how temperament promoted good adaptation in their group of "vulnerable but invincible" children. This example, as well as others, is discussed in later chapters.

Other Definitions of Temperament
We have described the Thomas and Chess view of temperament first and most prominently because, uniquely, it is clinically rather than theoreti-

Table 2.1
Examples of Individual Temperament Risk and Protective Factors

Dimension of Temperament	Temperament Risk Factor	Protective Factor
Activity	*High:* Interferes with social activities and task performance. May be confused with "hyperactivity," which is not just high activity but disorganized and purposeless activity. *Low:* Slow to perform tasks. Seems lethargic, "lazy."	*High:* Vigorous. Explores surroundings. Self-stimulates in dull environment. *Low:* Less obtrusive in restrictive circumstances.
Rhythmicity	*High:* May have problem if environment cannot provide needs on schedule. *Low:* Care requirements unpredictable.	*High:* Few surprises for caretakers. *Low:* May not be bothered by irregularities in caretaking.
Approach	*High:* Accepts negative factors too quickly. In danger in hazardous environment. *Low:* Slow to accept change. May avoid useful experiences.	*High:* Makes a rapid fit in positive setting. *Low:* Protective in perilous situation, like strangers in inner city.
Adaptability	*High:* In danger of incorporating negative influences in environment, such as antisocial values of peers. *Low:* Interferes with necessary adjustment to requirements of environment. Stress producing. "Difficult."	*High:* Generally an advantage. Accepts positive factors more quickly. In greater harmony with caretakers. *Low:* Protection against acceptance of negative influences.

Intensity	*High:* Abrasive. May evoke counterintensity. May mislead caretakers as to magnitude of issue or illness. *Low:* Needs may not be expressed with sufficient force.	*High:* Needs certain to get attention. Positive intensity welcome to caretakers. *Low:* Easier for caretakers to live with.
Mood	*Negative:* Unpleasant for caretakers, who may overestimate importance of issue or physical complaint. *Positive:* May be too positive about problems.	*Negative:* Few advantages. May evoke more positive involvement from caretaker because of concern. *Positive:* Generally welcome.
Persistence/ Attention Span	*High:* Attentive involvement in work or play may make child seem to ignore caretakers. *Low:* Less efficient task performance. Failure to perform as expected. But even very low attention span may not be considered an "attention deficit" if child functions well (as when there are compensatory factors like high adaptability and intelligence).	*High:* Greater achievement at various tasks and school performance. *Low:* May be more easily drawn out of activities or habits unacceptable to caretakers.
Distractibility	*High:* Easily diverted from tasks. Interferes with performance. Needs reminders. *Low:* May be oblivious to important signals.	*High:* High soothability an asset in young infants. *Low:* Can work efficiently in noisy places.
Sensory Threshold	*High:* May miss important cues from surroundings. *Low:* More perceptive of ambient noises, smells, lights, textures, and internal sensations. Infants more prone to colic and sleep disturbances.	*High:* More shielded from excessive environmental stimuli. *Low:* More aware of existence and nuances of thoughts and feelings of others.

cally derived and has been preeminent in clinical applications to date. Several differing conceptualizations of similar or related behavioral characteristics have been offered by developmental psychologists in the United States and Europe.

Arnold Buss and Robert Plomin (1975) proposed the formulation of emotionality, activity, sociability, and impulsivity (EASI) but later withdrew impulsivity because of lack of evidence of its heritability. Hans Eysenck (1982) in the United Kingdom speaks of three dimensions of personality: extroversion-introversion, neuroticism, and psychoticism, which resemble the qualities of sociability, emotionality, and the state of social adjustment, respectively. Hill Goldsmith and Joseph Campos (1986) have restricted their definition of temperament to the emotional sphere. Mary Rothbart and Douglas Derryberry (1981) prefer the dimensions of reactivity and self-regulation. Jan Strelau (1983) in Warsaw has evolved a regulative theory of temperament, derived from the Pavlovian typology and including components of energy and temporal traits. Marvin Zuckerman (1979) has drawn attention to the phenomenon of sensation seeking.

These alternative views have been the subject of extensive theoretical investigation but have been used minimally, if at all, in the identification and management of clinical problems in children (Kohnstamm, Bates, & Rothbart, 1989). We therefore use the familiar formulations presented by Thomas and Chess for the balance of the book.

ORIGINS OF TEMPERAMENT: CONSTITUTIONAL AND OTHER SOURCES

Much has changed from a generation or two ago, when all individual differences were thought to be the result of the imprint of the environment. Some early assumptions about the constitutional nature of temperament were that it should be present very early in life, strongly heritable, and stable over time (Buss & Plomin, 1975). However, as Rutter (1994) has pointed out, these may not be the right criteria. Genetic influences are not always maximal at birth and may increase as children get older, at least up until middle childhood. Second, some constitutional features are not genetically determined but result from early pre- and perinatal environmental factors, such as nutrition, hormonal activity, and infections. Finally, continuity takes different forms and cannot simply be equated to high correlations of the same measurement over time. In fact, some of the changes in the expression of temperament are apparently genetically induced.

A relatively new line of evidence supporting the "reality," or biological basis, of temperament is the growing body of studies that relates its behavioral manifestations to the underlying physiological functioning of the brain and other organs. Intriguing as these reports may be, they are presently too preliminary to offer any information that affects our diagnostic and management practices in the clinical and educational spheres. Those interested in finding out what is known about salivary cortisol levels, cardiac vagal tone, and electroencephalographic asymmetries should consult more theoretical books, such as Kohnstamm, Bates, and Rothbart's *Temperament in Childhood* (1989), Bates and Wachs's *Temperament: Individual Differences at the Interface of Biology and Behavior* (1994), and Kagan's *Galen's Prophecy: Temperament in Human Nature* (1994a).

Genetic Basis

What is the support for a genetic basis to temperament? Current evidence, according to Plomin (1990), indicates that inheritance plays a major role in human behavior. Summarizing family, adoption, and twin studies, he attributes heritability at about 50% for cognitive abilities and about 50% for temperamental qualities. He concludes that multiple genes with small effects seem to be responsible, rather than one or two major ones, and that nongenetic sources are at least as important (see also Plomin, Owen, & McGuffin, 1994).

Normal Variations

The figure of a 50% genetic basis is a summary of data from various sources. The magnitude of the percentage depends on the age of the person being assessed, the technique being used, and the particular characteristic under study. As for age differences, we should note that even identical twins, who later may display correlations as high as .8 or .9 with the co-twin, have few similarities in behavior as newborns, using the measures currently available (Riese, 1990). Either genetic effects on temperament are weakly expressed in the newborn or they are rendered undetectable by the preponderant pregnancy and perinatal influences on behavior. The rising co-twin correlations during the first several years are interpreted as steadily increasing genetic effects during that period (Cyphers, Phillips, Fulker, & Mrazek, 1990; Matheny, 1990; Torgersen, 1981; Torgersen & Kringlen, 1978; Wilson & Matheny, 1986). These effects are seen both as continuity and as synchrony of change. Detailed studies of continuing genetic influences beyond middle childhood are awaited. Existing clues suggest that, far from being diminished to insignificance, as some have thought, genetic influences undoubtedly continue to be active.

The estimate of a 50% genetic basis also depends to some extent on the technology of assessment; parental questionnaires tend to reveal higher identical-twin concordance than the brief observations usually used by researchers. Also, the evidence for heritability is stronger for some characteristics than for others.

The genotype of the individual child effects changes that go far beyond the mere inheritance of behavioral tendencies (Scarr & McCartney, 1983). It can alter the environment with which the child interacts, in several different ways: (1) *passively*, through environments provided by biologically related parents, with whom the child shares multiple genes; (2) *evocatively*, as when the child's genetically determined style modifies the responses of others; and (3) *actively*, as when differently endowed children select different surroundings with which to interact. An example of a passive effect of the genotype would be that of a parent who is highly active, owing to a genetic tendency, and who encourages the expression of activity in his similarly endowed child through stimulation. The genotype is working evocatively when a negative, inflexible child puts a strain on the parents and elicits from them less affectionate and accommodating child-rearing behaviors than would a more pleasant and gratifying child. The genotype is actively effecting change when a shy child deliberately avoids experiences that a bolder child would confront without hesitation, thus narrowing the range of challenges undertaken.

Gender Differences
The commonest chromosomal or genetic variation is, of course, gender difference. Contrary to our expectations, which have been shaped by cultural stereotypes, studies of the temperament of the two sexes demonstrate only negligible disparities (Maziade, Boudreault, Thivierge, Capéraà, & Côté, 1984). Newborn females were more irritable than males in one study (Riese, 1986). Several reports have agreed that in the early years of life females are a little more timid than boys and boys are a bit more active, but not to such a degree as to require different norms on temperament questionnaires. Even by the age of 8–12 years, the correlation of activity with male gender was only .18. Four other significantly dissimilar characteristics were measured at that small magnitude or less (Hegvik, McDevitt, & Carey, 1982). Suitable longitudinal studies have not yet clarified whether alleged sex differences in temperament between adolescent and adult males and females are related, if they exist, to intrinsic physical changes or acculturation.

Genetic and Chromosomal Abnormalities
Since normal genes clearly influence temperament, are genetic and chromosomal abnormalities associated with any specific patterns? At this time, the studies are too few, small, preliminary, and inconclusive for firm conclusions. Down syndrome, the abnormality most frequently evaluated, has not been confirmed to endow a child with the mild, pleasant temperament depicted by the old textbook stereotype; rather, children with Down syndrome exhibit few differences in temperament from the general population (see chapter 7). Other investigations have begun to appraise Klinefelter's, Turner's, Williams's, and fragile X syndromes. Although multiple minor congenital anomalies have not as yet been assigned a genetic or chromosomal basis, children with such anomalies have displayed lower persistence and attention span than controls at age

six years (McNeil, Blennow, Cantor-Graae, Persson-Blennow, Harty, & Karyd, 1993).

Ethnic and National Differences

Despite the strength and persistence of ethnic stereotypes, it has been difficult to establish whether distinctive ethnic traits, if they can be verified, are truly inborn. Moreover, researchers today tend to regard this as a politically hazardous line of inquiry. These questions will remain unanswered until measurement techniques are developed that allow standardized, culture-free observations. A reasonable observation for the present is that these traits are neither established nor disproven.

Nongenetic Physical Factors

Even the most distinguished developmental behavioral geneticists (Plomin, 1994) tend to regard the genes and the psychosocial environment as the only factors of consequence in the evolution of children's behavior, but that model is incomplete. If genetic influences account for about half of the origins of temperament characteristics, the other half must be divided up among a variety of other factors: the nongenetic physical factors and the psychosocial environment. Available information does not allow us to assign numerical estimates of their strength in determining temperament. We can only list these factors and discuss what we know about them.

Birth Order

Popular folklore has it that the first child in a family is the most difficult. However, this judgment is likely to be in the eye of the beholder, since no confirmation has come from the research. The parent may be more likely to evaluate the first child as more troublesome than average overall, but when the child's actual behavior, as reported by the parent, is scored on a standard temperament scale, the first child is no more or less difficult than later-born children. Another common opinion worthy of research scrutiny is that a difficult child is likely to be the last-born, because of parental fatigue.

Prenatal Environment

During the nine months that pass between conception and delivery, the intrauterine environment shapes the developing embryo and fetus in many ways. The fact that identical twins are not necessarily identical in behavior at birth is a reminder that a host of factors, such as the placement of the placenta and the blood supply, influence intrauterine development. The impact of these normal variations on newborn and later behavior has scarcely been acknowledged, much less investigated by researchers in the field. Better recognized and subjected to more scrutiny has been the exposure of the unborn child to abnormal chemical substances and infections. (See chapter 4 concerning these issues and other obstetrical and medical complications of pregnancy.)

Postnatal Physical Environment and Conditions
Numerous influences in the postnatal, nonhuman environment on the learning abilities and behavioral styles of children have received attention. Among the many pollutants we ingest or inhale, lead has been identified as a major offender. Although controversy still rages over some of the findings, it appears that even slightly elevated blood lead levels in early childhood are associated with intellectual and attentional deficits at 10–12 years (Bellinger, Stiles, & Needleman, 1992; Fergusson, Horwood, & Lynskey, 1993a). The effects of many other common pollutants, such as carbon monoxide and sulphur dioxide, await exploration. The possibility that temperament is altered by acute or chronic exposure to environmental allergens, whether by inhalation or contact, remains to be examined.

Other purely physical environmental factors have come under consideration. In a study of 82 toddlers, Theodore Wachs (1988) observed that greater household crowding increased the expression but not the incidence of a temperament of low sociability. Also, a new investigation indicates that children as well as adults exhibit more irritability and withdrawing behavior in the winter months, when they are exposed to less light (Carskadon & Acebo, 1993).

Few child health topics have provoked as much heated controversy in recent years as the assertion of Benjamin Feingold (1975) that coloring and flavoring additives in food are responsible for a variety of behavioral abnormalities such as "hyperactivity." Sober reviews of the evidence, however, generally refute the reports of such an association (Wender, 1986). The alleged deleterious effects of sugar have similarly been thrown into doubt (Wender & Solanto, 1991; Wolraich, Lindgren, Stumbo, Steginck, Appelbaum, & Kiritsy, 1994). Aspartame, the popular artificial sweetener (NutraSweet), "at greater than 10 times usual consumption has no effect on the cognitive and behavioral status of children with attention deficit disorder" (Shaywitz, Sullivan, Anderson, Gillespie, Sullivan, & Shaywitz, 1994). Likewise, food allergy "rarely is manifested exclusively or primarily in the form of disturbed behavior" (Goldbloom, 1992).

From these controversies we should not assume that children's nutritional status has no impact on their behavior. Observations of behavior in countries where malnutrition is endemic reveal a fairly consistent picture of a decrease in attention, in positive emotionality, and in activity in those who are malnourished (Worobey, 1993). While iron deficiency may contribute strongly to these effects, the fact that it is generally accompanied by inadequate intake of other nutrients makes it hard to separate out the results due specifically to lack of sufficient iron. The extent to which nutritional deficiency may be altering the temperament of children in the United States today has yet to be determined.

Some preliminary data suggest that breast-fed infants are more responsive, irritable, and active than those given formula. It is not known whether this behavioral change is due to the contents of the milk or the accompanying interaction with the mother, or how long these differences may persist (Worobey, 1993).

The list of drugs (such as phenobarbital) and foods (such as chocolate) that may affect an infant's behavior via breast milk is bewildering; decisions on what to eliminate from the mother's diet must be individualized on the basis of the nature of the substance, the dosage involved, and the tolerance of the individual infant. The interested reader is referred to "The Transfer of Drugs and Other Chemicals into Human Milk" (1994b) by the Committee on Drugs of the American Academy of Pediatrics.

Various physical conditions and medicines have been suspected of influencing behavioral style. Children who are unwell or tired usually show their condition in their behavior. Certainly sleep deprivation accentuates negative mood and low adaptability. Weissbluth (1989a, 1989b) reports that sleep loss affects attention directly and that indirectly it may produce, through an adrenally mediated stress response, a heightened alertness and increased temperamental difficulty. Decreased hearing due to serous otitis media (ear infection) can understandably diminish attentiveness, but enduring attention deficits long after the infection and fluid have cleared have not been displayed consistently (Arcia & Roberts, 1993). We cannot consider a woman's premenstrual syndrome symptoms to be her temperament, since they occur during only a small part of the month, but we note that poor concentration and irritability are believed to be due to transient hormonal changes. Among medicines, the antihistamines have most frequently evoked complaints of drowsiness and inattention, while the effects of theophylline and anticonvulsant medications are inconsistent and must be evaluated individually (Henretig, 1992).

Abnormalities of the Central Nervous System
In spite of the vast amount of research in the temperament field in the last three decades, scientists have almost completely ignored the question of its relationship to abnormalities of the structure or function of the central nervous system (see Bates & Wachs, 1994). This unfortunate oversight has generated much confusion.

Thomas et al.'s original NYLS (1968) of 133 children included three who had clinical signs of brain injury. Of these, two had easy temperaments and one was difficult, leading the group to conclude that cerebral insults probably do not impose any fixed pattern of temperament on their victims.

Margaret Hertzig (1983) of the NYLS group evaluated a separate sample of 66 premature infants and found that children whose prematurity was accompanied by abnormal neurological findings displayed more of the difficult temperament traits by three years of life. However, they failed to demonstrate unusual degrees of high activity, low attention, or high distractibility, contrary to the widespread assumption that children with brain malfunction differ from the norm in this respect.

Available data from rigorous studies are insufficient to settle this issue of a possible relationship between temperament and various abnormalities of the central nervous system: cerebral palsy, mental retardation, seizure disorders, meningitis, head trauma, or cerebral irradiation for malignancies like leukemia. Yet this ignorance has not stopped both laypersons and professionals of various disciplines from assuming, on the basis of no objective evidence, that children who are highly active, inattentive, or impulsive have the brain malfunction presently called attention deficit hyperactivity disorder (ADHD) (see chapter 9).

The Psychosocial Environment
As mentioned earlier, the general assumption of traditional developmental behavioral genetics has been that when behavior cannot be related to genetic processes, or when it changes, the only possible explanation lies in the psychosocial environment. In the previous section, we reviewed a long list of another set of influences, nongenetic physical factors, that possibly affect temperament. How much of the variance in behavioral style remains to be explained by the psychosocial environment? We cannot say. We have no trouble imagining that the child treated with affection and reasonable discipline will maximize a tendency to react with positive mood and flexibility. On the other hand, a child prolongedly exposed to an aversive setting is likely to move in the opposite direction. Socially desirable characteristics may be reinforced by approving caretakers, while the less favored ones are discouraged. But less desirable characteristics may also be reinforced by inappropriate parental tolerance or support.

As children grow older, they participate actively in the process of modifying the expression of stylistic qualities such as shyness or boldness when they are convinced that life will go more smoothly for them if they make such alterations. The subjective feelings of the child may not differ, but the outward expression, which is what the caretakers witness, may change substantially. Thus, a child's overt behavioral style can change in response to environmental pressures, but we do not have much information as to when and how this happens.

Social Class
A standard, commonly evaluated measure of the psychosocial environment is social class. Two studies with samples stratified for social class and with fairly homogeneous populations—in Quebec, Canada (Maziade, Boudreault, Thivierge, Capéraà, & Côté, 1984), and in Lund, Sweden (McNeil & Persson-Blennow, 1982)—found negligible differences. When studies examine more diverse populations with racial and ethnic mixtures, immigrant populations, and language barriers, the meaning of the social class differences revealed becomes unclear.

STABILITY OF TEMPERAMENT

We mentioned earlier that it is not necessary to demonstrate a high degree of stability or continuity of temperament to establish its viability as a real aspect of personality or a clinically significant force. Despite problems with definition and measurement, one can conclude that temperament, while not very stable in the newborn period, does become more so as the child gets older. By middle childhood, and presumably from then on, it is at least moderately stable. Temperament is never fixed at any time, nor is it completely changeable in any period.

These terms are not used in the same way by all the researchers in the field. McCall (1986) suggests that temperament be considered continuous if the same quality is exhibited across the time span in question, and that it be called stable if the individual retains the same relative rank ordering in the subject group over that period. Others may use the terms differently.

Another source of confusion is the problem in measurement. As a child ages and his or her brain matures, the repertory of reactions broadens. The same characteristic may require assessment from different behaviors, as with the shift in the area of activity when locomotion begins. Also, the same trait may assume different saliency or meaning in parent-child relations. For example, in the young infant distractibility is welcome because it is likely to mean soothability, but in the school-age child it interferes with application to tasks. The significance of different levels of rhythmicity changes as well: it becomes harder for parents to rate the regularity of bodily functions as the child grows older because they are decreasingly in touch with these matters.

Some researchers begin their determinations of stability in their subjects before birth. A new line of inquiry called behavioral perinatology contends that fetal and neonatal neurobehavioral functioning are continuous and that stable individual characteristics develop and can be identified before birth (DiPietro, 1993). The subsequent course of these differences, reflected in such phenomena as varying responses to uterine contractions, has yet to be followed (Emory & Toomey, 1991).

From the newborn period until later in childhood, modest short-term but minimal long-term stability has been demonstrated. For example, Birns, Barten, and Bridger (1969) found approximately .4 correlations between birth and four months for measurements of irritability, sensitivity, and tension. Yet extensive work with the Brazelton Neonatal Behavioral Assessment Scale (NBAS) discovered only "very low day-to-day correlations for most items, clusters, and factors" (Sameroff, 1978, p. 111). The only characteristic known by any measurement to be stable from the newborn period (up to two weeks after birth) to a point as late as 9–12 months is irritability (Matheny, Riese, & Wilson, 1985; Worobey & Blajda, 1989), and that is a low to moderate correlation (.32 and .46, respectively).

The exact course of increasing stability in temperament over the first years has not been worked out yet (Plomin et al., 1990, 1993). We can say that it is detectable by 18 months (McDevitt & Carey, 1981), and substantial by three years. Temperamental difficulty rated by parents at 18 months was correlated with ("predicted") adverse temperamental qualities of low adaptability and negative mood consistently on several subsequent determinations up to the age of 12 years (Guerin & Gottfried, 1994, in press). After the age of three years, the magnitude and duration of stability appears to increase dramatically (McDevitt, 1986). Stability from infancy to eight years (Pedlow, Sanson, Prior, & Oberklaid, 1993) and from 3–7 years to 8–12 years (Hegvik, McDevitt, & Carey, 1982) has been shown to be considerable. Measurements from middle childhood into adolescence and adulthood are awaited (Chess & Thomas, 1984).

Why is a phenomenon with such a strong genetic component not more stable? In the first place, the genes themselves are responsible for some of the changes as well as the continuities (Wilson & Matheny, 1986). Other changes apparently occur as the genes express themselves more fully over the course of the first few years of life, as demonstrated by the increasing resemblance of identical twins. Less mature infants tend to be less stable, as exhibited in a comparison of premature and term infants over the first two years (Riese, 1987). Recovering from perinatal complications, especially major ones such as intraventricular hemorrhage, may contribute to these changes (Garcia-Coll, Halpern, Vohr, Seifer, & Oh, 1992). (The possibility that changes in temperament are linked to the wearing off of the effects of drug use and abuse during pregnancy is considered in chapter 4.)

As mentioned earlier, the environment is certainly the reason for some of the observed changes in temperament, although documentation is sparse and it is surely not the only influence of consequence, as is commonly assumed. Either with their caretakers' help or on their own, children may learn to modify the expression of temperament characteristics that impair adjustment—for instance, suppressing either shyness in social situations or inattention in the classroom. Finally, it is well known that drugs like alcohol or methylphenidate (Ritalin) alter behavioral style, but only while the substance is present in the body.

How much does this issue of the degree of stability or continuity of temperament matter to professionals involved in the primary or consultative care of children? As the situation looks today, probably not much. It is important to our patients, students, and clients to the extent that it supports or interferes with the child's functioning *at this time*. Professionals need to know how temperament affects social relations, task performance, and other aspects of the child's life in the present. What the child's behavioral style will be ten years or five years or even one year in the future is of relatively little consequence. Professionals and caretakers alike are interested in solving today's problems, not in making predictions.

In one situation the changeability of a child's temperament does become a practical issue. Our main strategy in solving clinical problems with temperamental components is to attempt to alter the parents' handling so that the fit between them and the child will become more harmonious and the diminished stress will allow the problem to disappear. If all the reasonable environmental alterations have been accomplished and there is still a clinical problem because of the strength of the child's characteristics, then the question may arise as to whether it is desirable, possible, and ethical to try to change those characteristics. This can happen only if the trait is capable of such modification and there are available and acceptable means.

Except for the use of Ritalin to decrease inattentiveness in school, the research literature has largely ignored this therapeutic option. Peter Kramer's *Listening to Prozac* (1993) set off a flurry of speculations along these lines and much controversy. The possibility of using medications to alter normal temperament variations, as distinguished from treating psychopathology, is an immensely complex issue about which we are certain to hear more in the coming years.

THE PRACTICAL RELEVANCE OF TEMPERAMENT

Not only is temperament real, but it also matters in many ways for the caretaker-child relationship and for the caretakers and the children themselves as individuals (Carey, 1985b).

IMPACT ON THE CARETAKER-CHILD RELATIONSHIP

Any caretaker, whether a parent, teacher, or health care provider, needs little persuasion that child-rearing experiences are diverse. Feeding an infant who makes a face and spits out all new foods is not at all like performing the same duties with one who smiles and readily accepts these novelties. A persistent, intense, and active toddler requires a management plan different from that for the one who is timid and pliable. Trying to teach an inattentive, distractible child poses challenges not encountered by the teacher of the persistent and attentive one. Indeed, the whole fabric of daily life is affected by the behavioral style of the child and the way it molds these relationships.

Yet few researchers have analyzed these daily interactions, more energy having been expended in examining their consequences than their process. A few samples can be cited. Breitmayer and Ricciuti (1988) documented that as early as the second day of life an infant's emerging temperament plays a role in shaping the caregiving environment. Alert babies received the most social contact, active ones got the least, and irritable ones were soothed the most. Pnina Klein (1984) witnessed more sensory and social stimulation being given to easy babies at 6 and 12 months. More and larger surveys of this nature are needed to provide better details of these interactions. In the meantime, we cannot doubt that the effects of children's emerging and changing temperaments are extensive and powerful.

IMPACT ON THE CARETAKERS

Not only can a child's temperament alter the parent or teacher's response to the child, it can affect how caretakers think and feel about themselves. A number of recent investigations have documented this influence, using different measures of temperament and definitions of difficulty.

In a sample of 49 expectant parents formally assessed as to marital satisfaction prenatally and at four months postpartum, a difficult temperament in the infant at four months was associated with a decline in marital satisfaction both for fathers ($r = .52$) and mothers ($r = .58$) (McMillan, 1986). Twenty-two couples experienced more negative personality changes, especially in the sense of personal control, after the birth of a difficult infant (Sirignano & Lachman, 1985). Contrary to expectations, the presence of an aversive temperament in a group of 23 infants made their mothers less likely to return to work in the child's early years (Galambos & Lerner, 1987). Parental distress and diminished self-esteem have been noted with difficult temperament in newborns (Halpern & MacLean, 1993), in 20-month-old infants (Portales, Porges, & Greenspan, 1990), and in adolescents (Lerner, Castellino, & Perkins, in press). "Maternal distress, discomfort in the role of parent, poor spousal relationships and negative changes in way of life" were directly related to difficult infant temperament in a sample of 77 mothers (Sheeber & Johnson, 1992). Parents of easier children, like the Brown family mentioned at the beginning of this chapter, undoubtedly feel more enthusiastic about having another child than do parents of children whose temperaments have presented some problems. This possibility has not yet been systematically investigated, nor has the possible impact of a child's temperament on marital disharmony, separation, or divorce. The influence of a child's difficult temperament on the siblings has been assessed only to a limited degree.

THE IMPACT ON THE CHILD

We have been impressed with how much a child's temperament matters for everyday interactions with the caretakers and with the extent of the impact of that interaction on the caretakers themselves, but our chief concern is with how their temperaments affect children themselves. Much of the rest of this book deals with those influences and with how child care professionals can assess and cope with them. Virtually every aspect of a child's being is in one way or another touched or molded by temperamental features, including physical health, growth, development, social adjustment, and school performance.

ASSESSING AND COPING WITH TEMPERAMENT DIFFERENCES

A recurring theme in this book is that temperament differences in children can be clinically assessed and handled primarily by revising the management by the caretakers. The first step in this process is diagnosing the child's temperament profile, and we now review the various techniques for obtaining that profile.

TEMPERAMENT ASSESSMENT METHODS

The three methods available for obtaining data on behavioral style are interviews, observations, and questionnaires (Carey, 1992b).

Interviews

The best-known interview technique is the one described by the NYLS team (Thomas et al., 1963). Although it was sufficient for the needs of their study, neither it nor any derivative of it has found wide use, either in research or in clinical practice. The flexibility of the NYLS interview technique allows it to be more sensitive to varying situations, but it is also less capable of standardization. Its one- to two-hour length elicits a wealth of behavioral descriptions but renders it impractical in any clinical and most research situations.

Nevertheless, clinicians can, and often do, use the concepts in an abbreviated form in practical situations. A shortened interview of the clinician's own construction can yield usable data as long as he or she resists the temptation to generalize too readily from insufficiently comprehensive descriptions, such as one or two instances of a trait. The interview approach, adapted to the particular needs of the occasion, may be the most reasonable way to obtain temperament data when there is no need for a detailed analysis.

Observations

Teachers, day care workers, and some other child care professionals generally have extensive contact with their students and many opportunities to observe their behavior; they are in a good position to form sound judgments of individual children. On the other hand, physicians and psychologists usually witness only brief, sometimes atypical samples of behavior. At this time no standardized test or scoring method is available for making a comprehensive evaluation of a child's temperament in the clinical or educational milieu, or in any other setting. The few relatively brief observation protocols for research have not yet been modified suitably for practical use.

Questionnaires

In view of the limitations of measuring temperament in interviews and by observations, a series of questionnaires have been developed to obtain reports from parents. Parents are the experts on their own children and generally provide adequate information about them if asked the right sort of questions in the right way.

Several earlier scales intended for research with adults were developed by Eysenck in 1956, Guilford and Zimmerman in 1956, Thorndike in 1963, and Strelau in 1972. Some others for children were elaborated more recently by developmental psychologists but are intended for scientific explorations as well (see appendix 1).

For practical use we recommend the set of questionnaires, based on the NYLS dimensions, that are summarized in appendix 1. Along with three psychologist colleagues—William Fullard, Robin Hegvik, and Barbara Medoff-Cooper—we have produced a series of five such scales covering the age span from one month to 12 years (see appendix 2). Parents are asked to rate as to frequency about 95 specific descriptions of behaviors associated with the nine NYLS temperament dimensions in precise situations. The clinician then transfers these data to a scoring sheet and thence to a profile sheet, which displays the child's range of behavioral style characteristics compared with the norms. Appendix 1 also mentions three scales by Thomas and Chess and two by Keogh and Martin and their associates for use in schools.

These questionnaires using the NYLS formulation have several advantages:

1. They require only about 20–30 minutes for the parent or other caretaker to complete, making them briefer and more efficient than comparable interview or observation techniques. Scoring time by the professional or assistant takes only 10–15 minutes.

2. They are based on clinically relevant theory and measure nine characteristics that are all observable in children and have been shown to be related to clinical problems.

3. They rely on specific behavioral descriptions in particular situations ("The infant moves about much [kicks, grabs, squirms] during diapering and dressing") rather than on parental perceptions or general impressions ("Child is very energetic").

4. Their norms are standardized for the different characteristics and ages.

5. They have adequate psychometric characteristics as to retest reliability and internal consistency, as well as validity insofar as it can be tested in the absence of a standardized observation technique against which to compare the questionnaires.

Some uncertainties about these questionnaires, however, should be borne in mind:

1. Some researchers and clinicians have expressed doubts about the ability of parents with less than a high school education to respond adequately to these scales. Parents with less than average verbal skills may not be able to handle accurately the various shades of meaning. We must therefore advise caution in using these scales with such families. Furthermore, no study has investigated whether reading a questionnaire to a parent yields data of reliability and validity comparable to what is gained when a parent completes a scale unassisted.

2. Parents from cultures or subcultures different from those represented in the standardization samples might understand some of the items in unintended and different ways, introducing some confusing artifacts. We recommend restandardization whenever there is any question of a dissimilarity in the composition of the samples, even within the English language. Our recommendations for persons doing translations of the scales are included in appendix 3.

3. The issue of validity is not easily resolved. Behavioral scientists presently tend to speak of any parental judgments as "perceptions" and of their own data, no matter how brief and unrepresentative, as scientific "observations." It would be more accurate to say that perceptions are general or hasty impressions and that ratings are the result of multiple scored judgments of certain behavioral style patterns in specific settings. Both parents and professionals can have perceptions and make ratings. Since there is no comprehensive, standardized professional rating scheme against which to compare the questionnaires, we must settle for the briefer analyses available now. Every adequately designed test so far has demonstrated at least moderate validity of parental reports. Any further investigations of parental validity must use only contemporaneous data, consider specific behavioral patterns rather than general impressions, and compare the same content and dimensions of behavior in the reports of parents and other observers. These simple requirements have been overlooked in the few published reports claiming to discredit the validity of parental ratings (Carey, 1983). Clinical users of temperament questionnaires can therefore be reassured of at least a moderate degree of validity. Any tendency to distort can be minimized by the interviewing and observing that should always accompany the use of a questionnaire (Carey, 1992b).

4. Some academic psychologists interested in temperament research have published three critical reviews of temperament questionnaires in general (Hubert, Wachs, Peters-Martin, & Gandour, 1982; Rothbart & Mauro, 1990; Slabach, Morrow, & Wachs, 1991). Although we can agree that all the current scales have their shortcomings, these reviews suffer from a superficiality of analysis and the absence of a clinical perspective. For example, their comparisons of scales as to their reported internal consistencies do not recognize that internal consistency has been

artificially inflated by some authors by the juxtaposition of similarly worded items. These articles are more useful as surveys of what is available than for the pertinence of their analyses to the important issues discussed in this book.

RECOMMENDATIONS FOR ASSESSMENT

From this possibly confusing array of techniques and methodological issues we must select some general suggestions for use by professionals involved in the daily or episodic care of children. We do so acknowledging that temperament assessment is an imperfect science and art, although it should improve in the years to come. Moreover, what may work well in one situation at one time may change with an alteration of circumstances.

Routine Professional Care of Children

When there are no complaints from parents, other caretakers, or the children themselves, and no discernible areas of malfunction in the child, do we need to make a formal assessment of the child's temperament? No evidence has so far been presented to support routine evaluations of temperament in medical practice or in schools if caretakers are generally satisfied by a child's current behavioral status (Carey & McDevitt, 1989). The information obtained is not usually of sufficient value to justify the effort. At present the danger of misuse of these data by persons who do not understand them is greater than the possible benefits. Furthermore, we recommend that, if temperament assessments are made, they be arranged and scored by appropriate professionals rather than by parents, who may make mistakes or misunderstand the results.

Articles and books on temperament for parents usually present greatly simplified scales for them to use to evaluate their children. The advantage of making the subject easily accessible to parents is overshadowed by the risk of encouraging erroneous general impressions. Stanley Turecki offers at the very beginning of *The Difficult Child* (1985/1989) a two-page assessment questionnaire before introducing or explaining the details. By contrast, Mary Sheedy Kurcinka in *Raising Your Spirited Child* (1991) defines the temperament characteristics and provides between two and six situational descriptions of each before "getting a picture of your child's temperament" (p. 27).

When a Child Presents Clinical Concerns

When the caretaker is concerned about behavioral, emotional, or functional problems in a child, however, an assessment of the child's temperament is likely to make a substantial contribution to the diagnosis and management. A well-planned intervention should be based on a knowledge of the child's behavioral style in addition to the troublesome symptoms, the noxious elements in the environment, and their interaction. The extent of the temperament evaluation will depend on the nature and magnitude of the clinical concerns. A thumb-sucking or bed-wetting child will need less of a workup than the one failing at school or presenting oppositional behavior.

In our opinion, the most thorough appraisal is accomplished by having the caretakers complete one of the more sophisticated questionnaires, such as one in our series. The professional should supplement the questionnaire information with interviewing and at least some informal observations to round out the picture of the child and to learn more about how the caretakers feel about, and are interacting with, the child's temperament and other characteristics. The professional must be the judge of whether this optimal assessment is needed. If some data are needed but less than what is gathered from a questionnaire, we recommend using a detailed interview, one that asks about the child's behavior in a variety of situations (Johnson, 1992), rather than using one of the shorter, more impressionistic questionnaires developed by researchers. In other words, the amount of temperament data obtained should correspond to the magnitude and complexity of the child's problem.

CHAPTER 3

The Nature and Practical Relevance of Temperament: What Can We Do?

S EVERAL PROCEDURES have been worked out for the effective management of temperament differences and problems related to them,
as illustrated in the case studies of the two children introduced at
the beginning of chapter 2. Medical and psychological professionals did
not utilize this understanding in treating Jennifer, and her care was
unsuccessful.

As reported previously, Jennifer, the Browns' second child, was
much more difficult to manage than their first, leaving them perplexed and worried. Not wishing to seem like an incompetent
mother, Mrs. Brown had not complained to the pediatrician about the
baby's irritability, inflexibility, and other aversive characteristics at
either of the first two routine health care visits. By three months she
could no longer put on a brave face and pretend that she was completely satisfied and in control. The pediatrician assured her that the
physical examination was negative, offered the diagnostic impression
that milk allergy was responsible, and prescribed a change of feedings to a soy-based formula. The Browns were pleased to have such a
simple explanation and Jennifer did seem to be a little better for the
next two or three days. Very soon, however, it became clear that the
new formula was making no difference in Jennifer's behavior. When
Mrs. Brown telephoned the doctor the following week to report the
failure of the treatment plan, the doctor brusquely advised her that
everything possible had been done and that she would have to stop

being such a worrier. Feeling overwhelmed, the Browns next sought the advice of a child psychologist, who tested the baby, found her to be developmentally normal, and suggested to the Browns that they return for a series of counseling sessions to discuss their upset feelings. The Browns were left with the impression that either their observations of their temperamentally difficult child were distorted by some problems in themselves or that their pediatrician and psychologist were both inadequate in their appraisals.

By contrast, Ralph's parents received appropriate help with his challenging temperament from their pediatrician and her nurse.

The crying and low soothability of their baby Ralph led to great turmoil in the Jones family. The unfulfilled fantasies of domestic harmony had caused Mr. Jones to withdraw from the care of the previously valued child and from intimacy with his wife. The strain on the family relationships was bad and getting worse. At the four-month checkup, both the pediatrician and the nurse noticed that Mrs. Jones looked tired and despondent. The pediatrician sympathetically inquired about her situation and learned some of the details of the infant's behavior and the family's reactions. Being reassured that Ralph was physically and developmentally normal and growing well, the doctor urged Mrs. Jones to return with her husband for a 50-minute consultation the following afternoon. That additional visit proved to be the turning point. By having a more comprehensive discussion with the parents, the pediatrician confirmed her suspicions that Ralph was a temperamentally difficult but otherwise normal infant. She helped the parents to revise their understanding of the baby and their strategies of management. She persuaded them that Mrs. Jones should be relieved of the complete care of the child and that Mr. Jones should get involved again. She urged them to resume some of their former activities together outside the home, such as going to the movies and social events, which they had curtailed since Ralph's arrival. After just this one session, the Joneses viewed their child differently—as completely normal but presently hard to manage—and felt much better about themselves, still an attractive and loving young couple.

Briefer counseling was needed at some of the subsequent routine visits, but the appropriate professional intervention at a critical time changed the Joneses' lives dramatically.

These two case studies illustrate the variety of solutions that are commonly offered for the same clinical situation: a difficult or otherwise aversive temperament in a child. As with Jennifer and Ralph, the child-environment disharmony is often mismanaged as a physical disorder in the child or as the result of abnormal attitudes or practices of the parents.

Their stories demonstrate that temperamental difficulty is a variation of normal and that it cannot be cured in the traditional medical sense but can be mitigated by more appropriate understanding and management.

This chapter presents a general review of what has been learned about using our current knowledge of temperament for the benefit of children, their parents, and other caretakers. The principal applications of temperament theory and data in clinical and educational practice are: (1) general education of caretakers about temperament, (2) identification of a specific child's temperament profile when there is concern about his or her behavior, and (3) intervention when stress from the dissonance between the temperament and the environment has produced a clinical problem (Carey, 1982, 1985a, 1986, 1994).

GENERAL EDUCATION OF PARENTS AND OTHER CARETAKERS

Child health and education professionals should help the parents of the children in their care to understand the phenomenon of temperament at least in general terms. Too often young adults enter into parenthood poorly prepared. They are inadequately trained and informed and consequently may feel uncertain and helpless. One of the commonest of these failings, a lack of knowledge about temperament differences, is also relatively easy to remedy. Professionals can ensure that parents acquire sufficient information about the broad range of normal behavioral styles so that they have a background against which to view their own child clearly.

CONTENT OF EDUCATION

How much do parents need to know? They do not have to absorb all of the research information provided in the previous chapter, but they should be helped to become aware of the major points about the existence of largely inborn behavioral tendencies, their importance to children and their caretakers, and the current view that they are hard to change but can be accommodated by the caretakers to minimize stress and its consequences. Many parents have been exposed to only an environmentalist view of child development. They can be helped to appreciate that some behavioral predispositions are present in children from birth or soon after and that disagreeable behavior is not all directly attributable to faulty parental care or physical disorders in the child. They should become aware that simple child-rearing rules cannot be applied uniformly to all children with equal success. For example, they might find it illuminating to learn that an infant's slow approach to new foods or people may be a temperamental trait rather than a sign of parental inadequacy. Similarly, a highly active preschool child is more likely to be normal than to be overstimulated or to have a malfunctioning brain.

METHODS OF PRESENTATION

By what means can we help parents become reasonably knowledgeable about temperament differences? The most appropriate techniques depend on the setting, whether medical, educational, or community-based support groups.

1. The pediatrician, family physician, or nurse can present the concept of individual differences in general terms at various times, such as at a prenatal session, in the newborn nursery, during a well-child visit, or in the course of consultations for acute or chronic illness. Parents may understand it best as part of the instructions about feeding, sleeping, crying, and elimination.

   A group connected with the Kaiser Permanente Health Plan in California has built temperament education into the routine services offered by the pediatrics department of that large health maintenance organization (Cameron, Rice, Hansen, & Rosen, 1994). Although such education is unfortunately not common, the Kaiser system demonstrates that it is possible to persuade a vast health maintenance corporation that providing instruction and advice about temperament is not just an interesting frill but results in lower medical management expenses in the long run.

2. The education of parents by teachers in the regular school system is a largely unrealized opportunity for advancing parental understanding. The principal deterrent has been the general lack of instruction given to teachers themselves.

3. In view of the general inadequacy of medical and educational professional training at present, much of the task of parent instruction has fallen to other professional, semiprofessional, and voluntary educational and self-help organizations. Although we are acquainted with several of these, there are nowhere near enough of them to meet the needs of a largely uneducated public. These existing resources do demonstrate, however, how well temperament education can be done with limited resources. The Temperament Project (9460 140th St., Surrey, BC, Canada, V3V 5Z4), directed by Catherine J. Andersen (1994a) in Vancouver, British Columbia, and established by two perplexed mothers, is a nonprofit association with a program offering education and support for families of temperamentally difficult children. A volunteer professional advisory board reviews the program and instructional materials to ensure their quality. Parents commend the program for its information, for its help, and for the way it reduces the isolation felt by parents of challenging children. It has earned extensive community support from early childhood educators, mental health professionals, and social service agencies.

   The Temperament Program (1104 K Ave., La Grande, OR 97850), a county-run agency in rural eastern Oregon developed by the psychologist Bill Smith (1994), is primarily an early intervention service but also functions as an educational resource by offering parenting advice tailored to the individual needs of children and their families. The program's care, funded by the state of Oregon, is provided by specially trained parents, called temperament specialists, who are supervised by a licensed psychologist. Parents leave the program with a better understanding of their child, some effective coping strategies, and a resource book with further information relevant to their needs.

In the Minneapolis–St. Paul area, the educator Mary Sheedy Kurcinka (1991) and the psychologist Linda S. Budd (1993) have independently started or inspired several support groups. In the Philadelphia region, some organizations, such as the Parents' Network and Practical Parenting (an educational and counseling service run by our colleague Dr. Robin Hegvik), offer courses on a variety of topics, including one on the difficult child.

We are not aware of any reliable register of such services in other communities. Until one becomes available, parents will need to inquire through better-known community counseling services or through friends.

4. Videotapes and printed materials are available (see appendix 4). The California Department of Education issued in 1989 a videotape entitled *Flexible, Fearful, or Feisty: The Temperaments of Infants and Toddlers.* This is a small but promising beginning to what could become a major element in parental education.

How helpful is it for parents to gather only general information about temperament from lectures or books without more individualized data on their own child? One small study found that parents of difficult children were reassured to discover that they were normal, that their children's aversive characteristics were largely inborn and not the parents' fault, that their children also had a good side, and that the best strategy was to improve the fit. Beneficial effects on family life appeared to last for more than one year (Mettetal, 1994).

IDENTIFICATION OF A SPECIFIC CHILD'S TEMPERAMENT PROFILE

The second principal use of temperament information is in identifying a particular child's temperament profile, which provides the parents with a more organized picture of their child, a better perspective on how their child compares with others, and possible distortions in their perceptions. Despite the great benefits to parents of learning about and discussing the general nature and significance of temperament differences, they often need more specific help from a professional in understanding and managing their particular child. The process of determining a child's characteristics and discussing them with the parents may provide them with enough information and perspective to allow them to shift their supervision of the child in a healthy direction even without any intervention measures being taken by the professional.

Before the advent of refined interview and questionnaire techniques, general discussion of temperament was as far as the clinician could go with any accuracy, and most clinicians probably go no further even now. But since we now possess the technical skills to identify simply and fairly accurately the specific temperament pattern of any child up to 12 years of age, clinicians need no longer stop short of making such individual assessments.

There are two principal indications that a child care professional should attempt to identify a child's temperament pattern: (1) when the caretaker or a professional is concerned about the child's behavior or the parent-child relationship, and (2) when the professional detects a major discrepancy between the parents' general perceptions of their child and their more detailed descriptions or ratings of the child. As discussed in the previous chapter, we do not at present recommend routine individual measurements of children when these indications are not present.

CONCERN ABOUT THE CHILD'S BEHAVIOR
OR THE PARENT-CHILD RELATIONSHIP

If the parents or other caretakers express concern about a child's behavior, an assessment of the child's temperament profile can help in understanding the child's contribution to the problem. The diagnostic process should include an evaluation of both the child's behavioral adjustment and behavioral style. A behavioral adjustment disorder, which would mean a dysfunction in the areas of social relations, task performance, self-assurance, or thinking, feeling, or body function, can derive in part from a poor fit between the child's temperament and the environment.

On the other hand, there may be no dysfunction in any of these areas and the caretaker's distress arises entirely from the child's temperament. Almost any temperament characteristic or combination of them can generate anguish in a caretaker, but it is most commonly provoked by the difficult traits, the slow-to-warm-up pattern, or a low task orientation. Other common sources of discomfort to be looking for are high and low activity, high persistence, low distractibility (low soothability in infants), and high sensitivity.

The catalog of sources of parental concern about children's behavior should also include the possibility that their problem derives from misperception of a normal child who has no adjustment disorder or temperament risk factor. Such misperceptions are usually a matter of inexperience or psychosocial disturbance in the family (Carey, 1994).

When the parental concern arises from a mismatch with a child's temperament, the parents usually have either an inadequate under-standing or an intolerance of it. The objective of parent counseling is to deal with both of these issues. For example, most parents of difficult infants are aware that they are coping with a challenge, but they only dimly recognize the nature of the problem. When they learn that the infant's aversive traits are not their fault, they feel relieved of an enor-mous burden of guilt and can respond to their infant more appropri-ately with less anger and apprehension. The suitable handling therefore is parental accommodation, not behavioral management or psy-chotherapy, which would be called for when a child has a behavioral adjustment problem.

DISCREPANCIES BETWEEN PARENTS' PERCEPTIONS AND RATINGS

Sometimes parents give us general impressions of their children that are at variance with their own more detailed descriptions of what the child actually does. For example, a parent may report frequent, frightful, and deeply disturbing temper tantrums in a toddler that turn out, when more specifically elaborated on, to be mild, brief, and relatively uncom-mon. The professional's clinical task is skillfully to help the parent bring the two views closer together.

In chapter 2, we explained the difference between ratings and percep-tions of temperament. The term "ratings" refers to an average of multiple judgments by the parents as to the frequency of various behaviors, which are scored by the researcher or clinician and compared with established norms. "Perceptions" are quick or superficial impressions of the child's overall pattern formed by either the parent or the professional. Parental ratings and perceptions tend to agree, but as with the parent who misread the normal temper displays of his toddler, they can be different. These dis-crepancies may be clinically significant. If a parent's rating of an infant results in the child being scored difficult but the parent perceives the child as easy, the explanation could be anything from inexperience to denial to effective coping. The clinician's response must be individualized. Nothing is to be gained by insisting on affixing the label "difficult" to a child whose parents are coping satisfactorily and not feeling discomfort in the interac-tion. For example, a seven-month-old infant was rated difficult by his experienced, competent mother, but she offered a general impression of him as easy. When asked about this discrepancy, she replied, "He's hys-terical. He screams a lot, but we just laugh and he stops." We smile in our approbation of her attitude (McDevitt & Carey, 1981).

The opposite situation is less common but more worrisome. When a parent rates an infant as easy but perceives her as more difficult than average, be alert for a parental psychosocial problem or an inappropri-ate interaction (Carey, 1985a). Here a simple discussion of the child's behavior would be insufficient. Further investigation of the discrepancy is called for.

PRESENTATION OF DATA TO PARENTS

In forming conclusions about a child's temperament profile and presenting the results to the parents, great care must be taken to avoid potentially pejorative labels like "difficult" or "hyperactive." Such a profile is best conveyed in descriptive terms such as "relatively slow to accept changes" or "fairly active" rather than in diagnostic designations whose meaning and prognostic significance may be misunderstood by both the professional and the parent. Although some have recommended offering such results to parents in written form (Cameron et al., 1994; Little, 1985), the superiority of this approach over oral presentation remains unclear. The advantage of the written presentation is that the content can be retained in its exact form and referred to as needed later. In an oral presentation, however, uncertain points can be clarified, results can be phrased in language that is understandable to the listener, and clarifications can be made and misunderstandings corrected to ensure full comprehension.

THE GENERAL MANAGEMENT OF TEMPERAMENT VARIATIONS

How can child health and education professionals help parents cope with their children's temperaments? If the parental concern or perplexity derives from a lack of understanding or an intolerance of the temperament, our job is not just to educate the parent about general issues but also to offer specific suggestions as to how best to respond to their child. Various patterns of reaction in children call for different parental strategies to minimize stress and promote harmony. Although no one set of ideas fits all situations, the advice offered by Chess and Thomas (1992) in a recent textbook article gives us a practical summary of useful techniques (see table 3.1).

These suggestions do not exhaust the strategies available for accommodating more harmoniously the temperament characteristics sometimes found to be aversive. More suggestions will be made in subsequent chapters relative to specific situations.

These specific tactics should, of course, be embedded in an overall plan of management that recognizes the child's needs for: (1) guidance in the form of discipline and approval—that is, the enforcement of firm, consistent rules with an avoidance of physical punishment, with praise for good behavior, and with little attention to behavior that is only annoying; (2) affection, which includes acceptance and intimacy; (3) stimulation in the developmental and cognitive spheres; and (4) intrafamilial and extrafamilial socialization. (Chapter 5 discusses in greater detail the meeting of these requirements.)

MANAGEMENT OF A DIFFICULT TEMPERAMENT AND
OTHER TEMPERAMENT RISK FACTORS

Ten to fifteen percent of the population of children have temperaments that their parents rate or perceive as difficult. We turn now to a

Table 3.1

Children's Temperamental Qualities and Management Approaches

Temperamental Quality		Management Approach
Activity		
	High	Provide periodic opportunities for constructive high-speed activities. Demand motor quietness in socially appropriate places, but arrange that it be needed for short periods only.
	Low	Allow sufficient time for tasks so that child need not be rushed or scolded for slow pace. Do not denigrate slowness or allow quicker sibling to take over task. Compliment quality of completed task if genuine effort has been made.
Rhythmicity		
	Irregular	In early infancy, accommodate (eating, sleep). By toddler stage and older, accept lack of hunger, sleepiness, but impose social rules (next food at snack time, must be in own room if cannot sleep but allowed to play by self). Impose regular wakening time for school.
	Regular	In early infancy, accommodate. If irregularity is imposed by outside circumstances, make provision for actual regularity (bring food, diapers, pajamas, and so on). At older ages, warn child of impending disruption of usual schedule; commiserate.
Approach/ Withdrawal		
	Withdrawal	Be alert to the possibility that the activity refused by the child may actually bring pleasure; parent should be guided by awareness of child's interests. If this is the case, insist upon a time-limited trial.
	Approach	If suitable, express pleasure and interest. Be alert that the child's first positive response may be short-lived; if so, make it a learning experience ("We must remember," not "I told you so").
Adaptability		
	Slow	For mandated (school) or desirable (social exposure) activities, provide advance multiple opportunities for brief, graduated exposure. Do not force child into a "sink or swim" introduction to a shaky situation.
	Quick	For most part, an asset; enjoy. Be alert to child's selection of concepts and people for adaptation; find alternatives to adaptation to socially undesirable people or antisocial mores.
Threshold of responsiveness		
	Low	Avoid exciting stimuli immediately prior to and during sleep time (infants and toddlers). Provide nonirritating surroundings;

avoid high decibels, tight or itchy clothing, using degree of child's threshold as guide. Encourage positive aspects: empathy with people's feelings, reasonable preferences.

High Compensate child who misses cues by drilling in safety rules, social formulas—at developmental level.

Intensity of reactions

High Do not respond with counterintensity; wait out child's blast but consider the content. Make judgement according to actual reasonableness and state it with quiet persistence, whether denying or accepting child's demand. Do not assume that child's high intensity equals deep desire—it may be a trivial matter. Do not give in to "buy" peace.

Low Be alert to possibility that child's deep and valid interest may be expressed mildly. Take complaints of pain very seriously; investigate.

Quality of mood

Negative Do not feel guilty; it is not your fault. In making judgements, be aware of child's style of expressing positive involvement, e.g., persistence. Be alert to child's genuine distress, which may be camouflaged by a general negative mood.

Positive Appreciate your good fortune. Be alert to possibility that child may overvalue people and situations because of general positive mood. Teach (at developmental level) social, moral, and safety safeguards as a protection against undeserved positive judgments.

Distractibility

High Aim to compensate, not to change. Do not denigrate but redirect child's wandering attention without rancor. Help child set up reminders to return to task; act as a colleague. High praise for final accomplishment—if it is of reasonable quality.

Low If child continues task, seemingly ignoring another demand, insist but do not accuse of disobedience, as child really did not hear or notice.

Attention span and persistence

Low Quality and completion, not style of functioning, are the goals. Plan brief periods of task involvement (take into account both developmental stage and temperamental style). Rule: returning to task (after reminder) after each planned break is child's responsibility until completion; monitor nevertheless.

High Advance warning when task must be interrupted. Teach child to estimate time required; do not permit starting a lengthy task if time is brief, unless child accepts reality of need to stop short of completion.

Source: Chess & Thomas (1992), pp. 91–92; reprinted with permission.

review of some general strategies for managing them.

Before discussing specific plans, we would caution the reader that children are viewed by parents or other caretakers as difficult for a variety of reasons; temperament may or may not be a factor. Parents and professionals must therefore have come to some certainty as to the nature of a particular child's clinical problem. Besides temperament, the problems of a "difficult" child may arise from physical deviations (such as prematurity or recurrent middle ear infections), feeding issues (such as a normally decreased appetite or a selective diet), neurological variations (such as clumsiness), developmental disorders (such as retardation or a disability in information processing), or a behavioral adjustment abnormality (such as excessive aggressiveness or opposition). The successful application of the following plan depends on the presence of the typical temperament characteristics, such as low adaptability and negative mood, and on a recognition that other concerns may also demand evaluation.

Considering the frequency of aversive behavioral style characteristics, the reader may be surprised that no sensible, practical suggestions for management appeared until the mid-1980s. The main principles of guidance contained in the advice from Carey (1986), Chess and Thomas (1986), and Turecki and Tonner (1985/1989) were quite similar, despite their independent origins in different clinical settings. All three works describe the stages of: (1) recognition of the nature of the problem by the clinician, (2) revision of the parental understanding and handling of the child, and (3) other techniques that provide relief. These three Rs—recognition, revision, and relief—constitute a simple and easily remembered outline (Carey, 1986).

Recognition of the Pattern by the Clinician or Educator

Difficult temperament or other temperament risk factors may be identified by various professionals through observations, interviews, or questionnaires. Adequate appraisal should also cover other aspects of the child and environment, especially the vulnerabilities of the parents, the impact of the temperament on the child and the parents, and the possible secondary clinical problems resulting from these interactions. If the clinician does not recognize the existence and significance of temperament differences and does not take them into account in the clinical evaluation, an opportunity for specific, appropriate counseling will be lost. The clinician, whose own understanding and tolerance of the child's behavior is limited, is likely to give advice that is ill suited to the status of the child.

Revision of Parental Understanding and Handling

Helping parents reorganize their understanding and management of the difficult child has two components: (1) general counseling to supply parents with information, perspective, and confidence, and (2) specific counseling on coping skills.

As described earlier in this chapter, parents often lack background information on temperament differences, where they come from, how they affect the child, and how they interact with and have an impact on the caretakers too. Unwarranted parental feelings of guilt, fear, and anger must be dealt with appropriately, and misplaced blame—on themselves, on foods, on the pregnancy or delivery—must be corrected.

Once the parents have revised their view of the child, the outlook for the future can be discussed realistically. Parents should know that, although there are no simple prescriptions that work for everyone, experience tells us that, with suitable rearing, children with difficult or other abrasive temperaments generally do well eventually. Parents can learn to accommodate the aversive traits to minimize conflict without compromising the child's developmental requirements. Difficult traits often diminish in strength and pervasiveness as children grow older. A bothersome behavioral style can even become an asset later, as when the annoying persistence of the toddler is redirected into problem solving in school. The maturing child can learn to understand and suppress reactions that consistently get her into conflict with the people who matter to her. Maintaining hope in these possibilities can sustain parents through the turmoil of the present, as well as encourage them to remember their child's positive features and to express affection whenever there is the slightest reason to do so.

The aim of the specific counseling with parents is to help them improve their coping skills and to alter the parent-child interaction enough to accommodate the child better and reduce or eliminate excessive stress and the possible consequence of a secondary clinical disorder. Above all else, parents can use assistance in learning to be sensitive to their child's real and enduring needs rather than to the flamboyant and possibly distorted messages he or she sends from moment to moment. Parents should strive for a degree of detachment that enables them to avoid, as much as possible, overreacting to abrasive, difficult behaviors, such as intense, negative responses. This advice applies not only to current areas of conflict and stress but also to those anticipated in the future by the parent or counselor.

If the interaction has resulted in a secondary clinical problem in the health, development, or behavior of the child, the clinician's task is to separate out the temperament risk factors from the reactive disorder. The temperament is a variation of normal, but the secondary dysfunction is not and may require further treatment, such as discipline, behavior management, or psychotherapy. For example, low adaptability is a temperament characteristic. If through unfavorable interactions the low adaptability has resulted in poor peer relations, then there is a clinical problem as well. (This connection is described in greater detail in chapter 8.)

An opportunity may arise for direct discussion between the professional and an older child. The child who is helped to understand his own behavioral style and the stresses it provokes in his personal relationships and elsewhere is in a better position to handle and avoid these adverse consequences. This goal is best achieved when the parents aid their child in monitoring himself, but health care workers and teachers can initiate and extend the process. For example, the slow-to-warm-up 10-year-old who experiences abdominal pain before stressful events at home and at school would be aided if he could learn to recognize his stomach upset as an expression of his reaction pattern and to deal with it on his own without a call to the doctor or a visit to the school nurse.

Relief for the Parents by Environmental Intervention

Caring for a temperamentally aversive child can be exhausting for even the strongest and wisest of parents. The professional advising them can perform a valuable service by offering suggestions for respite from the stress: mobilize assistance from friends and relations; place the child in day care; take occasional nights and weekends away from the house or apartment to pursue pleasant, neglected activities; participate in organized parent support groups. Parents often feel reluctant to transfer the burden of the child's care to an outsider because the challenge seems too great to give to another person. Parents in this position should be urged even more strongly to seek recreational experiences for themselves, possibly in the home but preferably outside.

A recent report (Sheeber & Johnson, 1994) describes the success of a parent support and educational group: the parents of 21 difficult three- to five-year-old children met for nine weekly seminars—each lasting between one and a half and two hours—in which temperament and management techniques were described. Afterwards the participants, as compared with controls on the waiting list, reported "greater satisfaction in their relationships with their children, feeling more competent as parents, and experiencing more attachment to their children as defined by both feelings of emotional closeness and greater understanding of the child's needs. Mothers also reported reduced levels of anxiety and depression. At follow-up mothers reported feeling less restricted by parenting demands."

Is Referral Necessary?

A fourth possible step in the management of the child with a temperamental risk factor would be referral to a mental health specialist. This step is usually unnecessary. As long as the behavior causing the concern is a normal variation of temperament, the primary care physician, nurse, or educator should be able to deal with it. Even a mild to moderately severe secondary behavioral or functional problem, such as headaches related to stress, should not automatically require the services of a specialist. Referral is indicated only when the difficult temperament is compounded by an adjustment problem that is severe (dangerous to the child or to others), chronic (of several months' duration), multisymptomatic (for instance, chronic antisocial behavior in a dysfunctional family), or unresponsive to the measures taken at the primary level.

EASY CHILDREN

Positive and adaptable children usually bring joy and a sense of accomplishment to their parents because their rearing is relatively easy. But even they can generate problems. Easy children may cause distress by accepting too readily influences contrary to the preferences of the parents, such as quickly adopting the rough language or disapproved values of a neighborhood child. Also, the care of easy children may be complicated by the mildness of their complaints. Parents must be sure to take their softly expressed reports of pain as seriously as they do the shrieks of a more intense, difficult child. These children should not be ignored because they indicate their problems less vigorously. Care must be taken not to overlook their interests when they belong to groups with members who announce their interests more stridently.

INTERVENTION TO EASE TEMPERAMENT-ENVIRONMENT DISSONANCE

The third use for temperament information in child care, beside educating parents and identifying a child's individual profile, is intervention when dissonance in the interaction is leading to reactive symptoms in the child's health, development, or behavior. For example, an unadaptable child is pushed too hard by her parents to adjust rapidly to complex situations, such as the arrival of a sibling or placement with a rigid schoolteacher, with the result that the child becomes rebellious. The main strategy for the clinician would be to suggest alternative methods of parental management to improve the fit and restore consonance.

In this particular example, the clinician might suggest that the parents allow the child more time to make the necessary adjustments to novel situations. If the intervention is successful, the reactive symptom of rebellion should disappear. But the parents must also learn to live in greater harmony with their child's temperament in order to avoid problems in the future. This technique should be called "parent counseling" because its purpose is to help them change their attitudes toward, and practices with, their child. Since the emphasis is primarily on improving the interaction rather than on directly altering the personality of the parent or child, the technique cannot properly be called psychotherapy. A child's temperament is not a "disorder" in itself and is not changed by the intervention; it can be accommodated more comfortably by revised parental care.

Besides achieving greater consonance in the parent-child interaction, other techniques may resolve the accompanying behavioral or functional symptom: environmental alterations, such as removing or moderating noxious stimuli (a punitive teacher, for example); behavioral management of the child; psychotherapy for the child; correcting parental misperceptions; and medication. The collaboration of related professionals—physicians, psychologists, educators, or others—can be critical to a successful intervention.

This chapter began with the case study of baby Jennifer, whose difficult temperament went unrecognized by both the pediatrician and the psychologist, with the result that neither of these professionals gave suitable help to the Brown family. Their services were inadequate and perhaps even harmful. The Joneses, on the other hand, enjoyed the good fortune of receiving optimal medical care. Their pediatrician (and her nurse) did recognize baby Ralph's adverse temperament traits and helped his parents to revise their thinking about their difficult baby and how they handled him and to get some relief from the strain. This markedly superior care was delivered with only a small additional expenditure of professional time.

The general principles outlined in this chapter will be applied to a variety of specific situations throughout childhood in the remaining chapters.

CHAPTER 4

The Newborn Period

INDIVIDUAL BEHAVIORAL VARIATIONS are readily noticeable even in newborn infants. Although a newborn's particular behavior patterns may not be the same as the more stable ones that appear in later weeks and months, identifying them helps the parents to deal with them. Unfortunately, Nancy and her baby received no help from professionals in understanding normal newborn behavior.

Nancy was a 24-year-old single mother. Her pregnancy went remarkably smoothly, with no complications. She was, however, living alone. The baby's father was married to somebody else and had not acknowledged the situation to his wife. Nancy's own parents, who were struggling to achieve a position of respectability in the community, had distanced themselves from Nancy and offered her no support of any kind during the pregnancy. Nancy had decided that she would rather keep the baby than have an abortion. Her uncomplicated delivery produced a healthy seven-pound boy. At first Nancy was delighted, but soon her worries began to grow. Not knowing what was normal newborn behavior and with no one to help her learn, she was perplexed and concerned about the unfamiliar activities she witnessed: the baby's frequent yawning, trembling chin, hiccups, and spitting up. Maybe there was something seriously wrong with him, she thought. During her brief hospital stay, the nurses and the physician only told her not to worry. But she did worry, because she was so completely unprepared for the experience and so bereft of supportive people in her life. She felt depressed and overwhelmed.

By contrast, the experience of Polly and Jack exemplifies optimal professional services.

Polly and her husband Jack had done well with their two girls and wanted very much to have a boy to complete their family. Their success in producing and rearing the two girls made them fully confident that their final child would be just as easy. Unfortunately, Polly went into premature labor and delivered a baby son of just under three pounds. They were alarmed by the requirement that the baby be kept in an incubator and by the fact that he was not only small but also less active, less alert, less easily stimulated, sleepier in their arms, and different from their previous babies in other ways as well. Luckily, the medical and nursing personnel were able to help them through this potentially disturbing situation. Polly and Jack were encouraged to visit their infant son frequently, to take part in his care, and to obtain from the doctors and nurses the information and skills they needed to cope with the unexpected turn of events. After many days in the hospital, Polly and Jack took their baby home with a full understanding of what his various behaviors were likely to mean and a sense of confidence that they could manage his care well on their own.

With inadequate support from medical personnel and her family, Nancy was greatly upset by normal newborn behavior and was off to a bad start in her child-rearing experience. The education and training provided to Polly and Jack, however, equipped them to comprehend and handle the extra challenge of the difficult behavioral differences displayed by their preterm baby. This chapter reviews newborn behavioral differences, their origins, their evolution, and their management by clinicians and parents.

WHAT DO WE KNOW? BEHAVIORAL DIFFERENCES LARGELY TRANSIENT BUT THEY MATTER

Individual behavioral differences are easily observed and documented in newborn humans by attentive witnesses, professional or not. For example, some newborns are more active than others, and some are more alert. They vary in how responsive they are to stimuli and in how rapidly they habituate (decrease their responses on repeated exposure) to them.

T. Berry Brazelton (1994), a leading authority on newborn behavior, states: "The individual differences in neonatal behaviors reflect the variations in genetic endowment and intrauterine influences. As the neonate responds to labor, delivery, and recovery in the new environment, we can begin to predict how new experiences and learning will affect him or her and how the infant will interact with the new environment." We question, however, the assumption that genetic factors account for a substantial portion of behavioral individuality at this time of life. This chapter includes a review of the extensive evidence that intrauterine, perinatal, and newborn factors influence temperament variability in the neonate.

Any consideration of the general effects of an influence on newborn behavior or of the factors that produce individual differences must start by presenting the widely held view that assessments of an infant's behavior should begin with a recognition of his or her state. Levels of state are variously defined but generally consist of: quiet sleep, active sleep, drowsy state, alert inactivity, fussing, and crying. State is influenced by normal environmental factors (such as handling, light, sounds, temperature), normal internal physiological needs (such as hunger, satiety, a full bladder or rectum), and pathological conditions (such as drugs, asphyxia, toxemia, and other conditions to be discussed later in this chapter). The infant's state in turn affects physiological functions, such as heart and respiratory rates, as well as visual fixation, habituation, conditioning, and crying (Hack, 1992). "If state is accounted for, most of the infant's reactions to negative and positive stimuli from internal and external sources are predictable" (Brazelton, 1994).

GENETIC FACTORS IN NEWBORN BEHAVIOR

In chapter 2, we presented a review of the research data on the genetic effects on temperament in the newborn period. To recapitulate, despite the indications that 50% of the variance in temperament in later childhood is accounted for by genetic effects, little confirmation has been presented to date that these differences are expressed in the newborn period. The only exception is one study (which has not been replicated) that demonstrated that female newborns are more irritable than males (Riese, 1986); this difference has not been reported to endure past the newborn period. Either genetic influences are weakly represented then because of the limited repertory of neonatal behaviors or they are crowded out by the more transient intrauterine and perinatal influences. Or perhaps researchers have been measuring the wrong behaviors. In any case, the expression of the genes becomes more prominent during the weeks and months after birth.

PREGNANCY, PERINATAL, AND NEWBORN INFLUENCES ON BEHAVIOR

Prematurity

About 6% of newborn babies in the United States weigh less than 2,500 grams (five and a half pounds), the rate being double for African-Americans what it is for whites. Premature infants have shorter and less defined sleep cycles and display less auditory and visual habituation, less use of soothing, and different cry characteristics (Brazelton, 1994). They are also less active, less alert, less responsive to stimuli—including intrusive medical procedures—and, paradoxically, more sensitive to the same stimuli under some circumstances. These physiological distress signals of sensory overload include grimacing, gaze aversion, cyanosis (turning blue), and tachypnea (rapid breathing) (Gorski, 1992). Some of this behavioral disorganization may continue to be found in healthy premature infants even when they have reached their due dates (Als, Duffy, & McAnulty, 1988), but it is seen most often in those with chronic lung disease.

By the time of discharge from the newborn nursery and during the first year, the behavioral differences in premature infants, as compared with full-term infants, have been described as being more irritable and less responsive and having aberrant sleep and feeding patterns. The premature infant's cry may not be quantitatively greater, but it has a unique high-frequency quality that makes it more irritating and worrisome to parents. A continuing neurological immaturity of the preterm infant results often in reduced eye contact, greater passivity, delayed social smiling, and dislike of cuddling. Feeding and sleeping irregularities may stem from a combination of neurological immaturity and difficulty determining the appropriate timing and amount of stimulation (for further details, see Bernbaum & Hoffman-Williamson, 1991, chap. 12). These behavioral differences are likely to disappear during the early weeks and months of postnatal life, but the rate and sequence of such normalization is not well enough documented to report here.

SGA

The newborn infant who is small for gestational age (SGA) in addition to being premature may be different in other ways from the full-term (appropriate for gestational age, or AGA) infant. One line of evidence maintains that "infants with atypical patterns of fetal growth showed lower scores than did infants of appropriate growth on the NBAS [Newborn Behavioral Assessment Scale] orientation, motor, and reflex clusters and on 15 of the 18 supplementary scores" (Lester, Garcia-Coll, Valcarcel, Hoffman, & Brazelton, 1986). On the other hand, a comparison of temperament differences in the newborn period between SGA and AGA infants from the same twin pairs uncovered none of significance for preterm or full-term infants, except that full-term SGA infants were less irritable than full-term AGA infants (Riese, 1988). In a larger study of 70 pairs of full-term twins who were at least 15% discordant for birth weight, "the larger twin of the pair was more irritable, more difficult to soothe, more active while awake, more active during sleep, less reactive to visual and auditory stimuli and less reinforcing to the examiner than the smaller cotwin" (Riese, 1994). The explanation for the apparent discrepancy in these conclusions probably lies primarily in the fact that SGA infants are not a uniform population and differences in sampling will lead to varying results.

Very little research information is available concerning the evolution of newborn temperament differences into the subsequent months and years of life. Countless parents have witnessed and described the continuity or change in behavioral style of their premature infants, but little has been done to document the process with scientific rigor. One of the obstacles has been the absence until very recently of a means of measuring temperament during the first few months of life (Medoff-Cooper, Carey, & McDevitt, 1993). The presently available studies of the later course of temperament in premature infants do not begin until about six months.

When temperament is assessed by parent report from six months on, premature infants who have had an uncomplicated course are apparently no different from the general population as late as six years of age (Oberklaid, Sewell, Sanson, & Prior, 1991; Ross, 1987). However, the lower the birth weight and the greater the complications, the greater the risk that the child will emerge not only with cognitive and neuromuscular deficits but also with a decreased attention span (Hawdon, Hey, Kolvin, & Fundudis, 1990). A detailed investigation of 66 children who had been prematurely born found them to be more temperamentally difficult only if they had either localizing or nonfocal neurological signs (Hertzig, 1983). Prematurity may present an increased risk but not a certainty of aversive differences in behavioral style. Furthermore, the less favorable differences may moderate with time, as shown by a study of 41 infants of very low birth weight in which 32% were rated as temperamentally difficult at six months (corrected) but only the expected percentage of 12% were so rated at 12 months (Medoff-Cooper, 1986).

Several methodological problems have beset investigations in this area. Subject groups are not always defined in the same way. Control groups have not always been chosen carefully enough to allow meaningful comparisons. Also, the science and practice of neonatology have made enormous strides in the last 25 years, resulting in alterations in the details of management and outcome even within the same study population.

Obstetrical and Maternal Medical Complications

A multitude of obstetrical factors have been reported to affect newborn behavior. It is not possible to review exhaustively all the evidence presented in the professional literature. Such an attempt would push us far beyond the scope of this book. Furthermore, since most of these studies either do not extend their observations after the newborn period or have been unable to separate out the influence of confounding pre- and postnatal factors, it is often impossible to say whether the behavioral differences observed are attributable to the suspected cause or are of lasting importance. Obstetrical and maternal medical conditions that may be related to newborn behavior include: maternal diet, toxemia, hypertension, diabetes, intrauterine infection, and cesarean section.

Brain Hemorrhage

A perinatal complication increasingly found to affect behavior long after the newborn period is intraventricular hemorrhage in the premature neonate, particularly on the right side of the brain (Nass & Koch, 1987).

Such infants were less sociable and more difficult to soothe at three months post-term (Garcia-Coll et al., 1988). At one year of age, a group of six infants with pre- or perinatal unilateral focal brain damage on the right "showed marked affective impairment to positive, but not to negative, stimulation, when compared with age and gender matched controls who had comparable damage on the left side" (Reilly, Stiles, Larsen, & Trauner, 1994).

Maternal Drug Use

The maternal complication that has received the most intensive study is drug use and abuse during pregnancy. The substances most widely evaluated are cigarette smoke, alcohol, and cocaine. Despite the mounting evidence that these and other substances may be deleterious to the health and behavior of neonates and older children, firm conclusions are impeded by great methodological barriers. Often more than one potentially noxious substance is being taken in, making it hard to determine which effects are coming from the substance under study. Malnutrition and a variety of social stressors can further obscure specific causal relations. The time of use during pregnancy and the duration and magnitude of dosage must also be taken into consideration. Even when fetuses are exposed to the same amounts of the same offending agent, they can display different outcomes as infants.

Smoking

Although smoking during pregnancy is clearly established as a health problem for both mother and child, the possible effects on behavior in the newborn and older child remain uncertain (Naeye, 1992). A report from New Zealand that demonstrated a relationship between smoking during pregnancy (but not afterwards) and "small but detectable increases in the risks of problem behaviors" in middle childhood did not assess temperament as a possible intervening variable, either in early infancy or later (Fergusson, Horwood, & Lynskey, 1993b).

Alcohol

Fetal alcohol syndrome and fetal alcohol effects have been recognized and investigated since 1973. In addition to suffering from a range of major and minor physical defects and potential cognitive deficits, children whose mothers drank during pregnancy are reported to be more irritable than normal in infancy and to be more likely to develop attentional dysfunction during childhood (American Academy of Pediatrics, 1993). Studies have not yet documented a consistent appearance of this irritability in newborns who are not ill with physical complications.

Cocaine

The recent epidemic of cocaine and crack cocaine abuse during pregnancy has generated much clinical concern and confusion. In a comprehensive review of this vast literature, Volpe (1992) reached these conclusions about its neonatal neurologic and neurophysiologic features:

> A minority of infants exposed to cocaine have a neonatal neurologic syndrome characterized by abnormal sleep patterns, tremor, poor feeding, irritability, and occasionally, seizures; it is not severe, is most evident on the second day of life, and is relatively short-lasting. Newborns exposed in utero to cocaine also have abnormal electroencephalographic and brain-stem auditory evoked responses that disappear after one to six months.

Another review (Hawley & Disney, 1992) advises caution:

> Nevertheless, perinatal complications such as these do not inevitably lead to developmental delay or other dysfunctions. It is important, therefore, to avoid extrapolating from what cocaine-exposed children look like in the first few weeks after birth to predictions of the problems they might have as preschoolers and beyond. Existing measures of neonate and infant neurobehavior simply do not have this kind of predictive power.

More recent reviews continue to urge the same caution about making premature judgments (Gonzalez & Campbell, 1994; Zuckerman & Frank, 1994).

Maternal Feelings, Thoughts, and Behavior in Pregnancy

An abundant stock of folklore encourages us to believe that how a mother thinks and feels during pregnancy has an important impact on the behavior of the newborn child and later. Few studies have supported this assumption. Two recent investigations found more inconsolable, excessive crying in newborn infants of mothers who had been depressed during pregnancy (Zuckerman, Bauchner, Parker, & Cabral, 1990), and more crying during the standard neurobehavioral assessment in infants whose mothers had been classified with a Type A personality (Parker & Barrett, 1992). Whether these possible relationships are genetic, hormonal, or attributable to some other influence remains to be clarified.

During the course of a pregnancy, and especially in the eighth and ninth months, parents form fantasies of what their child will be like. These diverse images are derived from several sources, such as prior experience, reports of friends and relatives, reading material, and wishful thinking. Some observers have suggested that the ideas a mother forms of her infant's behavior before delivery ("internal working models") persist after delivery, deeply color her ratings of the infant's temperament, and perhaps even affect her behavior toward the infant to the extent that the fantasy becomes realized (Zeanah & Anders, 1987). The subsequent course of these fantasies has not been adequately documented but appears to consist mainly of a reshaping of the mother's image of the child under the influence of the actual behavior observed in the newborn and later.

Newborn Conditions

A variety of other conditions can affect the behavior of newborns and induce at least temporary variations: a transient disorganization of behavior after cesarean section; less responsiveness due to obstetrical medications; drowsiness when the mother is diabetic; decreased alertness during phototherapy for hyperbilirubinemia (newborn jaundice); and sleepiness and unavailability for social interaction after circumcision (Dixon & Stein, 1992). In chapter 2, we mentioned the small alterations in behavior that may be related to different types of feedings and the possible behavioral effects on infants of drugs ingested by the mother via her breast milk. Finally, we must acknowledge that the nursing care necessary for medical management of premature infants can be quite demanding for the infant and may inadvertently produce behavioral disorganization (Sell, Hill-Mangan, & Holberg, 1992).

TECHNIQUES FOR NEWBORN BEHAVIORAL ASSESSMENT

The New York Longitudinal Study (NYLS) group (Thomas, Chess, Birch, Hertzig, & Korn, 1963) began its temperament determinations in infants at about three months of age. The interview technique they used depended on descriptions of patterns by the parents, who had by then considerable experience caring for their children. This method worked well for these postnatal determinations, but success could not be expected in applying it to newborn infants. Parents have not had enough time to observe the typical reactions of their newborn infant, if they are established by then, and are often too tired or excited to be helpful witnesses. No technique has yet been designed for examining the NYLS temperament dimensions in the newborn period. Given the methodological problems, it seems unlikely that any such technique will be developed, unless one that relies on long periods of professional observations could be devised. It might also utilize and organize parental observations during prolonged newborn stays, as in the case of prematurity.

The Neonatal Behavioral Assessment Scale (NBAS) (Brazelton, 1973/1984) consists of 28 behavioral items, each scored on a nine-point scale, aimed at measuring the coping capacities and adaptive strategies of the newborn. "The test was expected to reflect the infant's inborn characteristics and behavioral responses that had been shaped by the intrauterine environment" (Brazelton, 1994). The developers of the scale hoped that a single assessment would suffice to give an adequate picture of the inborn behavioral characteristics of the newborn and allow reliable predictions of future behavior. Only small amounts of agreement were achieved, however, by repeated applications of the scale (Sameroff, 1978). This evidence of instability led to the revised view that the pattern of change is the most valuable information to be obtained from the use of the scale. Ideally, with measurements at ages two to three days, seven to ten days, and one month, a curve of recovery from the stresses of labor and delivery and adjustment to the demands of the extrauterine environment can be established (Brazelton, 1994). The scale has proved to be of great value in assessing the condition of newborn infants with problems like drug withdrawal but has not established itself as the definitive way to determine the enduring congenital components of temperament. Furthermore, it should be noted that only some of the behaviors assessed, such as irritability and consolability, can be considered temperament; others, such as motor responses and muscle tone, clearly are not. The trained, experienced tester takes at least 20 minutes to perform the examination.

The Assessment of Preterm Infants' Behavior (APIB) (Als, Lester, Tronick, & Brazelton, 1982) is a modification of the NBAS that assesses behavioral competence independent of the infant's gestational age at birth. The Newborn Individualized Developmental Care and Assessment Program (NID-CAP) (Als & Gibes, 1984) is a clinical adaptation of the APIB.

Two additional techniques for determining individual differences in the newborn period have appeared in the research literature. For the study of the neonatal behavior of twins, Marilyn Riese (1983) has produced and reported a system for rating the five dimensions of irritability, resistance to soothing, reactivity, reinforcement value, and activity. Michael Lewis (1992) has described a method for evaluating responses to stress in the three categories of threshold, dampening, and reactivation.

Two other newborn behavior tests devised by Frances Graham in 1956 and Judy Rosenblith in 1961 have seldom been used in research and probably not at all clinically. Other scales developed by Annelise Korner and her colleagues and by L. M. S. and V. Dubowitz are measures of maturity more than of temperament.

In conclusion, no formal scale for measuring temperament in the newborn period that is both appropriate in content and practical for routine clinical use has been established.

STABILITY OF INDIVIDUAL DIFFERENCES IN NEWBORNS

In chapter 2, we made the point that, whatever we may say about the stability of individual differences at later ages, temperament, at least as measured at present, has not been shown to be more than slightly stable in the newborn period. Most of the studies have compared results of the Brazelton NBAS performed in the days after birth with later determinations that use the same instrument (Sameroff, 1978) or shift to laboratory observations or parent questionnaires assessing different dimensions. Correlations have been of a low order or nonexistent. This is not to say that no continuity whatever can be demonstrated. (Pertinent reports are reviewed in chapter 2.)

The principal reason for raising this issue again here is to emphasize that many of the factors that influence individual behavioral differences in the newborn are transient and should not necessarily be expected to remain observable. Earlier in this chapter, we reviewed the great scope and variety of these factors. Some, like obstetrical medications, can be expected to wear off soon after birth. Others, such as the effects of an intraventricular hemorrhage, may or may not remain evident. Those of the severity of fetal alcohol syndrome offer a less favorable prognosis. Our point here is that the variable outlook for these influences makes predictions of behavioral style from the newborn period extremely difficult. Clinicians who make excessively gloomy predictions in the newborn nursery are neither supportive to the parents nor technically accurate.

In the midst of this theoretical discussion of the question of stability of newborn temperament characteristics, we should not lose sight of the fact that the behavior exhibited by the newborn *at the time* is what the professional caretakers and the parents must deal with whether it persists or not. Even when they know that a behavioral pattern will not persist, the behavior itself matters in the present for both the family and the infant. The clinician can discuss management strategies without making pessimistic predictions.

There are many ways in which a newborn behavior pattern matters to the infant, such as when the infant's sleepiness from obstetrical medication or a temporary behavioral disorganization after a cesarean section interferes with the start of breast-feeding. A less common but more dramatic example occurs when very low-birth-weight preterm infants are handled in ways that fail to be cognizant and respectful of their level of stimulus tolerance and result in less favorable respiratory status and feeding compared with individualized care (Als et al., 1986; Als et al., 1994).

In chapter 2, we described the ongoing impact on the parents of a child's temperament. This interaction begins, of course, as soon as the child is born. The newborn's characteristics have been shown to influence parental behavior as early as the second day of life. In one study, for example, not only were irritable infants soothed the most, but alert ones received the most nurturant and social contact, and active ones the least contact (Breitmayer & Ricciuti, 1988). If the parents cannot learn soon after delivery to observe correctly their infant's behavioral individuality, to understand it, and to respond to it appropriately, the resulting failure in their handling not only can lead to clinical problems for the infant but also may affect how the parents think and feel about themselves.

WHAT CAN WE DO? AIDING THE START OF THE PARENT-INFANT RELATIONSHIP

Chapter 3 outlined an approach to using general information and specific data about temperament to help parents deal with their children's individual differences. These principles start being useful immediately in the newborn period.

EDUCATION

Sources of parental education about newborn care in general and newborn behavior in particular are numerous these days throughout this country. The parents' own experience with small infants in their families or social circles is a good basis for this knowledge. There are many books and films that present information about what to expect in general, and a few mention the range of normal behavior. Prenatal classes usually include instruction in the standard care and typical behavior of the healthy newborn infant.

In spite of all these ways to educate themselves, however, parents arrive at this exciting point in their lives with highly varied and frequently insufficient amounts of preparation. Some new parents are well informed and equipped for their new adventure; others have only the most fragmentary understanding of the complexities of their new task. Many young adults begin their careers as parents with limited appreciation of the new stresses they are likely to encounter, such as sleep deprivation, emotional changes, and numerous disruptions of life as they have known it. Similarly, their understanding of infant behavior may be far from complete. This chapter began with the story of Nancy, a single mother with very little support of any sort who was so unready for her childbirth and parenting experience that she was frightened by her infant's normal behavior. No indoctrination is quite as thorough as prior experience, but even a multiparous mother may not be set for the unique challenges of a new baby if the family is troubled with social or financial adversities or the baby presents unexpected or unfamiliar difficulties.

Consequently, a major responsibility for parent education resides with all the professionals charged with assisting them at this time: physicians, nurses, and health educators. In addition to all the necessary details about such matters as feeding techniques and care of the navel, these professionals should help parents acquire a basic understanding of normal newborn behavior and the variations they are likely to encounter and should give them information about the more enduring phenomenon of temperament. For example, missing from most parent education is any reference to the average amount and normal range of crying to be expected in healthy infants or to the fact that some infants are more sensitive and irritable than others. Even without discussing the particular characteristics of the individual infant, the professional should be sure that parents are aware of the transient nature of much of newborn behavior; jitteriness or sleepiness in the newborn period does not necessarily develop into a lifelong trait. Newborn behavior is the preface to the book more than the table of contents (Bell, Weller, & Waldrop, 1971).

IDENTIFICATION

Newborn nurseries vary widely in how they assist parents in appreciating differences in infant states and understanding the behavioral individuality of their infants. No figures are available, but it would be fair to guess that in most nurseries little of this sort of help is provided. With the average newborn stay having shrunk from five days to about one or two in the last generation, owing mainly to pressures from insurance companies, the time available for such evaluations has just about disappeared.

Of the various tests of neurobehavioral function in the newborn period, the Neonatal Behavioral Assessment Scale (Brazelton, 1973/1984) is the best known and the most widely used. Some idealistic writers have urged that every newborn infant be given an NBAS rating because of its potential educational and diagnostic value. Administering this test has not become a routine practice for several reasons, the primary one being that the whole standard newborn physical examination takes less time than the 20 minutes required to perform the NBAS properly (Britt & Myers, 1994). A more effective use of this scale might be as a preventive measure in situations of unusual social stress (Nugent & Brazelton, 1989), with preterm infants (Widmayer & Field, 1981), or with infants identified by the nursing staff as difficult to manage. In any case, the NBAS is often the first test through which parents (and professionals) become aware of the existence, significance, and measurement of individual differences.

In the regular newborn nursery for full-term infants, any routine assessment of behavioral individuality by a formal test remains an impractical luxury. Nevertheless, skilled nurses and physicians can help attentive and interested parents make the most of the brief time together there by exchanging their observations and impressions of the infant. They can describe behaviors they have noticed and share information about the patterns displayed; nurses especially can offer guidance as to how best to respond to them. Even in a nursery stay of only one or two days, patterns of sensitivity, irritability, or soothability may be evident. In particular, nurses can demonstrate how to tolerate irritability and suggest strategies for managing it. Parents can be helped greatly by starting to learn to differentiate the various cries of hunger, fatigue, and discomfort. Soothing techniques suited to their particular infant can be demonstrated.

The longer hospitalization of the low-birth-weight infant allows more opportunity for professional observations and parental learning, and sometimes this opportunity is taken. The medical and nursing staff find it not only more possible but more necessary to identify the infant's unique behavioral characteristics. As mentioned earlier, sensitive individualization of the premature infant's management in the intensive care unit—that is, preventing inappropriate sensory input—results in less time on the respirator and better feeding behavior. Since doing the Brazelton examination or the Assessment of Preterm Infants' Behavior requires special training by a certified teacher, the practical clinical use of these tests has been minimal. However, the NID-CAP, the clinical adaptation, has been gaining in favor and use. Also, skilled and experienced newborn nursery nurses generally know their patients well and can make the necessary adjustments. They can help parents understand their infants by offering their observations and impressions, as well as by letting the parents participate in the infant's care and learn from their own observations. The parents of premature infants need guidance in appreciating that signs of immaturity of the nervous system, such as grimaces and gaze aversion, are not their fault and they should not feel distressed by them. For the sake of the developing parent-child relationship, these behaviors must not be misinterpreted as abnormality or as signs of rejection of the parents. The case study at the beginning of this chapter about Jack and Polly and their premature son is an example of how professional newborn services can work well to help parents recognize and meet the particular needs of their newborn child, especially when, as with prematurity, those needs are extraordinary.

INTERVENTION

Our concern here is with situations in which the behavioral characteristics of the newborn have resulted in a clinical problem and the nurse or physician wishes to intercede to improve the interaction and thus the outcome. As with older children, little can be done to change the reaction characteristics of the neonate; the remedial strategy must alter the attitudes of and handling by the professional and parental caretakers.

With both premature infants and full-term infants who were unusually stressed during delivery, it is important to make some evaluation of the state and reactivity of the infant. Careful observation of the infant's color, respirations, and alertness gives the clinician an idea of the infant's threshold for stimuli and at what point the infant is being overloaded. As mentioned earlier, an individualization of the infant's handling based on the observed reaction pattern can result in less stress for the infant and an improvement in weight gain, sensory integrity, and functional outcome. The interested reader will find more details of this strategy in the recent reviews of this growing literature (Brazelton, 1994; Gorski, 1992; Hack, 1992; Medoff-Cooper, 1994). We can emphasize the high probability that after discharge the infant will gradually become easier to manage in the near future.

An intervention is equally desirable when the newborn infant is normal but the parents are having trouble identifying, understanding, or tolerating some normal variant of behavior. Perhaps because of inexperience or psychosocial problems, the parents may be responding inappropriately to the individual needs of the infant and causing physiological disorganization, such as excessive crying or vomiting from overstimulation. After observing the infant and the parents both separately and together, the astute clinician will usually find a way fairly rapidly to help the parents modify their handling to make the infant more comfortable. Some proponents of the Brazelton scale urge that letting the parents watch the performance of the examination demonstrates the infant's abilities as nothing else can. Others find that less formal procedures achieve the same end.

Finally, as mentioned in chapter 3, an essential part of the professional's aid to parents in coping with challenging individual behaviors is helping them find relief through adequate rest, recreation, and support.

CHAPTER 5

General Parental Care: Infants, Toddlers, and Preschoolers

VARIATIONS IN CHILDREN'S TEMPERAMENTS make it impossible for parents to apply the same principles of child rearing to all their children with uniform results. They must make allowances for differences in their children's reaction styles: What is just right for one child may be ineffective or even abrasive for another. Parents may first encounter such variation when their second child proves from the very beginning to be quite dissimilar from their first one. Sarah's parents had such an experience.

Baby Sarah turned out to be rather different from her older brother, Jeffrey, who had been easy for his parents to manage. Shortly after taking Sarah home from the hospital, her parents realized that she was not going to be just another Jeff. Unlike Jeff, Sarah was highly sensitive to sounds, light, and touch. She cried and fussed more frequently and was harder to soothe when upset. Management strategies that had worked so well with Jeff proved ineffective with Sarah. Her parents usually found it hard to figure out what she needed; they decided that the best course of action was to pick her up and carry her as much as possible. This strategy did not work well, and Sarah's distress increased to the point where she was crying and fussing for six hours a day. Her parents were deeply disturbed by this situation and wondered what had gone wrong. They were feeling guilty about such incidents as the mother drinking one glass of sherry before she knew she was pregnant. His parents' preoccupation was confusing and disruptive even for the flexible young Jeffrey. A visit to the pediatrician confirmed that there was no physical problem with little Sarah and that it was "only colic." The doctor suggested a change in formula and remarked that the problem was not at all serious because it would clear up by itself by three months. With the new formula, Sarah did cry less for the next two days but then went back to the previous pattern. By three and a half months, her total crying time was down to only an hour a day, but she continued to be sensitive and irritable. Her colic was soon replaced by the problem of frequent awakenings with crying during the night. Her parents felt overwhelmed by the challenges Sarah presented.

Sarah, a temperamentally different infant, was poorly understood by her parents and by the pediatrician, and the medical advice was not at all helpful. On the other hand, the interpretation and handling of Debbie, who had perplexed her parents because of her different way of utilizing parental stimulation, was appropriate.

The Bryants were worried about their daughter Debbie. At 17 months, she was still not walking. Their family physician had been assuring them that she was completely normal, but still they were concerned. Every other child on their block was walking by about one year. Their older child, Bert, had started at 10 months. Discussion with the nurse-practitioner who performed developmental assessments in the doctor's office revealed that Debbie was doing everything else on schedule. In fact, in speech she was somewhat advanced, already saying simple three-word sentences, something her brother had not done until he was well over two years old. The parents were reassured to learn that speech acquisition is a much better measure of developmental status than gross motor achievements like walking. Debbie was a physically normal, apparently bright child, but not a particularly energetic one. She invested little energy in physical accomplishments and preferred to sit and chatter rather than to crawl about. One day, when Mrs. Bryant was cleaning up a spill on the kitchen floor, Debbie got up from her play and toddled across the floor to her mother, saying, "Debbie help Mommy." The parents were delighted by both the physical accomplishment and the positive sentiment she expressed.

Debbie's parents had not known about temperament's effect on the achievement of developmental milestones, but their health care adviser had made sense of it for them and given them reassurance that proved to be justified. Debbie was not understimulated, as one of the grandmothers had hinted, but was simply utilizing her parental stimulation differently.

This chapter discusses the ways children's temperaments may affect parental efforts to meet their physical, developmental, and behavioral needs, either facilitating or complicating the process. It offers suggestions for helping parents make appropriate adjustments to their thinking and handling in order to achieve a better fit with their child's particular requirements.

WHAT DO WE KNOW? EMERGENCE AND STABILIZATION OF TEMPERAMENT DIFFERENCES

In the previous chapter, we described the clinically important but often unstable behavioral differences that first appear in the newborn period. This chapter takes the reader through the next several years, the periods generally described as infancy, toddlerhood, and the preschool years, up to the start of formal education in kindergarten.

In chapter 4, we pointed out that the individual differences in behavior detected in the first days of life are largely a reflection of the conditions of the pregnancy and the perinatal period. In view of these origins, we should not expect initial manifestations of individuality to be strongly enduring. Current evidence indicates that behavior observed in the newborn period correlates only weakly with later behavior and that the continuities with newborn behavior diminish over time. As these transient effects wear off, they are replaced by more lasting individual differences. We do not know how and when the genetic effects first appear, but surely they are detectable in the early weeks of life and perhaps even to a limited degree in the newborn period. Just how this transition occurs is not well documented. Newborn behavior has been studied extensively, as has behavior from three months on, but the pattern of transition from one phase to the next is largely unexplored; what we know derives largely from the impressions of observant clinicians.

Similarly, there are insufficient data at this time to allow us to report at what point the genetically determined temperament characteristics become significantly stable. Available evidence indicates that stabilization begins in the early months of life and increases over time.

THE SHIFTING CLINICAL SIGNIFICANCE OF BEHAVIORAL STYLE DIFFERENCES

The increase in stability of temperament characteristics in this period does not necessarily increase or lessen their importance to child-adult interactions; nor does stabilization ensure that the significant areas of interaction will not change. What matters, as detailed in chapter 2, is the goodness of fit at the time, the consonance between the temperament (with its varying strength and durability), the other characteristics of the child, and the components of the environment.

At no other time in childhood is there a greater likelihood that the factors involved in the fit will shift. With increasing age, the same characteristic may take on a different meaning. For example, high distractibility, defined largely in terms of soothability in infancy, is generally regarded as a desirable trait in the first year, but in the school-age child, an inability to focus her attention can be an unwelcome obstacle to the completion of tasks. Persistence in the toddler can make his household explorations a recurring drain on the patience of the parent, yet the same trait in the young student can lead to academic accomplishment and earn praise from the teacher. A low sensory threshold can make an infant more vulnerable to the environmental stimuli that produce physiological disorganization, colicky crying, or a sleep disturbance, but as she matures, greater receptivity to environmental messages can enrich her experiences and promote cognitive development. Also affecting the influence of temperament during these first years is the child's interactions with a range of caretakers and subcultures: two different parents, a variety of substitute caretakers in the home and elsewhere, neighbors and friends, and eventually the whole new world of the educational system.

Our experience with standardization of our five questionnaires, covering ages one month through 12 years, has been that parents, at least the groups of them included in these surveys, shift in their reports of the most troublesome temperament characteristics (see table 5.1). Throughout the entire period, they told us that negative mood is especially annoying to them. During the first year, negative mood and low distractibility (or soothability) are cited as the two most difficult traits. Low distractibility then disappears as a source of friction, but high distractibility returns in the elementary school years as a problem in evaluations by teachers. In the toddler and preschool years, the difficult child syndrome, as described in the New York Longitudinal Study, achieves its period of clearest prominence; low adaptability, low approach, and high intensity join negative mood in the list of characteristics parents find hardest to manage. As the process of education begins, high activity and low persistence/attention span become sources of interactional stress.

Table 5.1
Characteristics Parents Find Hardest to Manage in Their Children

First Year	1–3 Years	3–7 Years*	8–12 Years
Negative mood, low distractibility (low soothability)	Low adaptability, negative mood, intensity, high activity, withdrawing	Low adaptability, low persistence, high activity, withdrawing, negative mood	Negative mood, low adaptability, low persistence, high activity, withdrawing

*Since the standardization for this age group did not include parental overall judgments of difficulty, these data are ratings by parents of children whose teachers were complaining about them. Source: Carey, McDevitt, & Baker (1979), p. 768.

Low rhythmicity does not appear on any of these lists, in spite of the clinical impression that it should. However, in our 8- to 12-year-old scale, the revision of low rhythmicity as low predictability does attract the unfavorable notice of parents. By that stage of middle childhood, negative mood and low adaptability have become established as the traits parents find most difficult to manage; perhaps they retain this prominence through the adolescent years and into adulthood. Despite the documented role of low sensory threshold in infant colic and sleep disturbances, parents do not complain about it much at any time. Comparable evaluations by teachers are described in chapter 9.

The Kaiser Permanente Group (Cameron, Rice, Hansen, & Rosen, 1994) has found some other combinations of characteristics particularly troublesome for parents: the high-intensity, slow-adapting child; the high-activity, slow-adapting child; and the sensitive, intense, withdrawing child (see appendix 4).

IMPACT OF TEMPERAMENT DIFFERENCES ON PARENTAL CARE

Before describing how a child's temperament supports or interferes with parental caretaking plans and interactions, we should first review the various dimensions of parental care. The parent's role in meeting a child's needs has been conceptualized several different ways. We find it most suitable here to think of the tasks of child care as satisfying the following requirements: (1) meeting a child's physical needs by supplying protection, food, housing, and health care; (2) meeting developmental, behavioral, and emotional needs by providing stimulation, guidance, and affection; and (3) meeting socialization needs by providing and teaching social relationships—both intrafamilial and extrafamilial (Ludwig & Rostain, 1992).

Rather than take the conventional approach of starting with problems in the child and working backwards to the causes in the child and family, we begin by describing these parental tasks and how a child's temperament may or may not be consonant with the specific objective. The clinical problems that may result are only mentioned here; we discuss them in greater detail later, especially in chapters 7 and 8.

Physical Needs: Food

No child care activity brings parent and young child together more than the act of feeding. At the outset, the child is totally dependent on the parent to supply the right kind and amount of nourishment in a manner and at times that are appropriate for the child. To facilitate this process, the parents must have some knowledge of suitable substances to provide and be able to read more or less correctly their infant's signals of hunger and satiety. In most circumstances, the infant emits cries of fitting intensity, character, and timing to evoke from the parents the offer of proper amounts of the foods required for maintenance and normal growth. A dysfunctional inadequacy of feeding may result in undernourishment or even failure to thrive; a dysfunctional overfeeding may lead to obesity or to bottle-mouth dental caries. Few clinical studies have been done to explore in detail this complex set of relationships.

Underfeeding

Some evidence suggests that some parents are less likely to feed an irrita- ble child—who may offer the caretaker less gratification for this time-con- suming procedure—but we can find documentation of this phenomenon only in the extreme. Theoretically, however, any temperament pattern might interfere with arousing and motivating the parent to provide appro- priate nourishment.

On the other hand, undernourishment may occur when the infant is unusually mild and uncomplaining to the point that a parent, especially one preoccupied with other problems, finds it easier to ignore the hunger cries. Although this possibility remains to be documented in ordinary liv- ing situations, it has been vividly demonstrated in harsh circumstances (see the discussion of starvation conditions in East Africa in chapter 7). The apparent paradox here may best be resolved by the conclusion that the interactional consonance of the feeding relationship is what counts. The child must be able to arouse the parent to sufficient involvement in feeding; the parent must receive sufficient cues from the child and grati- fication from the process to perform the task well.

Overfeeding

The best guide parents have as to how much food to give is their child's display of signs of satiety, such as turning the face away from the spoon or stopping sucking at the breast or bottle. If these messages are insuffi- ciently clear to inform the parent correctly and to override any precon- ceived ideas as to how much the child needs, there is some risk that the parent will coax an excess of food into the child. An irritable infant is par- ticularly likely to confuse the parent into thinking that hunger is still pres- ent and must be attended to. The consequent excessive weight gain and obesity are described in chapter 7.

Besides leading to obesity, immoderately providing a bottle to quiet an irritable infant may have other health consequences. Some parents allow their children to carry about with them or take to bed a bottle of juice or milk. This attempt to satisfy the complaining child may result in major decay of the upper central teeth, a condition called bottle-mouth caries (as described in chapter 7).

Other Feeding Problems

The child's temperament affects feeding interactions in many other ways. The infant with low biological rhythmicity feels and expresses hunger unpredictably, often confusing and annoying the parents. Infants with low approach and adaptability show these traits largely in feeding patterns in the early months of life: they are slow to accept new foods or changes in flavor, consistency, temperature, timing, place, or person doing the feeding. Distractible children may interrupt the process when ambient sights or sounds are competing for attention. Active babies present a moving target for parental efforts. Fussy infants, those who display intense and negative behavior, may mislead parents into thinking that the current feeding, whether breast or formula, is qualitatively inappropriate and must be changed, despite evidence that the child is physically thriving and showing none of the typical signs of milk allergy or lactose intolerance.

Physical Needs: Protection

Human infants are born into this world completely dependent on their parents for protection against the dangers it presents. These perils range from falls out of beds or off of tables to assaults by various predators. Underprotection means not providing, at the very least, a safe environment, one free of pests and toxins, and can extend as far as parents failing to shield a child from physical, sexual, or psychological abuse by themselves, other members of the household, or other caretakers. Overprotective parents, by contrast, are excessively concerned about their child's health and safety, for any of a multitude of reasons.

Protection from Injury

Earlier views of the origins of childhood accidents blamed all accidents either on the parents' inattentiveness or on the child's "accident proneness," which was thought to induce injury regardless of the circumstances. The current consensus of persons in accident prevention investigation is that diverse factors in the child, the caretakers, and the general environment are likely to contribute to an accident. The role of temperament in childhood injuries is treated more fully in chapter 7. Whatever may be the child characteristics most often associated with accidents, it is increasingly clear that some children are harder for their parents to protect from injury than others. Accident prevention plans must not ignore these contributions from the child.

Protection from Abuse

Child abuse is defined in different terms in each state, but we usually mean "injury of a child by a parent or other caregiver either deliberately or by omission" (Ludwig & Rostain, 1992). As with accidents, the current view of the causes of child abuse accounts for factors in the parents, the child, and the situation. Child-abusing parents tend to be lonely, unhappy, angry adults undergoing major stress. They injure their children in a burst of anger after being provoked by some misbehavior. Often they themselves experienced physical abuse as children. They are likely to believe that all misbehavior is deliberate and that severe punishment is necessary to teach children respect for authority.

The occurrence of physical abuse requires not only the particular parent but also a specific child and occasion. The child often has characteristics that make him or her provocative, such as negativism or a difficult temperament; some of the more offensive misbehaviors are intractable crying, wetting, soiling, and spilling. The occasion initiating the abuse is usually a family crisis; the most common crises include loss of a job or home, marital strife or upheavals, birth of a sibling, or physical exhaustion. (Schmitt & Krugman, 1992)

The child's contribution can be temperamental difficulty or any other stylistic trait that the parents find uncongenial or discordant. It can also be a nontemperamental difference, such as prematurity, a physical disability, or developmental delay. It is also possible that the child is provocative and oppositional as the result of prior abuse rather than owing to a long-established temperamental predisposition. Thus, the role of the child should be thought of as the last straw that makes an intolerable burden for the already seriously overstressed caretaker. Studies of abused children are reported in chapter 7.

Fortunately, not all the necessary ingredients for child abuse are usually present. Most temperamentally difficult children evidently do not find themselves in families with predisposed parents and crisis situations. Nevertheless, living with temperamental difficulty or other abrasive risk factors can be stressful and exasperating for parents and bring even the most humane and rational adults to the verge of committing violent acts against their children. A child's difficult temperament probably induces a greater amount of spanking and other physical punishments that fall short of producing the physical marks that usually define abuse.

Yet most parents are able to restrain the impulse to strike their child severely and manage to use other means of discipline. Professionals counseling parents of children with aversive temperaments would do well to respect and encourage the control they display in not letting themselves be aroused to excessive force by the provocative behaviors of their children. Special attention should be given to parents who are encumbered by unusual stressors that are weakening their parental skills. Also, ways may be found to minimize the child's output of irksome behaviors.

Overprotection

Sometimes parents provide a dysfunctional excess of protection. Worried by the disasters that may befall their children, they are overanxious about their health and safety. Overprotection has generally been attributed to inadequacies in the parents, especially when stressful events have unbalanced their judgment of the child.

An extreme form of this phenomenon is the vulnerable child syndrome (Green & Solnit, 1964). Following an acute illness, especially in the first months of life, the parents may be left with the impression, even when the child recovers completely, that he or she is somehow defective and extraordinarily vulnerable to stress and disease. When this attitude influences their handling of the child, usually by being inappropriately concerned about illness and by inadequately setting limits with the child, the child's behavior is adversely affected. We are not aware of any investigations that demonstrate a role for the child's temperament in these events, but it seems plausible that more irritable children would augment the parents' unfounded concerns about ill health and that inflexible children would be more prone to behavioral problems when parents are reluctant to set limits on unacceptable actions.

Physical Needs: Housing and Health Care

The child's need for adequate housing may be fulfilled in various ways—from the dysfunctional inadequacy of homelessness through the usual broad range of housing solutions to the dysfunctional excess of multiple residences due to complicated family circumstances. The possible impact of the child's temperament on this aspect of the parental role is considered in chapter 11.

Parents meet the health care needs of their children in many ways. They clothe them, bathe them, help them with bowel and bladder function until they can handle it independently, regulate sleep patterns, provide them with opportunities for exercise, and care for their illnesses and injuries. Professional involvement is commonly sought to supervise the overall process, to obtain immunizations against contagious diseases, and to help in the management of physical conditions beyond the competence of parents.

Most parents in industrial societies are able to furnish their children with acceptable levels of health care. Dysfunctional extremes are medical neglect and excessive medical care, including the Munchausen by proxy syndrome (fabrication of illness in the child by the parent to obtain unnecessary diagnostic procedures and treatment). Chapter 7 is concerned with the elements of children's temperaments that may obstruct or facilitate the administration of acceptable amounts and kinds of health care and may tend to push parents toward the dysfunctional extremes.

Developmental, Behavioral, and Emotional Needs

For normal development and behavior, the parents and other caretakers must provide children with suitable stimulation, guidance, and affection. We shall not enumerate the many child development theories that justify this particular set of requirements, since that would move us beyond the scope of this book. It is pertinent to note, however, that few of them incorporate an understanding and application of temperament differences. Our task here is to describe how a child's temperament interacts with ordinary parental management of his or her developmental and behavioral needs and how it may induce abnormal interactions that result in dysfunctional behavior. These clinical concerns are presented in greater detail in chapter 8 and elsewhere.

Stimulation

No coherent body of evidence substantiates a single temperament profile that best utilizes environmental stimulation and promotes development in all the possible child-rearing situations around the world. As in other aspects of child care, a good fit between the properties of the environment and those of the child must be the best arrangement. We may speculate that the optimal parent is one who understands and supports a child's current level of function and is eager and competent to help him or her consolidate the present achievements and move on to others at a higher level. The child best able to use what the caretakers have to offer would be one who is receptive to novelty, persistent at practicing new skills, and rewarding to the parents by being compliant and pleasant. An active child would be at an advantage, at least in acquiring early motor skills, because of the energy he or she puts into physical achievement.

Available research reports do corroborate this line of reasoning. In a group of 100 infants around six months of age, "there was a significant canonical relationship between cognitive development and the social and physical environments for those infants categorized as temperamentally easy but not for those categorized as temperamentally difficult. These data suggest greater reactivity to the environment by easier babies" (Wachs & Gandour, 1983). In other words, easier babies were better able to respond to and utilize the available positive stimuli in the environment. Another investigation of 60 infants concluded that, among infants reared in organized home environments, the active ones displayed higher cognitive functioning (Peters-Martin & Wachs, 1984).

Contrary to expectations, however, in a large, socially stratified sample in Quebec, the children rated with extremely difficult temperament at four to eight months displayed higher IQs than others at 4.7 years, but only in the middle and upper classes and "in families with superior functioning in terms of communication." The authors suggested that these "difficult infants activate special family resources, which stimulates intellectual development over the years" (Maziade, Côté, Boutin, Bernier, & Thivierge, 1987). One wonders also whether a difficult child with a high IQ may seem more or less hard to handle.

Child neglect is the failure of a caretaker to provide for the physical, developmental, and behavioral requirements of a child, including the need for developmental and cognitive stimulation. A temperamental predisposition leading to child neglect may be the one that in the particular set of circumstances fails to elicit from the caretakers a sufficient amount of the positive features of parental care. Studies of neglected children are discussed in chapter 7.

A dysfunctional excess of stimulation is called by various names, such as "hothousing" or parental perfectionism, and the affected children have been described as "hurried." The parents' oversupply of management, knowledge, and training emanates from several possible motivations. We are not aware of any data on specific temperamental predispositions in children that would make parents more inclined to this practice, but we may speculate about how temperament determines the impact of over-stimulation on the child. More adaptable and pleasant children should be more accepting of these inappropriate intrusions by the parents, while the more sensitive and reactive ones should experience greater emotional and physiological disruption in response to the pressures. In chapter 7, we return to the matter of physical symptoms that arise from reactions to environmental pressures. An example is colic, or excessive crying, in otherwise healthy and well-fed infants: excessive or inappropriately administered stimulation by parents is seemingly disorganizing for sensitive or irritable infants.

Guidance
An essential element in parental care is the guidance of the child toward socially acceptable behavior by example and teaching and by approval of what is right and disapproval of what is not. Much could be said about this process of discipline, but we must limit this discussion to how child temperament affects the interaction. Even more than in the parental provision of stimulation and affection, the negotiations of behavioral guidance are likely to be affected by the child's reactive style. How difficult or easy a child is makes a major difference in how rapidly and completely the parents are able to direct his or her development. One may object to a promiscuous use of the terms "difficult" and "easy," but they are in fact highly pertinent in this arena. For the parents whose child consistently refuses to accept changes, the experience of child rearing is vastly different from that enjoyed by the parents of a pleasant, flexible child. The course of toilet training is one of the familiar dramas influenced by a child's temperament. The rate of acceptance of family rules is another. There are "diverse pathways to internalization for children with different temperaments" (Kochanska, 1995).

Sometimes parental guidance is excessive. Inadequate approval, over-criticism, too much management, even psychological abuse, are distortions of the parental role that usually stem from problems in the parents and their social circumstances, but the well-informed clinician must not overlook the possibility that the child's temperament can provoke less laudable practices in the parents. When a stressed or unskilled parent is confronted by a child who stubbornly refuses to alter an unacceptable behavior, she or he may readily slip into an overuse of adult strength or authority, mounting criticism, or abusive language in order to achieve the modification.

The other extreme is the familiar situation of inadequate guidance: immoderate approval, or at least compliance, by the parents and insufficient limit setting. The children of such parents are overindulged and "spoiled." As with excessive guidance, the basis for this deviation in child rearing is generally to be found in the parents and their psychosocial setting, but children do sometimes contribute to the situation. Sometimes parents surrender to their child's demands and weaken or abandon the limits they have set because it seems simpler to give in to a stubborn child than to maintain a sustained strategy to overcome the resistance. The clinician's discovery of such a situation does not absolve the parent of responsibility, but it does provide a chance to suggest a different management approach, one that offers more support and less criticism for the parent.

Affection
Another primary developmental and behavioral need of the child that parents should be providing is the positive emotional support, intimacy, and acceptance variously referred to as affection or love. Parents are expected to love their children without qualification, and they probably do much of the time. However, all relationships are mutual, and the quality and extent of the interactions are strongly colored by how the child responds to the care offered by the parents. As discussed in chapter 2, children's reactions encourage some behaviors from their parents and discourage others. Some children are easier to love, and others less so, because of their temperaments. The pleasant, easy child gratifies the parents, rewards their expressions of affection, and increases the chances that their lovingness will continue. The more abrasive child dismays the parent and dampens the happy, friendly parental overtures. Many parents enter the child-rearing experience with an abundance of affection but are soon discouraged by the discovery that their child does not seem to reciprocate their feelings. Unconsciously, they may slip into a pattern of unaffectionate or even hostile interaction with their child. On the other hand, a parent with a minimal commitment to parenthood may be drawn closer into the relationship by a pleasant child who rewards the parent generously with smiles and friendly responses. The mental health consequences of temperament-environment dissonance are explored more fully in chapter 8.

Inadequate affection needs no documentation as a source of clinical problems. Without this essential ingredient, the developing child experiences difficulties in establishing a sense of self-esteem, in making intimate relationships with other people, and in feeling motivated to undertake tasks with enthusiasm.

A popular issue in the developmental psychology literature for the last decade has been whether a child's temperament plays a role in the formation of his or her emotional "attachment" to the parent, as judged by the Ainsworth Strange Situation Test. Although such a brief and possibly unrepresentative sample of the parent-child relationship used in the test undoubtedly draws heavily on the parental tasks outlined here, it seems likely that the test is also affected by the temperament of the child, particularly in the degree of distress the child demonstrates during the separation phase (Goldberg, 1991). Since this test is a research tool that has not been, and probably will not be, applied clinically, this academic dispute is of little direct interest to clinicians.

Is there such a condition as an excess of affection, as distinguished from overstimulation or overindulgence? One might classify incest as an excess of affection, but it is certainly not a true affection that respects the best interests of the child (Ludwig & Rostain, 1992). In any case, we are hard-pressed to find a means by which a child's temperament contributes to this tragic event. The blame lies completely with the perpetrator.

Socialization

Since the family is the basic unit of social organization throughout human society, children form their earliest important relationships in this setting and gain practical instruction in how the institution works. Within a functional family, they encounter a proper balance of parental participation that is neither too distanced nor overinvolved. Healthy extrafamilial relations occupy a point between excessive and deficient boundaries between the family and the rest of society. This important subject has not been scrutinized extensively with the impact of temperament differences in mind. Nevertheless, there is little doubt that a child's temperament, especially the sociability components, makes a substantial difference in how she experiences family life during childhood and helps to frame her expectations when forming such relationships as an adult.

How easily an older child accepts the arrival of a younger sibling and gets along with the new member of the family depends in part on his prior experience and parental management, but another strong influence appears to be his temperament before the arrival of the newborn. The supporting research data on sibling relationships appear in chapter 11. These and a handful of other reports consolidate the conclusion that family relationships are deeply influenced not just by parental and environmental contributions but by the temperaments of all the children as well. Parents may need help in understanding this important role of temperament.

WHAT CAN WE DO? FACILITATING EARLY PARENT-CHILD ADJUSTMENT

After the excitement and exhaustion of the birth of the new baby, the parents come home to settle into the complicated and fulfilling task of parenthood. The parents must make enormous adaptations to get the new relationship off to a good start, a fact that need not be belabored. Some parents come to this assignment better prepared than others, but all can benefit from professional assistance of one sort or another. These early months and years of life are a period during which physicians, nurses, child care workers, and others should make a major effort to ensure the welfare of the children with whom they come in contact. The main ways of achieving this goal in the area of individual differences are, as outlined in chapter 3, general education of the parents, sometimes the identification of the individual pattern of a specific child, and intervention when dissonance has produced reactive clinical symptoms.

EDUCATION

With a real baby in hand, the parents no longer have merely a theoretical interest in matters of child development and behavior, such as individual differences in behavioral style. The presence in the family circle of a new being, who may or may not exhibit the expected reactions, is likely to motivate parents to acquire more general knowledge about temperament.

The persons in the most advantageous position to help them with this education are the medical professionals with whom they come into regular contact in the course of health maintenance or supervision visits. Pediatricians, family physicians, and nurses have a unique opportunity to facilitate early parent-child adjustment by offering valuable information about temperament in one form or another. Later the responsibility shifts somewhat to day care workers and preschool teachers. Depending on the level of interest and educational background of the parents, it is appropriate to offer general comments and to suggest further reading or parent preparation classes; lengthy individual lectures for each parent are certainly unnecessary. (Some educational materials for parents are listed in appendix 4.)

IDENTIFICATION

Chapter 3 mentions the two main reasons to attempt to identify a child's temperament profile: (1) when the caretaker or professional is concerned about the child's behavior or the parent-child relationship, and (2) when the professional detects a significant discrepancy between the parent's perceptions of the child and the actual behavior as reported by the parent or witnessed by the professional.

Should the clinician use an interview, a questionnaire, observations, or some combination of these elements to identify a child's characteristics? As outlined in chapter 3, it may be possible to gain enough information from a series of well-chosen questions in the clinical interview to form a sufficiently clear picture of the child's temperament for the purposes of clinical counseling. A more comprehensive picture can be derived by using a temperament questionnaire. The clinician must decide whether the minimal expense and 10–15 minutes of professional (or secretarial) time to score the questionnaire are called for by the particular situation.

Unlike for the newborn period, several scales are available that measure temperament in the first few years of life. We are most familiar with, and therefore recommend, the series of instruments developed by our group: the Early Infancy Temperament Questionnaire (Medoff-Cooper, Carey, & McDevitt, 1993) for one to four months of age; the Infant

Temperament Questionnaire–Revised (Carey & McDevitt, 1978) for four to eight months; the Toddler Temperament Scale (Fullard, McDevitt, & Carey, 1984) for one to three years; and the Behavioral Style Questionnaire (McDevitt & Carey, 1978) for three to seven years. The reader will note that the interval from eight to twelve months is the only period not covered. Some have elected to use the Infant Temperament Questionnaire–Revised for this period, although it is not standardized for it. The strengths and weaknesses of these scales, as well as the characteristics of the other instruments available for this period, are reviewed in chapter 2 (see also appendixes 1 and 2).

Whatever the technique used, the purpose of identifying the child's temperament is to help the parents and clinician to view the child more completely and objectively. Frequently identifying the child's unique pattern is all the parents require to readjust their caretaking along more harmonious lines. A number of parents informed the senior author in the course of standardization of temperament questionnaires in his private practice that simply completing the questionnaire, even without knowing the results, had been an educational experience because it made them aware of new dimensions of their child's behavior. The case study about Debbie, the infant who was normal but not very energetic, is an example of how a knowledge of a child's temperament and its interaction with other events in her life enabled an astute clinician to understand the insignificance of her slow motor development and avoid the unnecessary intervention of laboratory tests and further consultations.

INTERVENTION

From the point of view of the physician or other child care professional, the first five years of life present an abundance of opportunities to intervene in parental care practices. The basic strategy lies in helping the parents to understand their child's characteristics better, to tolerate them, and to accommodate them so as to reduce or eliminate the stressful interactions that have produced clinical symptoms. Many parents blame themselves far too much and urgently need education about what we now know about temperament differences. The emphasis of such education is on changes the parents can make because we know so little about how to alter the temperament.

Some special cases may require the use of medication, such as a sedative for colic or sleep disturbances, but such measures are seldom appropriate. When children are coming to the end of this preschool period and entering school, they can begin to learn to suppress voluntarily the expression of the characteristics that are causing them trouble and interfering with their socialization or task performance, such as shyness or distractibility. The other treatment options of behavioral intervention or psychotherapy receive attention in chapter 8. Here our focus is on parental management.

Indications of a Need to Intervene

Taking a closer look at the indications for intervention in parental management in these years, we discover that the relatively simple principles just presented cannot be applied without consideration of the individual circumstances. Our diagnostic evaluation must determine (1) whether parental practices are appropriate according to general standards, (2) whether these practices are well suited to the temperamental pattern of the specific child, and (3) whether secondary symptoms attributable to the poor fit have arisen. We can discern three variations in these circumstances that deserve mention here.

In the simplest case, the parental practices arouse our concern but the child seems to be doing all right. There may be no "poor fit" and no symptoms in the child, but the parental care is inappropriate. If the parents are neglecting the child's physical needs, such as failing to provide sufficient nourishment or to observe safety measures in the home, the responsible professional is obligated to call this deficiency to the parents' attention, or perhaps even notify child protective services.

Indications that the professional should intervene in the developmental, behavioral, and socialization areas are less clear. If, for example, the parent seems to be overstimulating or overmanaging the child but the child shows no evidence of ill effects, then the parent's practice may be simply an expression of familial or cultural differences—in which case, the clinician has no grounds for interference. We must control our parochialism, which sometimes leads us into attempts to convert our patients and clients to doing things our own personal way. For example, a family of rock music enthusiasts may play their favorite records throughout much of the day and night, but the clinician's own distaste for the style does not make it inappropriate for this family, provided that the child is happy and doing well.

Intervention is probably appropriate, however, when the parental care being provided is not appropriate to a child's temperament, although it may reflect standard practice for the social group. For example, the parents may be stimulating their baby at a level as high as what they provided for a previous child or what their friends provide for their children—but at considerable risk to this particular baby, who may become overwhelmed by the overstimulation. If the parents do not understand that their infant should receive some variation of what they consider standard child care, we should help them recognize the unusual requirement.

Finally, intervention in child care practices is indicated when secondary symptoms have definitely developed as the result of the stress generated by a poor fit between the child's temperament and the parental handling. In the case study at the beginning of this chapter, Sarah's parents found that the excellent care they had given their first child was not working for her because of her different temperament. With her greater sensitivity, she could not tolerate a high level of stimulation. A more astute pediatrician would have detected this difference in Sarah and would have helped her parents find handling techniques better suited to her needs.

Specific Intervention Strategies

Sometimes a child's temperament plays a significant part in a family's distress, and understanding that contribution can lead to a corrective revision of the parental handling. For instance, when parents overuse bottles of milk or juice to quiet irritable infants, the infants may gain excessive weight, develop bottle-mouth caries, or take in a deficient amount of solid food. An appropriate intervention would consist of helping the parent to realize that much of the fussiness is not due to hunger and that other soothing techniques would be equally effective without physically harmful consequences—for example, rhythmic motions, physical contact, and soothing sounds (Sears, 1989, chap. 6).

With physiological disruptions like colic or sleep disturbances, the revelation of an unusual sensitivity in the infant should suggest different handling techniques that accommodate this characteristic, rather than useless gestures like changing the formula, as happened with baby Sarah. Recognition of a comparable predisposition in children with recurring headaches or abdominal pain would direct the plan of management away from a multitude of laboratory tests (CAT scans, electroencephalograms, and so on) toward developing insight and coping skills in the child and family.

We have mentioned that certain temperament profiles are very likely to predispose children to some clinical conditions, such as obesity, accidents, abuse, and neglect, but we have not been able to formulate rational interventions based on this knowledge. When the issue is obesity, the clinician can suggest less frequent use of the breast or bottle to quiet the irritable infant, but as the child gets older and gains freer access to food, parents can do relatively little to control caloric intake. Knowledge that a child has characteristics that make accidents more likely, as when a child is highly active, has not as yet been translated into a practical prevention program. Awareness that certain traits make some children more likely to be abused or neglected could lead the clinician to offer supportive services to their parents. But how does the clinician select from the large numbers of such children the ones who should receive the highest priority in the allocation of scarce resources? Moreover, the textbooks and manuals have little to say about how to appraise temperament factors in the interaction even after the abuse or neglect has occurred and rarely suggest that a recognition of them be included in the management plans. Our utilization of the concept of temperament risk factors and goodness of fit is clearly in a primitive state of development. Chapter 12 suggests some areas of effort that deserve urgent attention.

CHAPTER 6

Day Care: Preschool Child Care Outside the Home

W HEN CHILDREN ARE MOVED out from their homes into child care in the community, the challenge of meeting their developmental and behavioral needs is shared by a new set of persons. Like parents, these workers vary in the appropriateness and effectiveness of their child-rearing skills. Cathy's story documents how a day care worker's greater experience and detachment can improve parents' comprehension and management of their child.

When Cathy began her first term in day care at age three, her parents were a little apprehensive about how she would fit in. They knew her to be a rather "spirited" child who had repeatedly presented challenges in social relationships. She was explosive and irritable and did not easily or quickly fit into most social situations, although she did eventually achieve a reasonable degree of harmony in most of her personal relationships. Her parents' skillful management of her difficult temperament, however, had kept it from developing into a reactive social behavior problem. Her parents were astonished when the first report from her day care center was rapturously enthusiastic. Her teacher described her as a "little ray of sunshine." Her parents concluded that Cathy must be putting on her best behavior and somehow voluntarily suppressing her behavioral style at home when she went out into the world. Her parents were therefore dismayed but not surprised when one day the teacher reported that Cathy had had a temper tantrum because she could not have her way and had shoved another child. They asked the teacher whether they should seek psychological counseling because of this event, but the teacher assured them that Cathy was a "spirited" normal child who needed no such referral. In a parent-teacher conference, they exchanged information on ways they had found to help her with her temperamental difficulty. They also talked about her numerous more appealing features, such as her sense of humor and her enthusiasm. Cathy continued to make an overall satisfactory adjustment.

However, Harry's situation was less successful when his normal shyness was misinterpreted.

Harry's parents reported concern about him to their pediatrician because the day care center director had expressed the belief that he was "insecure." (This case is similar in some ways to that of shy Sally in chapter 1.) Harry had always been cautious about accepting new foods, clothes, places, and people, but he adjusted to novelty eventually, when he was allowed enough time. In the first three weeks of the fall session of the day care program, he had separated reluctantly from his mother in the morning and then remained on the periphery of most activities. While most of the other children talked and played, he watched quietly but observantly from the sidelines. He seemed interested and did not appear to be unhappy, but he repeatedly resisted invitations from the staff and other children to join in the activities. The young director of the center was worried that Harry might have a problem and felt obliged to call the parents in for a conference. She advised them to get psychological counseling because of the presumed problem of emotional insecurity. However, Harry's pediatrician knew Harry and his parents well and recognized that he was just showing his usual slow-to-warm-up pattern in a new situation. She encouraged the parents to acquaint the director with this temperamental pattern and to urge her to bear with Harry's timidity and gradually lure him into the games and projects. Within another three weeks, Harry was busily and happily engaged in the full range of the day care program. But he was never first in line for any new activity.

To put these two case studies into proper perspective, this chapter reviews the current status of day care in the United States, including its strengths and weaknesses. Then the discussion turns to a consideration of ways to enrich it. Although the leading professionals involved in "child care" outside the home believe that it is more appropriate to call it just that, rather than "day care," we shall refer to the arrangement as "day care" to distinguish it from parental child care.

WHAT DO WE KNOW ABOUT THE IMPACT OF TEMPERAMENT ON DAY CARE?

Despite the widespread use of day care for the children of the United States and some research interest in certain aspects of the rearing of our children in this kind of environment outside of the home, behavioral investigation in the area has almost completely ignored the impact of children's temperaments on the experience.

The transition from the home to the day care setting is usually a major adjustment challenge for the child. With most children, going into day care is the first time they have been away from their parents for periods of several hours in a nonfamily grouping. It is their debut into the wider world and their introduction to new caretakers with different styles and expectations.

A child may be overwhelmed by the number of other children in the group and unsettled by their diversity in appearance and behavior. Activities are likely to involve greater degrees of cooperation and organization than the child is used to, and some will test his or her ability to pay attention for longer periods of time. The physical environment is also unfamiliar, with different toilets, food, play areas, and rest places.

THE INCREASE IN THE USE OF DAY CARE AND ITS CONSEQUENCES

The rapid increase in the use of day care outside the home for young children is one of the distinctive social trends of our times. With the striking rise in the percentage of women participating in the workforce, many more children are experiencing alternative (nonparental) child care. In 1950 only 12% of married women with children under six years of age were working outside the home. The figure had risen to over 50% by 1985 and included about half of the mothers of infants and toddlers (Caldwell, 1992). Added to these numbers are the growing ranks of single parents who are obliged to find alternative care for their children during work hours.

Alternative child care arrangements vary from family day care in the private home of a relative or nonrelative to a wide assortment of organized child care facilities. A small number of mothers care for their young children themselves in the workplace. The quality of the care administered in these various situations remains poorly documented. Quality ranges from that found in the excellent centers where the physical, developmental, and behavioral welfare of the child is the paramount consideration, to that in the dubious places where abuse or neglect may be suspected or proven. Within any facility, of course, the quality of the individual workers is likely to vary.

Given the growing number of participants and the diverse nature of day care alternatives, it is not surprising that developmental psychologists, pediatricians, and others have expressed concern about the impact of this experience on our children and grandchildren. Although the early research in the 1970s found little reason to question the safety or developmental impact of the day care experience, doubts began to accumulate in the 1980s. These critical arguments were summarized in a recent literature review (McGurk, Caplan, Hennessy, & Moss, 1993):

1. Exposure to more than 20 hours per week of nonmaternal child care during the first year of life was reported to be associated with an increased probability of infants being classified as insecurely attached to their mothers at the time, using the Ainsworth Strange Situation Test.

2. Infants classified as insecurely attached to their mothers are believed on theoretical grounds to be at increased risk for subsequent maladjustment.

3. Children who as infants experienced more than 20 hours of nonmaternal care per week were described by some to display more maladjusted behavior than children who had received less nonmaternal care or none at all.

These studies, it should be noted, depend on data from the Ainsworth Strange Situation Test, a single brief set of staged observations used only by academic researchers and not at all by clinicians because it is unsuitable in practical situations and its results have not been clearly and consistently associated with demonstrable clinical problems.

The review article concludes that none of these points is sufficiently grounded in empirical evidence. In fact, most of the research in the field supplies a very different picture:

1. When alternative child care arrangements are reliable, consistent, and of good quality, there is little proof of adverse effects.

2. The within-group variance in children reared at home and in day care arrangements is marked.

3. Other variables, such as characteristics of the child, the family, and the child care environment, are more important for the developmental and behavioral outcome than whether the care is provided by the mother or somebody else.

THE LITERATURE ON DAY CARE

So far, the day care literature has only rarely considered temperament (for example, Anderson-Goetz & Worobey, 1984).

Each of the 50 states has its own standards for licensing, and most states have resisted the establishment of federal regulations. However, two important organizations have helped to ensure some uniformity in the quality of care. In 1985 the National Association for the Education of

Young Children was established as a voluntary national accreditation system; by 1992 it had approved over 3,000 centers. The American Academy of Pediatrics (AAP) has played an exemplary role in developing standards to guide health professionals in their dealings with day care centers, although its focus is on traditional pediatric topics such as nutrition, safety, infectious disease prevention, and record keeping. *Health in Day Care: A Manual for Health Professionals* (AAP, 1987) is presently undergoing revision.

In 1992 the AAP and the American Public Health Association jointly published the manual *Caring for Our Children: National Health and Safety Performance Standards: Guidelines for Out-of-Home Child Care Programs.* Chapter 7 of the manual examines special needs issues such as the care of seizures and prosthetic devices but says nothing about challenging behavioral variations.

In December 1994 *Pediatrics*, the official journal of the AAP, published a 134-page report, *Proceedings of the International Conference on Child Day Care: Science, Prevention, and Practice* (AAP, 1994a), which took place in Atlanta in 1992. Again, the principal topics were physical health issues, but the report did comment that "the contribution of child characteristics to the equation is important and understudied. While the effects of gender were considered in the past, it is time to explore the effects of age, health, and temperament of children as well as the effects of other psychological attributes" (p. 1070).

Shahla Chehrazi's book *Psychosocial Issues in Day Care* (1990) presents the separation of the child from the mother as the principal challenge for the child's adjustment. The determinants of the child's capacity to manage the separation are the developmental status of the child, the quality of the child's relationship with the parents, the child's previous experiences with separations, and the characteristics of the day care setting. No mention could be found in the almost 300 pages of this book of the important role of the child's temperament in the separation and adjustment experience.

A similar omission is evident in the early childhood education literature. The excellent volume *Making a Career of It: The State of the States Report on Career Development in Early Care and Education* (Morgan et al., 1993) declares that "quality in early care and education programs is directly linked to the training received by the practitioners." Its subsequent descriptions of the content and delivery of training, and the section on children with special needs, do not mention behavioral individuality of children as a topic worthy of attention.

On the other hand, it is reassuring to discover that *Young Children*, the official journal of the National Association for the Education of Young Children in Washington, DC, has an article on individual differences every year or two. Also, booklets published by the National Center for Clinical Infant Programs in Arlington, Virginia, directed at practitioners, educators, parents, and policy makers, make brief and general reference to individual differences as one of seven core concepts, but they offer no specific information or suggestions.

Promising Beginnings in Research on Day Care

Prominent among the few pertinent studies that evaluate temperament interactions in relation to day care are those that have investigated its possible role in the parents' decision about placing the child in nonmaternal care in the first place. Early estimates, backed by conventional wisdom, speculated that "difficult temperament in an infant might contribute to the likelihood that the mother would enter or reenter the out-of-home labor force. Mothers of easy babies, they suggested, might be equally likely to be employed for pay or be full-time homemakers, as their babies' adaptability ought to enable the mothers to select either option with good results" (Zigler & Hall, 1994).

One cannot easily discard such a seemingly sensible view, but the existing research points in the opposite direction. In particular, a later analysis investigated the relative influence of child, maternal, and demographic factors on the labor force participation of 93 mothers with young children in the New York Longitudinal Study. Multiple regression analyses revealed that child characteristics such as difficult temperament and physical problems were as potent as demographic features (particularly the number of children in the family) in determining the mother's return to the outside labor market (Galambos & Lerner, 1987). In other words, a difficult temperament in the child made these mothers *less* likely to leave the home for paid employment than when the child was an easier infant. Perhaps they felt that, as with a physical problem in the child, a difficult temperament was a special condition that required more maternal involvement. (These decisions were being made in the late 1950s and early 1960s, when the pressure to seek employment outside the home may not have been felt quite as strongly by middle-class mothers as it is today.)

As for problems on entering day care, in a sample of two-and-a-half- to three-and-a-half-year-old children, parental ratings of low approach before entering a group care experience were predictive of teacher evaluations of slower adjustment (Ratekin, 1994).

Several other studies demonstrate the wide range of day care topics available for study. Billman and McDevitt (1980) reported that more difficult temperament, as rated by the parents or the teachers, was related to "more rough-and-tumble and aggressive behaviors" in day care. "Individual differences in activity level, approach, adaptability, rhythmicity, intensity, and threshold influenced their behavior to age mates in the free-play nursery school situation. Interaction patterns could be partially predicted by assessing each child's temperament."

An exploration of the differing interactions of the shy boy and the shy girl demonstrated the advantages of the preschool setting for prolonged observations of the consequences of children's temperaments (Stevenson-Hinde & Hinde, 1986).

CLINICAL IMPRESSIONS AWAITING RESEARCH CONFIRMATION

A few other studies have begun the process of clarifying the importance of temperament differences in the day care setting. But they have generally been small, inconclusive, or insufficiently designed to yield findings that make significant contributions to our understanding or practical management. The role of temperament in a child's adjustment to alternative care arrangements is surely no less important than in the child's own home. It may even be of more consequence because of the greater call for adaptation to variety and change and for socializing and cooperative play.

Children cared for outside their homes continue to have the same needs as at home: physical needs; developmental, behavioral, and emotional needs; and the need to learn socialization skills (see chapter 5 for details). It seems quite reasonable to assume that these needs should be met in day care in much the same way as they are in the home. We await evidence as to what differences may exist.

Undoubtedly, individual children react differently to a particular day care center, and the same center may not have the same impact on different children. Day care workers, like parents, surely vary in their recognition and understanding of temperament differences and react to them in children with an assortment of responses based on opinions and feelings that may not be directly responsive to the needs of the child. The interactions must be similar to what happens at home, but the proof of this similarity by detailed studies is still awaited.

HOW SOME DAY CARE WORKERS USE A KNOWLEDGE OF TEMPERAMENT DIFFERENCES

On the basis of our current knowledge, we may conclude that what day care workers need to know about temperament is more or less the same as what parents need to know: an understanding of the relatively unchangeable nature of these normal differences and of the importance of the caregiver's acceptance of the child's individuality. Catherine Andersen (1994b) has summarized well some of the currently available tactics. For example, she suggests handling a child who is low in adaptability with neutral, noncritical labeling ("I know you need more time to get ready"); with empathy ("I didn't give you enough time. Here, let me help"); with specific strategies ("First eat your carrot. Then it will be time to go outside"); with praise ("Thanks for coming right away"); with planning ahead ("In five minutes we'll be having lunch. Time to put the blocks away soon"); and by not overreacting to the child's reactions (e.g., turning away from outbursts). She further suggests that a day care center can alter its program, as for an active child, by rearranging equipment, changing the program to allow more outdoor playtime, and flexibly altering caregiver expectations.

WHAT CAN WE DO? EDUCATING DAY CARE WORKERS AND PARENTS AND LEARNING MORE

We have described the undoubtedly important role of temperament differences in the adjustment of children to care outside of the home, the lack of a substantial body of research information to confirm fully this supposition, and the uncertain and possibly inadequate state of knowledge of these matters among the workers and perhaps even some of their directors and consultants. The case studies of Harry and Cathy at the beginning of this chapter are true stories. We do not know how common the two kinds of experiences may be. Several steps are necessary to improve the handling of children in day care.

SPREADING AND USING CURRENTLY AVAILABLE INFORMATION

The first step should be to make certain that day care workers and those who supervise and advise them are brought up-to-date with what we already know about the reality, importance, and management of temperament differences in children. Some professionals already have this awareness and information, but we do not know how numerous they may be. Reading reviews such as those described earlier and listed in appendix 4 is a good start in acquiring such information. Education begins with preservice and orientation components. In-service training sessions can easily refine and extend the subject matter. Discussion sessions with informed leaders help workers to appreciate how variations in behavioral style affect sociability, play patterns, and physical functions such as eating, sleeping, and elimination. The professional knowledge and skills of day care workers are enhanced by the use of examples of children currently in care to illustrate temperament traits, such as persistence and intensity, and the adjustment of child management strategies to individual behavioral styles. What works well for one child may not be so successful for another.

The in-service education of day care workers depends on the efforts of facility directors, but they in turn rely on their professional advisers—their supervisors, physicians, nurses, educators, early childhood educational consultants, and state regulators. It is incumbent on the advisers, therefore, to be certain to include information about behavioral individuality in the counsel they provide to workers in the field.

For example, in Pennsylvania a program called ECELS (Early Childhood Education Linkage System) has been providing health professional consultation, training, and technical assistance to improve early childhood education programs throughout the state since January 1990. This collaborative effort was initiated and is managed by the Pennsylvania chapter of the American Academy of Pediatrics, working closely with the governor's office, the state departments of health, public welfare, and education, the regional office of the U.S. Department of Health and Human Services, early childhood educators, and health professionals. ECELS now supplies five basic services in an estimated 12,000 programs to more than 300,000 children: (1) linkages with health professionals, (2) telephone advice about health and safety issues, (3) a free lending library of audiovisual materials, (4) a quarterly newsletter, and (5) arrangements for health and safety training for caregivers, licensing staff, and health consultants. This outstanding program has done an excellent job of improving the standards of care in several basic areas familiar to pediatricians, such as immunizations, written health policies, safety, and inclusion of children with disabilities. The immensity of the task and a shortage of funds have so far prevented the program from making any substantial improvements in the area of mental health in general or of temperamental differences in particular.

In this era of the dominance of television, videotapes could play a much larger role in this educational process. Issued in 1989 by the California Department of Education, the 29-minute tape *Flexible, Fearful, or Feisty: The Temperaments of Infants and Toddlers* is a helpful first attempt at presenting a brief explanation of the phenomenon and some vivid pictorial illustrations of the several characteristics, but it is only a sketchy beginning and unfortunately blurs some of the concepts. Other tapes produced more recently elsewhere are listed in appendix 4.

FINDING A GOOD FIT BETWEEN DAY CARE CENTER AND CHILD

Since both children and day care facilities have their special characteristics, the fit between the two will vary. Children bring to their day care programs the full range of temperament characteristics. Day care settings are also highly diverse, with varying total enrollments, teacher-child ratios, rates of staff turnover, educational qualifications of the director and the workers, sophistication on matters of child development, personal commitment to a high quality of care, and the content and flexibility of the standard program offered to the children. We can surmise that temperamentally easy children tolerate a broader assortment of arrangements, and that the difficult ones are more likely to have greater problems in adjustment and excessively stressful experiences in less supportive and nurturing environments.

Professionals who advise parents about day care, such as pediatricians and early childhood educators, should urge them to consider the fit of the prospective program with their child. Parents should take the time to select the best arrangement, not just the most convenient or the most socially desirable. Obvious basic requirements to review are the qualifications of the director, licensure, size and location of the facility, class size, staff turnover, cleanliness, safety precautions, toys and play equipment, meals, and transportation provisions. Perhaps the most important information is gained when the parent observes firsthand the existing relationships between the caregivers and the children already in care. Do they display an appropriate measure of sensitivity, stimulation, guidance, and affection?

When the child starts a day care program, the transition can be made smoother if he or she is prepared in advance for the separation. The first three to five visits to a day care home or center can be kept fairly short. Depending on the child's temperament, the initial visit can range from 30 minutes to about two hours. The time can be gradually extended. The parents should review the arrangements periodically to make sure that the fit continues to be good and that the child's needs are being met (Stuy, 1994).

SHARING INFORMATION IN PARENT-CAREGIVER CONFERENCES

Parents and alternative caregivers who share in the rearing of a child can form an alliance with the aim of promoting the child's physical, developmental, and behavioral needs and emotional well-being. Parents can help the day care workers by letting them know about their experience with the child, including illustrations of the temperament characteristics they have observed so far. After the child has been in the day care setting for a while, the teacher can offer his or her own observations of the child to inform the parents of the behavior away from home and discuss any discrepancies. From this exchange, the teacher learns about the child's background and gets a better idea of what to expect in the future. The parents may have their understanding of their child greatly enriched by learning how the child functions in a different environment, as viewed by an objective, trained, and experienced observer. One cannot say how often formal parent-teacher meetings should occur; an ongoing interchange to keep both parties informed would probably be best. Day care workers can also perform the valuable function of informing parents when the child exhibits behavior that is not just a variant of normal but suggestive of behavioral maladjustment, such as excessive aggressiveness (Muir & Thorlaksdottir, 1994).

CITIZEN ACTION TO IMPROVE DAY CARE

"What seems to be required is a flexibility in the development of child care arrangements that ensure that children are reared in love and security in contexts and under conditions that promote their well being and which foster the emergence of enduring relationships with parental and non-parental caregivers alike" (McGurk et al., 1993). Zigler and Hall (1994) "do not feel sanguine about the potential effects of substitute child care in its present state in the United States, particularly where infants and toddlers are concerned." They call for a higher degree of involvement and commitment by the federal government and propose a legislative agenda consisting of several items: (1) continuation and expansion of research in child care; (2) a nationwide, federally mandated set of standards for child care quality; (3) a national parental care leave law (passed by Congress in 1993); (4) implementation of a child or family allowance policy similar to those currently in place in Canada and many European nations; and (5) an integrated network of child care services organized through the school system.

We are all concerned about the well-being of our children in day care. Our duty as citizens is to make certain that our representatives in Washington are aware of the problems and our concern and are working toward appropriate solutions.

INCREASE QUALITY AND QUANTITY OF DAY CARE RESEARCH

To date, most of the research about day care has been concerned with theoretical rather than practical issues. For example, some investigators have been interested in documenting the differences and similarities between parents' ratings and perceptions of temperament as compared with those of alternative caregivers. Others have been preoccupied with the question of the adequacy of the child's "attachment" to the mother when in day care placement. But day care is here to stay, and research should be redirected away from theory building and toward answering the multitude of practical questions.

What kinds of children do better in what kinds of care arrangements? Does a child's temperament influence his or her behavior with peers and child care professionals in the day care situation in the same ways as in the home? How can we deliver day care that best meets the needs of parents and children? What happens when there is a poor fit between the child's characteristics and the handling provided by the day care facility? How is this dissonance best detected? Will the management principles that seem to work for parents in the home also prove effective in the day care setting? What do day care workers generally know about important mental health matters, including temperament differences? Where do they get such information, and how successfully do they apply it? What is the best way to augment that knowledge? What benefits can be demonstrated for its use? What are the consequences of day care workers not having this knowledge? For aggressive or noncompliant behavior, what management strategies beside time-out are suitable? How can parents and day care workers best collaborate for the well-being of the child?

Only some readers will be in a position to initiate and pursue research projects to answer these questions. However, everyone working in the field is urged to generate hypotheses that can be passed on to investigators, who can systematically examine whether the hypotheses can be supported by objective data collection with appropriately large numbers. Many valuable research discoveries elsewhere have resulted from the careful scrutiny of such clinical impressions.

Day care is only one of many areas in which our knowledge of how the environment interacts with temperament is insufficient—but perhaps no other area involves so many children at such a vulnerable age.

CHAPTER 7

Physical Health Care

At first sight, the role of temperament in physical health care might seem to be small and inconsequential. Closer inspection reveals, however, that normal behavioral variations influence the frequency of some physical problems and the outcome of others. This short narrative about Max exemplifies how temperament can predispose a child to a variety of physical conditions.

It seemed as though little Max had more than his share of problems. He was quite colicky during the early weeks of life, until his parents discovered the importance of not being overresponsive to such a sensitive baby. At seven months, he taxed his parents' patience with recurrent night waking, which persisted until their physician advised them to follow a plan of gradual withdrawal of their involvement with him at night. At 18 months, he sustained a laceration of his scalp during vigorous play with an older sibling. When he was two years old, his parents decided to have him start playing with children his own age in a child care center down the street. When his mother tried to lead him into the center, he pulled away from her with such force that his elbow joint was partially dislocated. The joint was easily restored to the normal position by his doctor, but the family and center director wondered if he was ready for this experience.

Max was a sensitive, irritable, and inflexible child, but he had no ongoing adjustment or developmental problem. In fact, his boisterous laugh and emphatic expressions of affection made him lovable to his parents and popular among his peers. His skillful handling by his parents, who came to understand his temperament, undoubtedly helped him to cope with the problems he had experienced and possibly averted others. Although he would probably continue to be a challenge for his parents and other caregivers, the prospect was for a good overall adjustment in his physical health and behavior.

On the other hand, the history of the twins Tim and Tom illustrates how variations in behavioral style can lead to differences in the outcome of the same physical illness by inducing modifications of the medical management.

Tim and Tom had a great deal in common, but they were dissimilar in an important dimension. They were four-year-old identical twins who shared a bedroom, meals, clothes, friends, and infections. Most people found it hard to tell them apart. Yet they were different enough in their behavioral styles to have affected the management of their ear infections. When Tim's eardrums began to become inflamed, he was prompt in letting the world know. He screamed loudly and prolongedly in a way that was difficult for his parents to soothe. His evident degree of discomfort was impossible for his parents to ignore, with the result that they tried to obtain medical consultation as rapidly as possible. By contrast, Tom almost always had the same cold and about the same amount of redness of the eardrum. His infection was usually discovered only because the parents took both of the twins to the doctor's office for convenience and because experience had taught the doctor and the parents to be cautious with Tom. Tim usually continued to complain longer and more vigorously than his brother after the antibiotic had been started. This apparent continuation of discomfort had meant that Tim's treatment had frequently been shifted to a different antibiotic two or three days later, and it was probably why he was scheduled for an operation to insert ventilating tubes in his eardrums.

Objective measures had not been able to demonstrate more disease in Tim's ears. Could it be that he was headed for surgery simply because he complained more?

A review of the literature about the wide extent to which temperament affects the incidence, outcome, and management of certain physical conditions will be followed by a consideration of how we can use this information clinically to facilitate health care.

WHAT DO WE KNOW? TEMPERAMENT'S ROLE IN SOME PHYSICAL PROBLEMS

The interaction of a child's temperament with the environment affects much more than just his or her behavioral adjustment. Many people are aware of its significance for social relationships but are not yet informed about its impact on physical health.

Yet there is a long tradition associating temperament with physical health; the theories of the ancient thinkers Hippocrates and Galen ascribed both the individual's health and temperament to the particular mixture in the individual of the four basic humors: blood, yellow bile, black bile, and phlegm. The humoral theory has been discarded and consigned to the history books; it has been replaced by a new body of evidence based not on inspired speculation but on scientific observation.

In chapter 2, we reviewed our current state of knowledge about the influence of a child's physical state on his or her temperament. In this chapter, we present a summary of what we have learned about the effects in the opposite direction—the impact of the child's temperament on his or her physical health. This chapter will be of primary interest to health care professionals but also to others who care for children.

TEMPERAMENT AFFECTS VULNERABILITY TO AND INCIDENCE OF SOME PHYSICAL PROBLEMS

General Mechanisms

Before enumerating the physical conditions apparently induced or shaped by temperament interactions, we should consider the general mechanisms by which these results come about: evocation, perception, and reaction. Until more detailed study of these underlying phenomena has been undertaken, the conclusions presented here must be regarded as tentative.

As discussed earlier, especially in chapter 5, a child's temperament may evoke from the environment certain interpersonal or other forces that might not otherwise be noticeable or prominent. The irritable infant may evoke physical abuse from the overstressed parent with insufficient self-control. Irritability and other characteristics may also alter the character of parental involvement in feeding, stimulation, guidance, and affection.

Second, a child's temperament affects his or her perception and experience of the surrounding persons and things and thereby the nature and force of the environmental impact. A child's sensory threshold, as we have defined it, determines the amount of stimulation required to evoke an observable response. A child's threshold for the *perception* of the stimulus is variable too and may differ from the threshold for the *response*. For example, an infant's sensitivity to ambient sounds can be a major factor in the sleep disturbance of night waking. The qualities of attention span, distractibility, adaptability, and intensity may also be significant mediating factors in the impact of the environment and thus in the magnitude of the physical consequences.

Third, children's temperaments shape their responses to the people and things in their daily lives, especially those that induce stress. The overt behavioral components of their child's reactions are what parents have always seen and what scientific observers have been noting in the last few decades. However, underlying overt responses are the vastly complex physiological reactions, which have only recently come under scientific scrutiny. Research is uncovering individual differences in psychobiological reactivity in areas such as the cardiovascular, immunologic, and neuroendocrine systems and suggesting that these different levels of reactivity may be responsible for differing responses to stress (Boyce, Barr, & Zeltzer, 1992). For example, a slow-to-warm-up child under pressure to adjust to a new situation might be more likely not only to avoid the novelty but also to mobilize the sympathetic nervous system and to experience some physical disturbance, such as abdominal discomfort. We do not know now whether temperament determines the physical reaction, whether the effect is in the opposite direction, or whether temperament is the more visible component of a child's general reaction to a stressor.

In addition to the environmental forces and the individual child's characteristics, the child's developmental stage has an impact on the causation of physical conditions. A useful illustration is constipation with encopresis: this condition is largely a disorder of middle childhood and is not seen as often in early infancy and adolescence.

Infantile colic illustrates how these mechanisms of the temperament—evocation, perception, reaction, and developmental stage—combine to affect the child's physical condition. A more irritable, less soothable infant can induce her parents to change the caretaking practice they established with their previous child by getting them to pay attention to her much more quickly when she cries and to handle her much more. Also, the colicky infant is likely to be more sensitive than average to the disorganizing effects of excessive or inappropriate parental handling. The intensity and duration of her crying response to these factors also reflects her temperament. The colic occurs only in the first three or four months of life. Children express a state of overarousal in different ways at later ages.

The physical conditions in which the child's temperament may play a role can be classified as: (1) organic, (2) feeding and growth problems, and (3) functional, that is, involving physiological functions such as elimination, sleep, and pain. When we mentioned some of these problems in chapter 5, we were discussing the influence of a child's temperament on the parent and on the parent-child interactions. The emphasis here is on the effects of temperament on the child's physical status.

Organic Physical Conditions
The early research in this area has focused on several rather dramatic conditions.

Accidents
Temperamental difficulty was found to be related to lacerations requiring sutures in infancy in an American general pediatrics practice (Carey, 1972) and to hospitalization for all kinds of injuries in the first five years in a cohort of 1,855 Finnish children (Nyman, 1987). The most extensive study of this phenomenon, the Louisville Twin Study (Irwin, Cataldo,

Matheny, & Peterson, 1992), recognized contributions from the mother, the father, the household, and the child. Boys experienced a higher rate of injuries. Injured boys were "more withdrawn, negative in mood, less attentive and adaptable and more likely to have irregular sleep habits (*r* values between .20 and .58)." Injured girls were distinguishable only by being less attentive and more negative in mood.

It is too simple and inaccurate to propose that a single temperamental trait or set of traits makes a child "accident-prone" in all situations and at all ages throughout childhood. It has generally been assumed that activity level alone is the main source of trouble, but activity has not emerged from the research with the expected salience. The common thread of the several available studies seems to be that the characteristics that put a child in conflict, or out of touch, with his or her setting are those that raise the likelihood of the child being injured. Temperamental difficulty and inattentiveness are the most commonly observed of these behaviors. A difficult or inattentive child in a home with potential hazards and an emotionally overwhelmed, unenergetic caretaker is in particular danger of sustaining an unintentional injury. But the specific characteristics associated with injury seem to shift with different ages and situations. To these points the senior author must add his clinical impression that in pediatric practice it is often hard to establish the quality of the immediate interaction that resulted in the accident.

Child Abuse
In chapter 5, we discussed child abuse in terms of the stresses experienced by parents, the possibility that stress pushes them toward violence against their children, and the possible contribution of the child's temperament. One encounters great methodological complexity when starting from the outcome of an act or acts of abuse and then looking backward to establish the possible role of the child's temperament in the tragedy. Ideally, we would investigate the child and the interaction before the abuse occurs, but this is almost impossible to arrange. By the time a child comes to clinical attention, the experience of the abuse may have altered his or her behavior. Nevertheless, investigations performed after the abuse has taken place often reveal the existence of difficult temperament in the child (Engfer, 1992; George & Main, 1979).

Child Neglect
The role of temperament in child neglect has been examined only to a limited degree. We found one study: a sample of 160 neglected children were documented to have, among other contributing factors, more difficult temperaments than did matched controls (Brayden, Altmeier, Tucker, Dietrich, & Vietze, 1992).

The general picture, however, is likely to be more complex. In more favorable circumstances, the same temperament pattern may result in the opposite result—increased parental involvement, as detected in the

Quebec study (Maziade et al., 1987). Also worthy of investigation is the possibility that other temperament patterns may lead to child neglect. The slow-to-warm-up child may so persistently refuse opportunities to utilize the available advantages of the setting that the parent may suspend efforts to broaden the child's social and intellectual acquaintance, thereby, in effect, neglecting the child's development. Parents of easy children often have expressed to their pediatricians, apparently in jest, the concern that their children require so little attention, perhaps they are not getting enough. We do not know how often easy children are so deprived, but parents who express such a concern would seem unlikely to be truly neglectful.

The temperamental predisposition conducive to child neglect may be the one that in the particular set of circumstances fails to elicit from the caretakers a sufficient amount of the positive features of parental care.

Bottle-mouth Caries

The rampant decay of the upper central incisors in toddlers remained a mystery until about 25 years ago, when an association was detected with prolonged exposure to bottle feedings in the day or night. A survey of 24 such children uncovered several predisposing factors, such as single-parent households, "sleep difficulties," and a "strong temper" (Marino, Bomze, Scholl, & Anhalt, 1989).

The response of health authorities has been to blame mothers for allowing such decay to happen. Although parents are in a position to exercise a nearly absolute control over the practice, we must remember that certain children are more liable than others to induce parents to provide the bottle, regardless of what may be in the best interests of the child. The irritable child, especially when persistent and hard to distract or when wakeful, can usually be quieted at least temporarily by the insertion of a bottle of juice or milk into his mouth. Again, we note that a child's temperament does not automatically bring on the physical problem; only under certain circumstances does it set up an interaction that leads to the problem.

Feeding and Growth Problems

As with organic physical problems, the issues that have attracted research interest in the feeding and growth domain have been the more extreme ones.

Nonorganic Failure to Thrive

The term "failure to thrive" is generally used to describe infants and toddlers who do not grow at the expected rate for their age and sex and who are abnormally below the fifth percentile in weight. A variety of possible contributing factors have been identified, but the ultimate cause seems to be an inadequate intake of nutrition, in the context of a dysfunctional parent-child interaction. "The parent does not 'read' or respond to the infant appropriately, and the infant has difficulty in eliciting attention and appropriate care from the parent" (Casey, 1992). Parental factors in the relationship can be personal (e.g., depression) as well as external (e.g, unfavorable living conditions). The child's contribution to the interaction has been increasingly recognized in recent years, but as yet there is no agreement as to the most likely specific factors. Commonly cited are the immaturity, temperament, or appearance of the child.

As mentioned in chapter 5, any pattern that interferes with arousing and motivating the parent to provide an appropriate amount of feeding might theoretically be involved. The research information to date favors the possibility that difficult temperament is the most common such pattern, especially negative mood. A study of 28 children ages 6–36 months with nonorganic failure to thrive found that they "expressed less positive affect . . . and more negative affect in feeding than normally growing children" (Polan, Leon, Kaplan, Kessler, Stern, & Ward, 1991). A study of nine such one-year-old infants found them to be "more fussy, demanding, and unsociable . . . also less task-oriented and persistent" than matched controls (Wolke, Skuse, & Mathisen, 1990). Such results must be interpreted with caution because of the possibility that a child's negative mood may be a result of undernourishment rather than a preexisting factor. We must, however, continue to look for evidence of other incompatible "fits," such as the child of easy temperament who may be ignored by the highly stressed parent.

Survival in Famine

The possibility that the uncomplaining, amiable infant may also be vulnerable to failure to thrive is underscored by a single but rather striking report. Under conditions of severe drought and starvation in East Africa, a previously identified group of temperamentally easy babies largely perished while most of the difficult ones survived (DeVries, 1984). The parent-child interactions were not observed by the person reporting this tragedy, but we may reasonably assume that, with a scarcity of food supplies, the more irritable infants were fed more often than the milder, less complaining infants. We feel compelled to conclude that there is some "survival value" in difficult temperament under such highly adverse circumstances. It would be hazardous to attempt to transpose this finding to less extreme living conditions without supporting evidence, but it does seem possible that an uncomplaining infant may risk being underfed in more ordinary circumstances.

Obesity

Although a standard definition of obesity has been hard to achieve, generally accepted criteria usually include measures like weight for height above a certain amount (typically, above the 95th percentile) or triceps or subscapular skin folds in excess of the 90–95th percentile. The ultimate cause of obesity, of course, is an excess of caloric intake over caloric expenditure, but most would agree that there are many contributing factors. Some evidence points to child temperament, in both infancy and middle childhood, as one of the elements in this complex picture.

In a sample of 200 normal 6–12-month-old infants, those whose mothers rated them as temperamentally difficult and especially negative in mood, or perceived them as generally more difficult than average, gained significantly more weight for height than the rest of the normal subjects (Carey, 1985c). The study did not include calculations of caloric intake, but it is reasonable to assume that the fussy infants were fed more in an attempt to quiet them. Also, in a group of 138 normal 8–12-year-old children, those with difficult temperaments gained weight for height more rapidly, and 21 who were actually obese (above the 95th percentile in weight for height) were rated by their parents as less predictable and less persistent. However, by middle childhood, when children are feeding themselves, the interactional issues are different (Carey, Hegvik, & McDevitt, 1988).

There is reason to believe that temperament contributes in some degree to obesity, but available data suggest a relatively minor role. Since overweight infants usually shed their fat during the second year, early extra feeding probably contributes only minimally to obesity in later childhood or adulthood. However, becoming obese by middle childhood carries a much less favorable prognosis: approximately half of such children will remain obese into and throughout adult life.

Functional Physical Conditions
In functional conditions, physiological function is disrupted to some degree, but with no observable structural changes.

Colic
Infantile colic, or primary excessive crying in young infants (Carey, 1992a), is a poorly defined and incompletely understood phenomenon. There is no standard definition of colic, but in formal presentations the colicky infant is most commonly understood to be one who is otherwise healthy and well fed but cries for a total of more than three hours per day and during more than three days in any one week in the first three or four months of life.

The standard pediatric texts describe the cause of colic as unknown and its treatment as ineffective, but more recent articles offer a richer insight and are more sanguine about the possibility of successful management. Of the many factors that may be involved when a physically normal infant cries more than three hours a day, two stand out as possible explanations: a physiological or temperamental predisposition in the infant and inappropriate handling by the parents. The vulnerability in the infant has been identified as a difficult temperament or a low sensory threshold, at least when the temperament is assessed at about four months of age (Carey, 1972). More recently, temperamental difficulty, as rated by the parent on a 17-item questionnaire at two weeks of age, before the onset of the excessive crying, was demonstrated to predict the duration and frequency of subsequent crying (Barr, Kramer, Pless, Boisjoly, & Leduc, 1989). Still awaited are studies that explore the behavioral style characteristics between 2 and 12 weeks, when the colic is present. In any case, it is clear that not all difficult babies become colicky, and not all colicky babies have difficult temperaments.

Inappropriate parental handling may be due to psychosocial problems but is probably more commonly the result of normal inexperience or anxiety. Parents do not always know at first which methods are most effective for quieting babies in general or theirs in particular. They may have trouble understanding their child's expression of needs and may respond with unsuitable manipulations. Excessive and inappropriate handling of the infant is frequently observed both as a causal factor and as a response to excessive crying. Clinical management (to be discussed in more detail later in this chapter) is aimed at helping the parents read their infant's needs more accurately.

Sleep Disturbances
As the relatively undifferentiated states of the newborn become more clearly established sleep-wake cycles by three or four months, a variety of influences are shaping them. In addition to varying patterns of circadian rhythms and parental handling, temperament helps to organize and maintain the development of sleep habits. It may influence the parent-child interaction in all three ways suggested above: (1) by eliciting changes in parental behavior, (2) by affecting the impact of the environment on the child, and (3) by determining the child's response to the caretaking provided. "It is often difficult to determine whether disturbed sleep was caused initially by a specific temperament trait or by a parent's behavior (in response to a trait or independently) because interactive effects always evolve" (Weissbluth, 1989b).

Marc Weissbluth (1989a, 1989b) has outlined ways in which temperament interactions may be disruptive to sleep, some of them derived from his own observations, some from those of others. An arrhythmic temperament with an irregular response from the parents leads to an erratic sleep schedule. Temperamental difficulty, especially intensity and negative mood, when responded to with oversolicitousness by the parents, encourages night waking and crying. Children with the problem of night waking are evidently not waking up any more than those who are regarded as sleeping well, but they do not manage to soothe themselves back to sleep without disturbing someone (Minde, Popiel, Leos, Falkner, Parker, & Handley-Derry, 1993). The less adaptable child with parents who do not strive to establish nap routines will be likely to have fewer naps. The child with a low sensory threshold, as well as the one with difficult temperament, would also be prone to develop night waking (Carey, 1974). The persistent child with indulgent parents may be prolonging bedtime routines to an unreasonable extent. The principal consequence of all of these situations is a sleep deficit, which directly impairs attention and learning and indirectly triggers a stress response that makes the child become "overaroused, more difficult, and more emotional" (Weissbluth, 1989b).

Recurrent Abdominal Pain

This troublesome symptom can be brought on by a multitude of factors. Emotional stress occupies a prominent place on the list, but only recently has there been an appreciation of the contribution of the child's temperament to the interactions generating that stress. In a cohort of 1,855 children in Helsinki, the 51 children of up to five years of age who were examined at the hospital for what turned out to be recurrent (or "functional") abdominal pain had been rated by their mothers at six to eight months as significantly more intense and negative than their unaffected peers on the original Infant Temperament Questionnaire (Huttunen & Nyman, 1982).

An examination of 494 six-year-old schoolchildren in Northumberland, England, developed this theme further (Davison, Faull, & Nicol, 1986). Defining recurrent abdominal pain as "three or more episodes of incapacitating pain over not less than 3 months," and using a temperament questionnaire that measured only withdrawal, activity, irregularity, mood, and overall difficulty, the investigators demonstrated a significant relationship between the occurrence of the pain and general difficulty. They noted that the pain occurred primarily at the beginning of the school year, when the children were getting used to the new class routines, and abated as the school year progressed, while the temperamental traits persisted. They concluded that the behavioral style of these children made them especially vulnerable to the stress of adaptation to changes at school.

Recurrent Headaches

Headaches are also common in children and adolescents and present an even greater diagnostic challenge. Stress is widely recognized as a precipitating factor in both migraine and tension headaches, but little consideration has been devoted to the probable role of a child's temperament in mediating that stress. Using 23 volunteer primary school children, as judged by their parents on the Adelaide Parent Rating Scale, investigators in Australia (Kowal & Pritchard, 1990) discovered that the subjects complaining of headaches did not experience a greater number of external stressors than controls did. They did, however, appear to be "distinguished by a more vulnerable physiological constitution" in that, along with some other behavioral differences, they were more "shy or sensitive" than the controls. If this finding can be strengthened by replication, clinicians should direct their attention as much to the reactive style of the child with headaches as to the type and magnitude of the environmental stressors.

Encopresis and Enuresis

Another distressing symptom is presented by the child who regularly soils his clothing with feces, owing to fecal retention (and leakage), after the age of four years. A generation ago, apparently because of the absence of an obvious physical cause and the difficulty of removing the problem by brief counseling, this condition was widely regarded as evidence of a severe emotional disturbance. Well-designed studies in the 1970s failed to support that assumption. At present the evidence strengthens the position that several factors in the child and the situation contribute to the problem (Levine, 1992b). An unproven clinical impression is that these children may not have a greater number of behavioral disorders, but they may have more temperamental difficulty. Normal stubbornness (low adaptability) may promote their resistance to developing suitable toilet habits and to using the new and unfamiliar remedies offered by the parents or physician.

Our thinking on enuresis has gone through an evolution similar to that on encopresis in that it used to be blamed on emotional problems and is now seen as arising from a number of other factors. Since bed-wetting occurs during sleep, it has not seemed as plausible a venue for the interplay of temperament and environment.

Other Functional Problems

The interaction of temperament with other functional conditions, such as breath holding, tics, and anorexia nervosa, has yet to be subjected to research scrutiny. One cannot conclude that temperament has no role in a problem without doing specific measurements of it. For example, it is a mistake to say that temperament is not involved in breath-holding spells just because the subjects present no differences on an irrelevant measure like the Child Behavior Checklist (DiMario & Burleson, 1993).

TEMPERAMENT AFFECTS REACTION TO AND OUTCOME OF PHYSICAL ILLNESS AND ITS MANAGEMENT

The case study of Tim and Tom illustrates how a child's temperament can affect the outcome of an illness, quite apart from what the precipitating factors may have been. The experience of numerous parents and clinicians verifies the view that some sick children command more attention than others. The sensitive, inflexible, negative child is prone to complain early, loudly, and extensively. Such a child is more of a challenge and a burden for the parents to manage during illness as well as in health. Such a child probably has the advantage of getting medical attention earlier, but the protracted complaining may result in more medical or surgical treatment than is truly necessary. We left unanswered the question of whether Tim may be getting a superfluous operation as the result of his endless whining. Probably he is.

Meanwhile, the mild, adaptable, and pleasant child, such as Tom, usually expresses distress more slowly and less dramatically. When this child feels sick, he may go quietly to his room and lie down without audible crying. For parents, the care of such a child is far less taxing, but it may take them longer to recognize that he is sick and requires some special attention. Such a delay could even have serious consequences, as when a child with an inflamed appendix about to rupture calmly insists to the parents that the pain is not bad at all (see the story of Fred at the beginning of chapter 10). Physicians and other health care personnel can also be misled by the low volume and lack of persistence of the mild child's complaints. These clinical impressions of the important role of temperament are backed up by a few studies.

Response to Illness and to Procedures
A survey of 65 five-year-old children receiving routine diphtheria-pertussis-tetanus booster injections revealed substantially more distressed behavior in those who a month earlier had been rated by their parents as more temperamentally difficult on the Behavioral Style Questionnaire. The highest correlation was between the mother's rating of low adaptability and the expression of distress ($r = .43$). Parental predictions of how their child would react, undoubtedly based on a long acquaintance with his or her behavioral style, were slightly higher ($r = .52$ for the fathers) (Schechter, Bernstein, Beck, Hart, & Scherzer, 1991).

A survey of the reactions of 137 three- to seven-year-old children to the uniform pain stimulus of a presurgery venipuncture demonstrated a significant relationship between lower sensory threshold, as rated previously by the parent on the Behavioral Style Questionnaire, and a higher level of pain reported by the child (Lee, 1993).

Utilization of Medical Care
A review of 200 infants in a private pediatric practice revealed that difficult infants, as defined by the original Infant Temperament Questionnaire, paid more visits for any sort of illness or injury in the first two years than the easy ones. Perhaps they had more problems, but they may also have provoked greater anxiety in their parents or physician since they complained more (Carey, 1972).

A survey of 140 families in a health maintenance organization revealed a significantly higher rate of utilization of medical services by six- to nine-year-old children who were more negative in mood or lower in distractibility on the Middle Childhood Temperament Questionnaire (Wertlieb, Weigel, & Feldstein, 1988). In a study such as this, it is hard to distinguish between more illness and more utilization of care.

Analyses of children with diabetes mellitus have illustrated the importance of both parental and child characteristics and the degree of discrepancy between them in maintaining adequate blood sugar control and compliance with specific medical care directions. Using the Dimensions of Temperament Survey (DOTS) (Lerner et al., 1982) for both parents and children, investigators have documented both poorer blood sugar control and poorer compliance with routines especially when children were low in attention span, and poorer control when the parents rated themselves as low in flexibility and negative in mood. Furthermore, the greater the discrepancy between the mothers' ratings of themselves and of their children on the several dimensions of temperament, regardless of the specific direction of the differences, the more likely the child was to be having problems in the management of the disease (Garrison, Biggs, & Williams, 1990).

Response to Hospitalization

Admission to a hospital and being subjected to the separation, unfamiliarity, and frightening and painful experiences often encountered there would challenge the adaptive capacities of any child. Certainly a child's prior adjustment, the amount and quality of preparation, and the nurturing support by the hospital staff all make a difference in his or her behavioral and emotional response both at the time and in the weeks after discharge. A more comprehensive view of the situation recognizes that the child's temperament also has a major impact on the nature of the response.

For 47 four- to twelve-year-old children admitted to the hospital for tonsillectomy, their previous adjustment and the parent-child relationship were important in predicting the effects of the hospitalization on them, but so also were each child's rhythmicity (or predictability), approach, adaptability, and mood, all rated on the Behavioral Style Questionnaire or the Middle Childhood Temperament Questionnaire prior to admission (Carson, Council, & Gravley, 1991). In another group of 75 school-age children, the characteristics of mood and approach were the most consistent predictors of their behavioral response to hospital admission (McClowry, 1990).

In a sample of children who had just had genitourinary surgery, the ones who were given the most medication by the nurses on an as needed standing medication order were those who before admission had been rated by their parents as the highest in the temperamental characteristic of intensity (Ruddy-Wallace, 1989). Evidently, the more forceful the complaints, the more the patient was judged to be suffering.

Temperament Affects Behavior Problems in, and Management of, Chronic Illness and Developmental Disabilities

At this time we have no reason to suspect that a child's temperament has anything to do with causing chronic illness or developmental disabilities. Nor is there much support for the contention that some of these clinical problems are accompanied by distinctive behavioral styles. We can say with certainty, however, that temperament is a major factor in the management of the chronically ill or developmentally disabled child and in his or her behavioral adjustment.

Do Specific Temperament Patterns Exist?
A recent literature review notes that most of the very few studies in this area have been concerned with children with Down syndrome (Huntington & Simeonsson, 1993). The authors conclude that, "although it has often been inferred that young children with disabilities differ from nondisabled peers in behavioral style, the above review provides little support for differences as a function of specific impairments. Few consistent findings appear across studies" (see also Goldberg & Marcovitch, 1989).

One of the impediments to uniformity of results has been the varying selection processes used to assemble study populations. Investigators have frequently overlooked the self-selection that takes place in clinic samples and may make them differently representative of the heterogeneous general population of individuals with the same problem.

The explorations of Down syndrome fail to uphold the traditional view of such children as unusually mild and pleasant but rather give a mixed picture of a fairly ordinary range of individuality, including some rated as difficult. While these children are being rated like normal ones, with the possible exception of lower persistence, they may be perceived as easy (Huntington & Simeonsson, 1993). But the inconsistency of the findings of these studies should restrain us from assuming that the matter is settled.

Children with other forms of developmental delay have been evaluated sparsely but seem to be equally diverse in temperament. The 52 retarded five- to twelve-year-old middle-class children living at home and evaluated by the New York Longitudinal Study group did not differ appreciably from comparable controls in numbers of the difficult characteristics. However, children who were both retarded and difficult were especially hard for their parents to manage and even more prone to develop behavior disorders (Chess & Korn, 1970).

As for other developmental disabilities, such as cerebral palsy, sensory impairments, and communication disorders, or chronic illnesses that do not involve the central nervous system, such as diabetes and heart disease, we have some information about how temperament matters for them, but little indication of whether these conditions have any special set of distinguishing traits.

Growing Evidence of the Importance of Temperament
In recent years, evidence has been accumulating to support the view that the significant factor in behavior problems in children with developmental disabilities or chronic illnesses is not primarily the nature or severity of the clinical problem but the child's temperament. In other words, these children develop dysfunctional behavior for the same reasons as do completely normal children.

A meta-analysis of 38 studies of children's adjustment to physical disorders and disabilities concluded that, among the various contributing factors, the "child characteristics show the strongest correlation to adjust-ment, but these measures may be contaminated because items on some of these scales (e.g., self-concept, temperament) sometimes overlap with those on measures of total adjustment" (Lavigne & Faier-Routman, 1993).

For example, 44 mildly retarded middle-class children observed over a six-year period in New York displayed a higher rate of behavioral prob-lems than a comparable control group, but for those with a difficult tem-perament, the risk was even higher (Chess, 1977). For 35 six-year-old California children with delays of unknown etiology, "the child variable most strongly associated with behavior problems was temperament, or behavioral style" (Keogh, Bernheimer, Haney, & Daley, 1989).

A similar picture emerges for children with chronic physical disabilities and illnesses. For 34 children between three and eight years of age with myelomeningocoeles (spina bifida with hernial protrusion of the spinal cord and its coverings), greater problem scores on the Child Behavior Checklist "were associated with lower levels of family cohesiveness, lower self-coping ability, greater temperamental difficulty and lower dis-tractibility" (Lavigne, Nolan, & McLone, 1988). In 42 children with con-genital or acquired limb deficiencies, more emotionality on the EAS Temperament Survey of Buss and Plomin (1984) "predicted greater inter-nalizing and externalizing behavior problems and less social compe-tence" (Varni, Rubenfeld, Talbot, & Setoguchi, 1989). With diabetes melli-tus, temperament variables predict not only metabolic control but also a child's psychological adjustment; in an analysis of 117 such children ages 5–18 years, lower flexibility and higher activity, as determined on the Dimensions of Temperament Survey, were related to more problems on the Child Behavior Checklist (Weissberg-Benchell, Glasgow, & Wirtz, 1993).

One could safely venture the speculation that children involved in extensive or arduous therapeutic procedures for their chronic illness or disability would demonstrate an increase in adherence and success in proportion to their endowment with the characteristics of adaptability and persistence. Support of this view comes mainly by extrapolating from data collected in schools. Specific clinical explorations are awaited.

WHAT CAN WE DO? USING TEMPERAMENT DATA TO IMPROVE DIAGNOSIS AND TREATMENT

We hope that the following set of recommendations will be useful to clin-icians in the diagnosis, management, and prevention of physical prob-lems in children. We intend these suggestions to apply to the full range of health care professionals working in private practices, health mainte-nance organizations, or various clinics: pediatricians, pediatric nurse-practitioners, general practice and family physicians, other nurses, psy-chiatrists, and allied health professionals such as psychologists, social workers, and physical and occupational therapists. Although the physical settings and methods of financing the health care may vary, the principles we discuss should apply throughout the field. Our message can be summarized as: (1) know about temperament differences in general; (2) identify the temperament pattern as part of the diagnosis, management, and prevention of physical conditions; and (3) use this general and specific temperament information in managing interventions with children in whose conditions it plays a significant part.

LEARNING ABOUT TEMPERAMENT DIFFERENCES

Before we can expect health care professionals to make suitable use of the sort of information reported in the first part of this chapter, there must be a major effort at all levels of health care education to inform them of what they need to know. This education should begin in the professional schools, continue during postgraduate training, and be maintained by continuing education exercises. Health care professionals must be made aware of our current knowledge about the nature, clinical importance, and practical uses of temperament information. It seems likely that very little such instruction is currently taking place.

Believing in the value of helping parents become well informed, we also urge professionals to lose no opportunity to participate in the general education of the public on these matters. The most direct and powerful way is within the professional-parent or professional-patient relationship. As described in chapter 3, a family's understanding can often be augmented or revised by the right comments from the clinician or educator. Also, we now can turn to various books, pamphlets, and other educational aids for elaboration, but nothing is quite so meaningful to parents as information that is immediately applicable to their family's situation.

IDENTIFYING TEMPERAMENT PATTERNS IN DIAGNOSIS, MANAGEMENT, AND PREVENTION

It is not enough for the health care professional simply to know about temperament at a theoretical level. To make this information of clinical value, the clinician must routinely apply it in his or her thinking about the diagnosis, management, and prevention of practical problems encountered in medical practice. From the research data reviewed above and our own clinical experience, we suggest the following guidelines.

1. *Recognize temperamental vulnerability.* The presence and magnitude of symptoms in the child are not necessarily proportional to the importance of the distressing situation. Normal individual variations in temperament make some children more, and others less, sensitive and vulnerable to stress-producing or uncongenial environments. The

presence and severity of the child's complaints may be as much a reflection of the child's reactivity as a sign of the child's prior adjustment or the virulence of the present environmental factors.

For example, a seven-year-old boy with recurrent abdominal pain in a family undergoing episodic marital disharmony may or may not be reflecting preexisting emotional disturbance or an especially bitter parental conflict. He may be overreacting to a situation that his siblings are handling without physical symptoms. Knowledge of the boy's behavioral style should put these various elements in proper perspective. But such an enhancement of diagnosis happens only if the clinician is thinking comprehensively and has in mind the possibility of a temperamental contribution. If such a vulnerability or predisposition is revealed by the diagnostic workup, an essential part of the treatment plan would be helping the child to develop ways of handling the stress to minimize or abolish recurrences of the disturbing abdominal discomfort. The clinician would also, of course, direct attention toward the parents' relationship and their interactions with the patient.

2. *Consider temperament's influence on a child's response to physical symptoms.* If the parents or clinician know the child to be one who complains too much or too little, or if the physical findings are inconsistent with the subjective reports, the clinician should be sure to consider the possible role being played by the child's behavioral style. If a child with only minimal redness of the eardrum is screaming loudly, it could be either that he is seeking attention or that a major infection is about to begin, but the parent and clinician should also recognize that he may be a normal child who is sensitive and highly reactive to pain. Management plans must be adjusted to the real needs of the child rather than to the amount of complaining.

Most observant parents learn before long that some children's complaints need not be taken very seriously most of the time, while with others it is prudent to listen carefully to any mention of indisposition. For those parents who do not achieve this insight on their own, their medical clinicians can help them become more in touch with the real needs of their child. As children get older, they can be taught to describe more specifically the relative intensity of the discomfort of the symptom and not to exaggerate or minimize symptoms.

3. *Remember temperament's role in adjustment to chronic illness or disability.* Pediatricians and other primary health care providers are especially important here because of their early and ongoing contact with the child and the family.

What the family needs, first of all, is to learn from the pediatrician to regard the child as an individual who has human worth as does any other child, rather than as one of "those children" undeserving of professional time. The physician who inquires about and points out the child's personal characteristics, talks to the child, and responds with understanding to parental questions conveys the message of individualization. (Szymanski, 1992)

Parents who recognize and accommodate individual differences in their children can expect to manage them more easily and encounter fewer behavior problems.

4. *Modify the environment to control stressors.* Whether a clinical problem exists or not, the clinician should identify the environmental elements that are particularly incompatible with the child and weigh the possible value of attempting to alter them. They may be specific to the child or more general. A simple example of changing the physical environment is attempting to control the noise disturbing the sleep of a sensitive child.

Modifying the environment also includes altering the reactions of the parents and health care providers. We mentioned earlier that children's temperaments can evoke a variety of responses from the people around them. They can arouse from parents behavioral reactions that might otherwise remain quiescent. For example, an irritable infant would be annoying for any parent to care for and might induce a parent to withdraw affection and become punitive. If the parent were severely taxed with personal and social pressures, this behavioral response elicited by the baby could even reach the point of physical abuse. The clinician becoming aware of such a situation of parental vulnerability and infant provocation should seek to reduce the chances of violence or other unacceptable parental care by helping the parent understand the fussiness, find effective ways of coping with the unpleasantness, and obtain help and support from other resources.

Practically all children find some of the challenges presented by the health care system frightening or at least distasteful. An outstanding example is hospital admission. Since children can be expected to respond differently to this challenge, parents and hospital personnel should bear in mind the importance of providing support suited to the needs of the particular child (McLeod & McClowry, 1990). Difficult and shy children are not the only ones with specific requirements; special attention should also be paid to easy children, whose mild expressions of sensations and emotions may mask their feelings and cause nursing attention to be directed elsewhere.

USING TEMPERAMENT DATA IN INTERVENTION MANAGEMENT

In addition to thinking in general terms about the role of temperament in physical health care and specifically in individual case evaluations, we urge the logical further step of including the resulting insights in the actual management. It would be an unfortunate omission to undertake the process of intervention counseling without using the understanding achieved up to that point. Despite the enriched view we now have on the origins of conditions like abuse, neglect, accidents, recurring pains, and colic, recommended plans of therapy usually fail to include the necessary ingredient of helping the parent or child to recognize and cope better with the temperamental predisposition that may have been partially responsible for the clinical problem. Verification of this omission can readily be made by inspecting pediatric texts and similar volumes devoted to clinical management.

As outlined in chapter 3, we recommend a two-part intervention when an incompatible temperament-environment interaction has produced secondary clinical problems. First, the clinician should try to help the caretakers to alter their handling of the child to accommodate better the child's individual style and eliminate unnecessary friction between them. If that amelioration is successful, the conflict and stress should be greatly reduced and the secondary clinical problem is likely to diminish and disappear. The other part of the process is helping the caretakers to understand and learn to live more harmoniously with the child's temperament. If they do not increase their comprehension and tolerance of the temperament, further secondary problems may arise in the future as new developmental stages are reached and new challenges encountered. Max's story illustrates how new problems may arise if the parents are not made aware of the possible additional pitfalls awaiting children with certain predispositions. We shall illustrate this point by discussing the management of some of the conditions mentioned earlier.

When child abuse might occur or has already been documented, it is not enough to direct the therapeutic efforts at the offending parent and his or her psychosocial liabilities. Help should also be provided for developing a higher level of understanding of and tolerance for the child's aversive characteristics. This step is seldom listed in the standard recommendations for management. In cases of child neglect or failure to thrive, the caretaker should be made aware that certain characteristics of the child may be making the relationship unattractive and not motivating the caretaker to put forth the right quality and quantity of care to stimulate optimal interaction, growth, and development.

The same counsel can be given for the various body function problems in which temperament may play a part: colic, sleep disturbances, encopresis, and recurrent pains. We cannot alter the temperamental or physiological predisposition (except possibly with sedative medication). We can only try to make the environmental input better suited to the individual child's pattern. But the parents should know about their child's predispositions for two reasons. Such knowledge helps them to realize that the clinical problem has been caused in part by the child's vulnerability to it and is not necessarily the result of something they did wrong.

Second, parents who have been educated as to what sort of child they have are better able to anticipate and avoid some of the comparable problems that may lie ahead.

Colic provides a good illustration of the potential of this educational process. Most standard pediatrics textbooks describe colic as mysterious recurring bouts of abdominal pain of unknown cause for which no remedy is effective. However, this traditional view has no scientific foundation and fails to recognize what we have learned about the condition in recent years. In fact, colic is probably the earliest instance in human life of a poor fit between the infant's predispositions and the handling attempted by the parents (Carey, 1992a). The condition of excessive crying in otherwise healthy and well-fed infants is not well understood, but it seems likely that it involves a temperamental predisposition coupled with excessive or inappropriate handling by the parents, who have not yet learned to read the infant's needs well and respond to them effectively and harmoniously.

Management begins with a complete medical and social history and physical examination. Effective counseling should cover the following points: (1) the infant is not sick; (2) all infants cry some during this period (the average is two hours a day at two weeks, almost three hours a day at six weeks, then decreasing to one hour a day by twelve weeks); and (3) the excessive crying can be reduced to acceptable levels within two or three days with some simple changes. The parents are taught to be better observers of the state of their infants and to read their needs more accurately. With more soothing and less stimulation, infants do decrease their crying rather dramatically in this interval in about 90% of cases. Others take a little longer (Carey, 1992a). Under the best of circumstances, the parents not only learn how to manage their infant more successfully at the time of the colic but carry the lesson forward as they move on to new challenges. If Max's parents had really understood their child after the colic episode, they might not have slipped into a similar trap with the night waking and would have been better able to halt the problem before it became well established.

CHAPTER 8

Developmental Variation and Behavioral Adjustment Problems

Problems in behavioral adjustment and mental health were the first areas explored by research on the impact of temperament, and over the years these issues have been the most extensively assessed. The following account of Charlie's reaction to the birth of a younger sibling demonstrates that recognition of the temperamental component of a clinical problem can improve the accuracy of the diagnosis and the effectiveness of the intervention.

Charlie's parents had managed him fairly successfully during the first two years of his life, even though he was clearly temperamentally challenging, primarily in his intolerance of novelty and changes in routine. Because of his generally happy adjustment, his parents had expressed no concern about him to their pediatrician. But then their second child was born, and the father's business began to keep him away from home much more than before. Charlie was upset by the sibling competition and became angry and aggressive. His mother, exhausted by her new responsibilities and inadequately supported by her absent husband, overreacted and became impatient and punitive. Charlie rebelled further: He emptied jars of food on the floor and smeared cosmetics on the walls. In desperation, his mother asked the pediatrician for help. Since the ingredients of the troubled situation were clear to the doctor, he could give advice on altered management in the first counseling session. After discussing the dynamics, the pediatrician advised the mother to spend more time alone with the jealous Charlie and to alter the unacceptable behavior with some simple behavioral modification techniques. Charlie's behavior improved rapidly, and no mental health specialist referral was needed.

Knowledge of Charlie's difficult temperament helped in two ways: It explained why he reacted so extremely to a relatively ordinary situation, and it set limits on expectations for the intervention outcome. He remained a child with low adaptability and other difficult traits, but the behavioral problems disappeared. Subsequently, with better preparation, he uneventfully tolerated the arrival of another sibling (Carey, 1982). Similarly, a recognition of Gerry's poor fit with her second-grade teacher clarified the diagnosis of her deteriorating school performance and gave specific direction to the management.

Even though Gerry was scholastically highly competent and well motivated, she got into trouble with a behavior problem in school partly because of her difficult temperament. She had had some trouble settling down at the beginning of her kindergarten and first-grade years, but resourceful, experienced teachers allowed her to get used to the novelty gradually and she continued to make normal educational and social progress. However, in second grade her rigid young teacher could not tolerate deviations from her highly structured program. Gerry was frustrated, had frequent temper tantrums, and was threatened with expulsion from class, and her scholastic achievement deteriorated. Her hardworking, highly achieving parents were unable to understand how a child of theirs could fall into such a state. The mother guiltily felt that her return to full-time employment may have been responsible for the turmoil.

In Gerry's case, intervention consisted of: (1) giving her parents a better perspective on her low adaptability and teaching them how to recognize and deal with that characteristic at home; (2) relieving the mother of her guilt feelings; and (3) a parent-teacher conference, in which the parents provided the teacher with insight into Gerry's behavioral style and suggested a revised plan for handling her.

The tension at home was rapidly relieved, but owing to the teacher's continuing inflexibility, Gerry's school performance and comfort in the classroom during the rest of the school year improved only partially. The teacher believed that her teaching style was the correct one, since several other parents had commended her for her unyielding organization, which was just what they thought their own children needed. In the following year, with another mature and understanding teacher, Gerry flourished and joined the program for academically talented students.

Once again, the knowledge of a child's temperament aided the diagnostic process by explaining the magnitude and direction of her behavioral reactions and by guiding management plans and expectations (Carey, 1982).

For the clinician to attempt to prevent behavioral problems or to intervene successfully, as happened in both of these cases, he or she must be acquainted with the available information on how temperament may contribute to such problems and how this understanding modifies their management.

WHAT DO WE KNOW?
TEMPERAMENT'S INFLUENCE ON DEVELOPMENT AND BEHAVIORAL ADJUSTMENT

In this chapter, we shift our focus from the physical care of the child to the role of temperament in a child's development and behavior. This is the area of children's lives with which the New York Longitudinal Study and most of the other clinical research in this field has been primarily concerned. For that reason, we have more detailed data and a few more suggestions for management than for other areas. In chapter 5, we reviewed the ways in which a child's temperament supports or interferes with the parents' performance of their child-rearing functions; now we consider at length how a child's temperament affects his or her behavioral adjustment, either directly or via interactions with the parents and other caretakers. Our interest in this chapter is the social adjustment of children; we evaluate their scholastic performance and issues of attentional dysfunction more extensively in chapter 9.

THE ROLE OF TEMPERAMENT IN DEVELOPMENT

As conceptualized by Thomas and Chess (1977), a child's developmental level, abilities, intelligence, and special cognitive skills belong to a domain separate from those stylistic aspects of behavior we refer to as temperament. They do deserve to be considered and evaluated separately because they have different origins, manifestations, and consequences. It does not follow, however, that they demonstrate no relationship whatever with temperament. We all know that at varying developmental stages children express their temperamental traits differently, depending on their available repertory of abilities. The persistent infant who gropes prolongedly for a toy just out of reach may become the school-age child who works for hours without rest to complete a homework project. Similarly, there is increasing reason to believe that a child's temperament may accelerate or delay the achievement of developmental milestones and affect how he or she utilizes the new skills.

This possibility that temperament affects development has not been explored extensively. We have enough data to suggest that such a connection is real and should be investigated further. Let us review what studies have shown us so far. In brief, they suggest that, in infants and toddlers, the most important temperamental traits are those in the difficult-easy cluster and activity, while persistence/attention span and adaptability seem to have the most influence on the development of the school-age child.

An early report in the difficult-easy sphere found more advanced development in three- and four-year-old children who were rhythmic, adaptable, approaching, positive in mood, and persistent but low in activity (Moller, 1983). Another investigation affirmed a significant canonical relationship between cognitive development and social and physical environments for infants rated temperamentally easy but not for those rated difficult. These data suggest that easy babies are more likely to utilize favorable stimuli from the environment (Wachs & Gandour, 1983).

But clearly there is more to this interrelation than the greater receptivity of easy babies. In a large longitudinal study in Quebec, difficult temperament in infancy was unexpectedly related to higher IQs at 4.7 years, but only in middle and upper socioeconomic classes and in families with superior functioning in terms of communication. The authors interpreted these data as supporting the hypothesis that under optimal circumstances the intellectual development of difficult infants is stimulated because they activate positive family resources (Maziade et al., 1987). The underlying theme here is apparently that the child's temperament, whether difficult or easy, matters for the developmental status of the child when it interacts with the environment in such a way as to give him favorable stimulation for advancement.

Higher activity has been associated with more advanced development in a series of reports (Carey, 1972; Escalona, 1968; Matheny, Brown, & Wilson, 1971). More recently, another inquiry revealed a similar relationship between greater activity as rated on the Rothbart Infant Behavior Questionnaire and higher scores on the Bayley Scales of Infant Development at four, eight, and twelve months (Fagen, Singer, Ohr, & Fleckenstein, 1987). Yet we also note that another survey found that "active infants' cognitive functioning was higher when these infants were reared in organized environments" (Peters-Martin & Wachs, 1984). These authors present the case for an "organismic specificity model . . . integrating individual characteristics as well as environmental factors into an understanding of development." They support the view that temperament mediates the impact of the environment on the individual.

The question of the association between temperament and cognitive abilities in the school-age child remains unresolved. We return to this issue in chapter 9.

The Kauai longitudinal study (Werner & Smith, 1982) affirms the likelihood that, at least under the most unfavorable circumstances, all of these temperamental traits may have an impact on cognitive function. Of a sample of 698 children born on that Hawaiian island in 1955, 201 were

considered by the investigators to be vulnerable for behavioral and learning problems because they had experienced four or more major physical
or psychosocial risk factors by their second birthdays: chronic poverty,
little maternal education, moderate to severe perinatal complications,
developmental delays or irregularities, genetic abnormalities, and
parental psychopathology. Stressful postnatal events included prolonged
separation from the primary caretaker in the first year, serious or
repeated illness, parental illness or divorce, and 11 other adversities. Two-
thirds of these vulnerable children developed problems in behavior or
learning by eight years of age. Yet 72 of them did not have any such problems and were described as "vulnerable but invincible." In this group, the
investigators discovered certain protective factors in the child, the family,
and outside the family circle. The most prominent factors in the children
themselves were the temperament characteristics of high activity and
high sociability (good-natured, affectionate, responsive), as rated by
maternal impressions at one year, and qualities such as the ability to
focus attention and control impulses, as observed by elementary school
teachers. Other ingredients in promoting successful learning and acceptable behavior were: (1) at least normal intelligence and adequate sensorimotor, perceptual, and communication skills; (2) family features such as
affectional ties, which provided emotional support; and (3) extrafamilial
factors that rewarded individual competencies and determination and
provided belief systems by which to live.

A summary of the information on temperament's impact on development and cognition must be tentative for the present. It seems clear that
sometimes a child's behavioral style directly influences her rate of development without much environmental interaction. The vigorous child
probably drives her development ahead by concentrating energy on
physical skills. In other cases, the force of the temperament will be felt
only with the collaboration of certain environmental elements. For example, the adaptable child may increase his vocabulary more rapidly only
when the caretakers supply him with rich and appropriate models to
copy and incorporate.

Little can be said with certainty about the maximum size and duration
of temperament's effects on the rate of development. No case has been
made for a major deficit in development being linked to temperamental
difficulty or easiness or to the amount of activity, although the potential
connection deserves evaluation. These differences may amount to no
more than variations within the range of normal, such as late walking in
an inactive and otherwise normal child, like Debbie at the beginning of
chapter 5. Perhaps temperament affects the speed and thoroughness of a
child's exploitation of what the maturation of the nervous system has
made available. However, an ongoing rejection of novelty could result in
such an accumulation of lost opportunities that a child's development or
intellectual progress could be significantly altered in the long term.

One can speak with greater assurance about the influence on cognitive development, for better or worse, of the quantities of certain temperament characteristics, especially attention span/persistence, distractibility, and activity. We examine this connection at length in chapter 9.

THE ROLE OF TEMPERAMENT IN BEHAVIORAL ADJUSTMENT

The Elements of Behavioral Adjustment

Before giving a systematic presentation of the role of temperament in a child's behavioral or emotional adjustment, we should define what we mean by "adjustment." A comprehensive view of the child encompasses:

1. Physical health, including both organic and functional aspects, nutrition and growth, and neurological status
2. Development, consisting of the full range of capacities
3. Behavior
   A. Behavioral style or temperament
   B. Behavioral performance or adjustment
      1. A child's relations with people: His or her degree of social competence or undersocialization
      2. Performance of tasks, especially schoolwork, and play: The extent of the child's task mastery or underachievement
      3. Self-relations: Whether a child is self-assured or troubled with problems in self-esteem, self-care, and self-regulation
      4. General contentment: Whether a child has a sense of well-being or disturbed feelings (e.g., anxiety, depression), thinking (e.g., phobias, obsessions), or physiological dysfunctions (e.g., sleep disorders or recurrent pains)
      5. Adaptive or coping style: Those typical strategies for handling life's problems ("defense mechanisms") that are derived from our capacities, temperament, and experience, such as direct engagement or avoidance (Carey & Levine, 1992)

Parents and other caretakers present clinicians and educators with varying kinds of concern about the behavior of the children in their care. Three levels must be distinguished:

1. *A behavioral or emotional problem.* This kind of problem is a significant disturbance in one of the five areas of adjustment listed earlier: relations to others, performance of tasks, self-relations, general contentment, or coping style. The problem may be minor (nose picking or nail biting), major (severe depression or anorexia nervosa), or moderate (aggressiveness or noncompliance with parental requirements). This last group—moderate behavioral or emotional problems—is the focus of this chapter. A child's temperament may or may not play a significant role in the development of such problems.

2. *A temperament risk factor without a behavior problem.* If a child has one of the aversive temperament profiles, such as the difficult or slow-to-warm-up clusters, the parents may be distressed about their handling of the child and may complain to a child care professional, but there may be no secondary problems in behavior, feelings, or physical function. Some parents can deal successfully with these characteristics, especially if they understand them, have good coping skills, and are well supported. Other parents experience more anguish with the same behaviors, particularly if they are inexperienced, have unrealistic expectations, or are encumbered by personal tensions or social burdens. Even extremes of temperamental difficulty are not the same as behavioral disturbances, nor do they necessarily lead to them. A survey in Quebec disclosed that, while a disproportionate number of children referred for psychiatric care had extremely difficult temperaments, many of those referred did not, and many with the risk factor were free of symptoms of disturbance (Maziade, Caron, Côté, Boutin, & Thivierge, 1990). Similarly, temperamental shyness can and should be distinguished from a pattern of unsociable behavior, although the one may be the origin of the other (Asendorpf, 1993).

3. *A parental misperception of behavior.* What does it mean when caretakers express concern about a child's behavior but the child presents no behavioral adjustment problem or obvious temperament risk factor? There are two principal explanations. Perhaps most common is parental inexperience or misinformation. Parents may not understand the normal variations of behavior, such as the toddler's efforts to achieve some autonomy or his normally decreased appetite, and they may misinterpret these behaviors as deliberate opposition to parental care. On the other hand, parental depression or hostility, marital discord, or other personal problems may be responsible for the parent's inability to appreciate the normality of the child. Experience has taught us that an easy child perceived as difficult is in far greater jeopardy than a difficult child regarded as easy.

We would add the caution that the clinician's failure readily to detect a problem hardly means that one does not exist. Sometimes an expression of concern about the child serves as the "ticket of admission" for the parent who wants attention for some other personal or family problem.

Temperamental and Other Factors in Behavioral Problems

Having described the functional areas in which behavior problems may occur and the differences between them and temperament, we turn to what the current evidence says about how such disturbances are caused. In chapter 2, we covered in some detail the concept of goodness of fit, especially as a mechanism through which temperament contributes to a child's behavioral adjustment. Before recapitulating the principal evidence supporting this influence, we will review the factors that contribute to a child's behavioral and emotional status, lest the reader arrive at the unintended conclusion that we are proposing that all children's behavioral disorders are due to temperament and its interactions with other factors.

Recent reviews of risk and protective factors for the adjustment of children agree that the three primary elements are the child, the family, and the extrafamilial physical and social situation (Garmezy, 1985; Rutter, 1987; Werner, 1994; Werner & Smith, 1982).

The Child

We explained in chapter 2 that a normal temperament profile and a normal environmental situation can produce a healthy or a pathological interaction depending on qualities of the temperament, other characteristics of the child, and various aspects of the environment. Risk factors such as temperamental difficulty predispose to unfavorable outcomes in certain situations. A child's temperament becomes a source of problems mainly when it interacts stressfully and incompatibly with his or her other characteristics and environmental factors, resulting in secondary or reactive disordered behaviors.

How does this interaction come about? Chess and Thomas (1986, 1992) have proposed that the poor fit generates excessive stress and conflict (with or without anxiety) against which the child uses both direct efforts at solution and various defensive strategies, such as denial, suppression, or avoidance. Several outcomes are possible: full mastery of the situation and achievement of goals, or the less successful outcomes of partial achievement, increased anxiety, or a disorganization of behavior. While the functional area in which the symptom develops tends to be the result of environmental influences, the form appears to be related to the child's temperament pattern (Thomas, Chess, & Birch, 1968, p. 159). For example, Gerry's behavior problem involved dysfunctional behavior at school because that was where the unreasonable pressure was being applied; her low adaptability determined the character of her reaction.

Also, behavioral adjustment is compromised if the temperament characteristic, along with other components, becomes augmented through experience into an established nonadaptive coping style, as when a shy child excessively and consistently avoids novelty. However, we find little evidence to support the thesis (Stevenson & Graham, 1982) that temperament is just a smaller and subclinical amount of the same kind of behavior one observes in greater quantities in recognizable disturbances.

Other child factors are developmental delay, other disabilities of the central nervous system, and chronic or recurrent physical illness. We believe that of the many children now given the label of attention deficit hyperactivity disorder (see chapter 9), a small number may really have deficits in attention and excesses of activity that diverge not only quantitatively but qualitatively from the normal range and are in fact based on a disordered function of the brain. No tests are available to distinguish which children might be so affected.

The Family

Conditions like family cohesion and harmonious function or marital discord and parental psychopathology are too well known to require extensive elaboration here. These influences may be so powerful, as with physical or psychological abuse, that they leave their imprint on the child regardless of his or her temperament. However, as we shall see in chapter 11, even the impact of these damaging experiences can be exaggerated or mitigated by a child's behavioral style.

The Extrafamilial Physical and Social Situation

Risk and protective factors outside the home embrace the local and wider cultural factors such as socioeconomic status, housing conditions, and the quality of the neighborhood and schools. As with family influences, these can also be sufficient cause in themselves to produce significant behavior problems in the child despite various protective mechanisms in the child or family (Rutter, 1987). Yet their effects may also be magnified or minimized by the child's temperament. Temperamentally easy children may even be more vulnerable to pathological environmental influences because they are more receptive to them, a possibility not yet adequately explored. (This division of environmental influences is slightly different from what was presented in chapter 2 concerning the "cultural niche," but similar elements are represented.)

Temperament and Mild to Moderately Severe Behavioral Problems

The great majority of studies of the connection between temperament risk factors and behavior problems have followed the early lead of Thomas and Chess in investigating the consequences of temperamental difficulty in its various forms: the original difficult cluster, the similar slow-to-warm-up profile, and various other components of temperament, such as behavioral inhibition (or low approach). Over 30 studies around the world have taken up this theme. They are not easily compared because they have used different age groups, cultural settings, measures of temperament, time intervals, and times and measures of outcome. But they are in overall agreement that temperamental adversity is a definite risk factor for unfavorable behavioral adjustment. Rather than recount in detail all the available reports, we shall select from the long list those that seem to have the most to tell us about clinical applications.

As described earlier, the New York Longitudinal Study of Thomas, Chess, and their colleagues followed a cohort of 133 middle- and upper-middle-class children from New York City from three months of age up into adult life. Their subjects' temperaments were assessed by means of a rather long semistructured interview, which was done periodically starting at three months, continuing for the first five years of life, and done again by questionnaire at 17–24 years. The children's behavioral adjustment was determined at regular intervals, starting at two years, by means of parent interviews, observations in the standard psychometric test situation, and teacher interviews and school observations, the overall diagnoses being made by a child psychiatrist.

As we know, the behavioral problems of these children demonstrated a substantial role for temperament risk factors. The frequency of behavioral problems ran highest in those judged temperamentally difficult (71%), and next highest in the slow-to-warm-up group (50%); only a few of the easy children experienced such disorders (7.5%) (Chess & Thomas, 1984, pp. 186–191). This pattern persisted until about the age of nine years, when temperament began to be less instrumental in the onset of new behavioral problems through adolescence.

Of the 44 problems arising between the ages of two and nine years, there were about six new cases a year (about 5% of the population each year), with a peak of 10 between ages five and six. Most of these were diagnosed as reactive behavioral disorders, and a poor fit involving the child's temperament was usually a factor. Between ages nine and 12 only one new behavioral problem of any kind arose. By adolescence, more than half of the behavioral problems of childhood had improved or resolved completely, but one-third of them (16, or 12% of the population) were unchanged or worse. Although new problems increased again between 13 and 16 years of age to 12 cases, or about three or four per year, only two of them were diagnosed as reactive to experience. The others were various other conditions, including depression and conduct disorders.

In other words, in early and middle childhood temperament appeared to play an important role in the generation of behavior problems, some of which continued into adolescence, but it was much less involved in the production of new problems in adolescence. It seems that if temperament-environment dissonance is going to lead to a behavioral problem, it has already done so by puberty (Carey, 1992c).

Some cautions are necessary in interpreting these important findings. The NYLS group had a rather affluent sample; they were examining children whose lives were not uncomplicated but who also were not subjected to the physical and social consequences of a less privileged existence. Our understanding of the favorable outcomes of so many of the behavioral problems must be tempered by recognition of the ready access these families had to psychiatric consultation, through the study personnel and elsewhere.

In the almost 30 years since the first published results of the New York Longitudinal Study, confirmatory reports have appeared with increasing frequency. Early among them, Graham, Rutter, and George (1973) encountered more behavior problems in 60 children of four to nine years of age if they had one year earlier been determined to be low in rhythmicity, malleability (adaptability), and fastidiousness (not well defined) and to be negative in mood. McInerny and Chamberlin (1978) discovered more aggressive and resistant behavior at two years in 22 children—out of a population of 118—who had been rated difficult by their mothers at six months. Terestman (1980) evaluated a subgroup of 58 of the NYLS children when they were in nursery school and found that the ratings of negative mood and high intensity made in that setting (as opposed to parental judgments at home) were the best predictors of behavior problems during the next five years. Huttunen and Nyman (1982) documented an association of high intensity and negative mood, as reported at about six months, with hospital clinic visits for behavior problems in the first five years.

In the last dozen years, further investigations have confirmed the risk of having a difficult temperament. For example, Earls and Jung (1987) conclude from their epidemiological survey on Martha's Vineyard that "temperament characteristics of poor adaptability and high intensity of emotional expression [at age two years] more powerfully predict behavior problems [at age three] than do indices of the interpersonal and material home environment. Beyond the influence of temperament, marital discord operates rather selectively in boys to heighten the risk for a poor outcome."

The important series of papers emanating from Michel Maziade and his group in Quebec have already been cited. They concluded that extremely difficult temperament in infancy by itself had no strong direct association with clinical outcome at four years. However, extreme temperament in infancy might indirectly affect outcome through its association with temperament at four (Maziade, Côté, Bernier, Boutin, & Thivierge, 1989). (Their definition of extremely difficult temperament was fulfilled if the child was rated higher than the 70th percentile on four of the five characteristics: withdrawal, low adaptability, intensity, negative mood, and low distractibility.) This conclusion fits with our clinical impressions that long-term predictions from infancy are of questionable value.

By contrast, those children identified at age seven as having a difficult temperament had by age 12 more clinical disorders that qualified for a *DSM-III* diagnosis. The rate of clinical disorders among children in superior functioning families was lower than for those in dysfunctional families (Maziade, Capéraà, Laplante, Boudreault, Thivierge, Côté, & Boutin, 1985). Their first factor cluster (the five NYLS difficult traits minus rhythmicity) was associated with "externalizing" behaviors (such as conduct and oppositional disorders) outside the home and "internalizing" symptoms (anxiety and depression) in the home (Maziade et al., 1990). This work has been summarized in a recent review chapter (Maziade, 1994).

Using a different formulation and measurement of temperament, John Bates and his colleagues have arrived at a slightly different position. Their longitudinal research with their Infant Characteristics Questionnaire

(ICQ) showed that "maternally perceived difficult temperament" (defined primarily as frequent, intense expressions of negative emotion), low adaptability to new people and situations, and resistance to management of activity were all related in varying degrees to later internalizing and externalizing behavior problems at three to six years (Bates, 1989). The use of these highly impressionistic questionnaires and the subdivision of temperamental difficulty into these components make these findings hard to compare with the work of other researchers.

Several reports from the Australian Temperament Project are especially noteworthy. One reconfirms earlier data from elsewhere that what matters for the generation of behavior problems is the mother's perceptions of, and reaction to, the child's temperament more than the actual rating (Oberklaid, Sanson, Pedlow, & Prior, 1993). Another report pointed out that children with stable behavior problems, in contrast with more transient problems, were more likely to have ratings and maternal perceptions of difficult temperament (Prior, Smart, Sanson, Pedlow, & Oberklaid, 1992). Also, a Temperament Project report supported the conclusion that "aggression (with or without hyperactivity) emerges when difficultness in infancy interacts with a stressed environment" (Sanson, Smart, Prior, & Oberklaid, 1993).

Some have pursued with special interest research on the slow-to-warm-up or shy temperament characteristics. For example, Simpson and Stevenson-Hinde (1985) called attention to the fact that, "while shy scores of boys were associated with negative family interactions, shy scores of girls were associated with positive interactions."

Jerome Kagan has taken the NYLS characteristic of approach/withdrawal, expanded it as uninhibited/inhibited types, and investigated it extensively. He and his coworkers have evaluated the genetic origins, physiological basis, varying clinical manifestations, and clinical consequences of this characteristic (Kagan, 1994a, 1994b; Kagan & Snidman, 1991). For example, uninhibited children may be more prone to develop conduct disorders. Also, findings from a recent analysis of a longitudinal cohort indicated that "inhibited children are at high risk for developing childhood-onset anxiety disorders and provide additional support for the hypothesis that behavioral inhibition is a predictor of later anxiety disorder" (Biederman et al., 1993).

The inhibited are described as "reactive" when presented with unfamiliar visual, auditory, and olfactory stimuli in the laboratory at four months of age: they become fretful and motorically active. Evaluated again in the laboratory at 14 months, the reactive infants generally showed fear responses when they encountered unfamiliar people and experiences and unaccustomed tastes (Kagan, 1994b). The true practical significance of this body of work has yet to be established. It may be that the earlier reactivity and the later inhibition are simply different aspects of the same temperamental shyness. Furthermore, the phenomenon under study started out as just initial approach/withdrawal but may have expanded to incorporate elements of adaptability, negative mood, and intensity. If that is so, this group may, in fact, be describing a broader cluster of difficult temperament characteristics. Some clarification is needed before this promising line of work can bear fruit at the clinical level.

In addition to the long-term follow-up into adulthood by the NYLS group (Chess & Thomas, 1984), two reports derived from the Berkeley Guidance Study are of interest. Caspi, Elder, and Bem (1987, 1988) reevaluated 30 years later children in that study who had had temper tantrums or were shy at age eight to 10 years. Men with a history of tantrums (38% of the male population) "experienced downward occupational mobility, erratic work lives, and were likely to divorce. Women with such histories (29% of the sample) married men with lower occupational status, were likely to divorce, and became ill-tempered mothers." Although shy girls (32% of the female sample) were more likely than their peers to follow a conventional lifestyle, shy boys (28% of the sample) "were more likely than their peers to delay entry into marriage, parenthood, and stable careers; to attain less occupational achievement and stability; and—when late in establishing stable careers—to experience marital instability." To summarize, "Ill-tempered children became ill-tempered adults," whereas "childhood shyness did not produce pathological or extreme outcomes, but it did have significant consequences for later adult development."

Without trying to review all the remaining studies that testify to the importance of temperament for social adjustment, let us just point out a few additional areas of influence. In the first place, temperament affects a child's adjustment at school as well as at home, despite the differences in the challenges children face in the educational arena (Keogh, 1986). (These complex issues are presented in greater detail in chapter 9). Also, as discussed in chapter 7, temperament is related to behavioral outcome just as much for children with developmental disabilities and those who were low in birth weight (Goldberg, Corter, Lojkasek, & Minde, 1990). Furthermore, although investigations have not been undertaken in all the varied cultures around the world, the relationship has been confirmed where it has been sampled, even in a social setting as different from our own as rural India (Malhotra, Varma, & Verma, 1986).

Temperament and Major Behavioral Problems

The role of temperament in the more severe problems, such as depression, conduct disorder, and anorexia nervosa, remains unclear. On the basis of their NYLS data on 133 children, Chess and Thomas (1984) concluded that there was little evidence of its participation, but their sample was too small to resolve the matter. Before temperament can be fully excluded as a predisposing factor in major behavioral problems, larger numbers of such patients must be subjected to study (Maziade, 1994). Some studies have hinted at such a connection. A British survey found several significant adverse temperament differences in a randomly selected group of 38 excessively aggressive secondary school boys (Kolvin, Nicol, Garside, Day, & Tweddle, 1982). The apparent biological predisposition of some children to develop conduct disorders in conjunction with environmental factors may include a temperamental component, such as being "hyporesponsive to intense and punishing stimuli" (Lytton, 1990). Aside from the question of how temperament may predispose to problems of this sort, temperament may also add to their persistence or severity and therefore affect their management.

Temperament and Other Areas of Behavioral Adjustment

Earlier in this chapter, we described five main areas in which behavioral adjustment can be appraised: relations with people, task performance, self-relations, general contentment, and coping style. The bulk of the preceding review of the literature has been concerned with the first of these areas—problems in social behavior. This was the field first described by the New York Longitudinal Study and most extensively pursued by those impressed by the importance of that work. However, it would be a mistake to suppose that this is the only domain of consequence for temperament interactions. We presented in chapter 7 the increasing body of data demonstrating a considerable impact on the physical health of children. Chapter 9 will discuss the similarly impressive role it plays in school function. Let us at this point review what we have learned about the part played by behavioral style in the areas of positive social adjustment, self-relations, and coping style.

From the mass of data, albeit imperfect and still rather fragmentary, one gains the perspective that the interactions of children's temperaments with their adjustment in these various areas is more a linear process than a categorical one. It seems to be not just a matter of certain aversive behavioral style characteristics leading to specific diagnostic categories that are easily distinguishable from normal, the way the varicella virus produces chicken pox in susceptible individuals. The more difficult a child's temperament, the smaller the range of environments that can accommodate him or her and the greater the risk of a dissonant relationship.

There also seems to be an association between certain characteristics and positive aspects of development. For example, if having a moderate amount of persistence results in a higher degree of scholastic adjustment than having less, it is likely to follow that having a high amount of that characteristic will be of benefit to the child even more than a moderate amount. Of course, this principle must be tempered by the recognition that the consonance of the temperament-environment fit is more important than the absolute amount of the characteristic. Let us evaluate the bits of evidence supporting this view.

Positive Social Adjustment: Social Competence

Research on conscience development has emphasized the contribution of

parent socialization and neglected the influence of the child's temperament. In a recent review,

> two developmental processes that result in the formation of two
> respective components of conscience are proposed: (1) development of
> the tendency to experience affective discomfort, guilt, and anxiety
> associated with wrongdoing; and (2) development of behavioral con-
> trol—the ability to inhibit a prohibited action, to suppress an antisocial
> or destructive impulse, and to perform a more prosocial/desirable
> behavior. . . . The present framework proposes that conscience
> emerges as an outcome of intricate, developmentally changing inter-
> action between children's individual temperamental qualities and
> parental rearing styles. (Kochanska, 1993; see also Kochanska, DeVet,
> Goldman, Murray, & Putnam, 1994)

Some have taken a rather different line of inquiry: exploring the role of
children's temperaments in their humor expression. In a sample of 158
four- and five-year-old nursery school students, "children who were
more active and approaching were reported to laugh more frequently
and more often try, verbally and behaviorally, to initiate humor." Mood,
persistence, and threshold displayed significant but less extensive links;
on the whole, the associations were "extremely limited" (Carson,
Skarpness, Schultz, & McGhee, 1986).

A vast body of literature has appeared in the last 20–30 years on the
phenomenon of the "attachment" of infants. The Ainsworth Strange
Situation test, an artificially staged laboratory test, supposedly determines the security of an infant's emotional attachment to the mother and
is thought by its developers to be entirely a reflection of the quality of
parental care. A controversy has raged over whether what the test measures as attachment is really the child's temperament, or is at least in
some degree influenced by temperament. This possibility is supported by
various lines of evidence, including the demonstration of a relationship
between neonatal irritability and the later attachment classification.
"Negative emotionality in infants seems to be more responsible than
maternal behavior for the development of an anxious attachment relationship" (Van den Boom, 1989). It is not clear just what the test is sampling in the few brief minutes it takes to administer. Although the infant's
emotional affiliation with the mother is undoubtedly critically important,
these uncertainties and the lack of any adaptation of the test for practical
use make the whole dispute largely irrelevant to child health care clinicians and educators. Clinical applications have yet to be demonstrated.

Self-relations

The self-relations aspect of behavioral adjustment has scarcely been
explored. One examination of 186 college students compared their self-
ratings on the Dimensions of Temperament Scale and the short form of

the Texas Social Behavior Inventory. Significant correlations were found between self-esteem and adaptability (*r* = .53), attention/distractibility (*r* = .35), and reactivity (*r* = .19). "Temperament may mediate how each individual perceives and experiences social demands and constraints, thereby influencing the level of positive regard and success during development" (Klein, 1992).

In another investigation of 91 adolescents, positive self-esteem was associated with certain personality characteristics, including assertiveness, cheerfulness, social poise, persistence, stability of mood, and predictability (Block & Robins, 1993).

Adaptive or Coping Style
Coping style or ability usually refers to an individual's strategies for handling the problems of life. Although no one definition of its origins and components is commonly accepted, it seems reasonable to consider coping style a measure of behavioral adjustment as well as a factor in producing it. It encompasses elements such as developmental level, cognitive skills, defense mechanisms, prior experience, and behavioral style. We have suggested that temperament undoubtedly contributes to the formation of a child's adaptive style but that it is not the same phenomenon. We would expect to find a relationship between the two but not an identity. For example, an easy child would be assumed to accept strangers readily, but not if that child has repeatedly experienced frightening encounters with unfamiliar people.

A survey of 60 nine- to twelve-year-old children examined two possible factors in coping ability. Creative thinking, as defined by the Torrance Tests of Creative Thinking, particularly in the areas of fluency, originality, elaboration, and resistance to premature closure, was strongly associated with greater coping ability. So also was temperament, as measured by the Middle Childhood Temperament Questionnaire, in the dimensions of higher activity, more predictability, more positive mood, and greater adaptability. Creative thinking and temperament appear to have been independent contributions to coping, since they were largely unrelated to each other (Carson & Bittner, 1994).

Some Perspective on the Clinical Presentation of Behavioral Problems
The preceding review of the literature on the impact of temperament on behavioral adjustment may leave the reader overwhelmed and perplexed as to the frequency and variety of ways these issues present themselves in the daily practice of a child care professional. It is hard to say how often temperament affects behavioral adjustment, but we may be certain that, once the phenomenon is understood, it will be recognized as a leading source of friction between caretaker and child.

We can, however, offer some perspective from the recent report of a survey of the senior author's pediatric practice (Carey, 1994). On the termination of this long-established practice in 1989, it was necessary to review practically all the active patient charts (perhaps 1,200) in order to prepare individual transcripts to send to other physicians. This was not a truly quantitative population analysis in that selection processes had operated at several points: the parents' decision to participate in the practice, their presentation of their problems to the physician, the variable recording of these discussions by the physician, and the fact that, even two years after the practice was terminated, some records had still not been requested. Nevertheless, several reaction patterns turned up with such frequency that they would surely stand out in a more rigorous cross-sectional study.

The principal finding of this survey was that, when parents were concerned about their children's behavior, temperament data were usually helpful. When there was a mild or moderately severe behavioral adjustment problem, information on the child's temperament clarified the diagnosis and guided the management. When there was parental concern about behavior but no adjustment problem (involving social competence, task performance, self-assurance, or general contentment), the temperament itself was often the source of the concern (Carey, 1994).

The survey found three principal types of situations that bothered parents:

1. *Acute social behavioral problems.* Acute behavior problems were those of at least moderate severity and of fairly abrupt onset. They were frequently exhibited by children with difficult temperaments who had been doing satisfactorily under normal circumstances with competent parental handling but had reacted to heightened stress more dramatically than others, such as siblings or classmates, who had tolerated it without such a disruption. The presence and magnitude of the symptoms may be attributable more to the reactivity of these children's temperaments than to the pathogenicity of the events or the children's biological vulnerability. A good example is Charlie (described at the beginning of the chapter), a difficult child who did well until he was apparently overwhelmed by the arrival of a younger sibling and his mother's unsupportive response.

2. *Recurring behavior problems.* For some children, behavioral symptoms and parental concern about them are not so sudden and dramatic but rather are more chronic or recurrent. The child's temperament is likely to remain somewhat stable, but because of shifting combinations of developmental status and environmental factors, she may have separate periods of behavioral dysfunction related to the temperament-environment interactions. Between those episodes, her behavior may evoke no distress in the parents. The story of Max at the start of chapter 7 illustrates this situation.

3. *School performance problems.* School problems present a different picture. Schools do not send all bothersome children to physicians for evalua-

tion. They are likely to refer those who do not adapt themselves to school routines and pay attention to their work and for whom the teacher would like some remedy such as methylphenidate (Ritalin) to increase compliance. It was no surprise that the charts reviewed invariably showed that the children referred from schools had either difficult temperament, "low task orientation," or some combination of these features. The case study of Gerry describes a school behavior problem that was generated by the crisis of a difficult child being subjected to unreasonable expectations by an inflexible young teacher. The full range of school problems is explored in chapter 9.

WHAT CAN WE DO?
TECHNIQUES FOR PREVENTING AND
HANDLING BEHAVIORAL PROBLEMS

This chapter has presented in great detail a review of the growing multitude of studies that demonstrate a relationship between temperamental predispositions and the appearance of dysfunctions in the full range of behavioral adjustment. Few of these reports have been interested in offering suggestions as to how child health care and educational professionals could use this information to solve or ameliorate these concerns. Our business here is to describe what we know about handling behavioral problems, especially those in which the child's temperament plays an active role. First we survey the available suggestions; then we present our own set of recommendations for professionals wishing to make helpful interventions. Since we have already discussed the preventive measures of parental education and more specific counseling based on the child's individual pattern (see chapter 2), we shall not revisit those subjects here.

WHAT THE PROFESSIONAL LITERATURE SAYS

Although Chess and Thomas (1986) have explicitly described the therapeutic approach they followed in managing the problems encountered in the course of the New York Longitudinal Study, and their 50% success rate with parent counseling alone, some commentators in child psychology and psychiatry research have recently suggested that we do not know enough to make effective interventions.

Chess and Thomas (1986, chap. 11) devoted 32 pages to a lengthy presentation of their procedure in handling behavior problems, specifically those defined in the then-current edition of the official terminology (*DSM-III* [American Psychiatric Association, 1980]) as adjustment, conduct, and anxiety disorders. Illustrations made the presentation more vivid. "In the NYLS sample, parent guidance was recommended as the primary therapeutic approach in all children identified as suffering from a behavior disorder" (Chess and Thomas, 1986). This technique was safe, efficient, and usually effective, since most cases involved goodness of fit.

Their strategy was to identify the particulars of the individual problem as precisely as possible and then to advise the parents to change specific aspects of their functioning with the child, that is, to improve the fit. The advice was not simply couched in generalities but was tailored to the particular situations in which friction was evident. They considered this approach an appropriate one regardless of the possible presence of psychopathology in the parents. The parents were treated as "therapeutic allies" who worked with the counselor, rather than as a part of the problem requiring change before the child could improve. This plan was "moderately or highly" successful after two or three guidance sessions in about 50% of the cases, especially when the problem was of recent onset, there was no elaboration of defense mechanisms, the nature of the dissonance in the fit was fairly obvious, both parents were informed, stable, and cooperative, and there were no additional complicating factors, such as a learning disability. Improvement was as likely in the presence of temperamental difficulty as with easier profiles. The parent counseling was not so fruitful when less of, or the opposites of, these conditions were present. Also less responsive were the cases involving children who were low in persistence and high in distractibility (four out of 133 subjects). The children who did not improve were usually referred for psychotherapy.

Thomas, Chess, and Birch (1968) first publicized their management techniques and their success with them over a quarter-century ago. Yet since then little further research information has been offered by other investigators that either confirms or disputes their findings. An enormous amount of research time and resources have been expended on such theoretical matters as predictions and factor structures. Many clinicians have informally recounted their gratitude at the way these NYLS insights have enriched their therapeutic attempts and benefited countless children, but published systematic surveys of the work of others are hard to find. From academic commentators have come some surprisingly critical judgments. Despite his great erudition, Michael Rutter (1989) judged that, "in spite of all we know, there is no straightforward fashion in which measurement of a person's temperamental qualities can lead directly to particular clinical interventions." John Bates (1989) expressed a similar skepticism: "Temperament concepts are not fully validated, so when used in a clinical context, they should be used hypothetically, as a relevant and partly true fiction." Another observer (Carek, 1992), revealing no evidence of having applied the published techniques in practice himself, opined that the goodness-of-fit model "has its limitations and . . . has been relatively exhausted." All these views indicate inadequate clinical experience in applying these concepts and an unfamiliarity with the clinical literature (Sheeber & Johnson, 1994).

RECOMMENDATIONS FOR SELF-HELP BY PARENTS

While the pursuit of theory building, as opposed to problem solving, has preoccupied academic researchers, practitioners in the field have often recognized the value of the Thomas and Chess orientation and have adapted it to their clinical needs. As mentioned in chapter 1, a few books have been published by practitioners eager to share with parents their particular interpretation of the NYLS view of children. The best known of these, Stanley Turecki and Leslie Tonner's *The Difficult Child* (1985/1989), has proven to be very helpful for many parents, especially when their professional advisers are not fully aware of the phenomenon of temperament and therefore have been insufficiently helpful to them in understanding and managing their child's temperament characteristics. *Raising Your Spirited Child* (1991) by Mary Sheedy Kurcinka is an equally valuable but longer and more detailed presentation for parents. Publications of the Preventive Ounce and the Kaiser Permanente Group in California are awaited. A somewhat different conceptualization forms the basis of *Living with the Active Alert Child* (1993) by Linda Budd (see also appendix 4).

The Difficult Child introduces an algorithm called "The Expert Response: A Decision Tree for Parents." Although it is intended for parents and not professionals, we describe it here so as to contrast it with the algorithm for professionals we offer later in this chapter. Turecki's algorithm begins with "problem behavior" and goes through six steps, two of them requiring yes/no decisions. To paraphrase:

1. Can I deal with it now? If no, a minimal response and disengagement. If yes, go on to next step.

2. Become the leader. Stand back. Get neutral. Think and evaluate.

3. Frame the behavior. Recognize the pattern. Focus on behavior, not motives.

4. Is it temperament? If yes, management. Sympathetic attitude. Establish eye contact. Use a label. Apply a technique. If no, move on to step 5.

5. Is it relevant? If no, minimal response and disengagement. If yes, move on to step 6.

6. Effective punishment. Stern attitude. Be brief. Be direct.

The greatest strength of Turecki's presentation is that it helps parents to distinguish between temperament and reactive behavior problems. It assists them in recognizing that shyness and moodiness are manifestations of temperament that should be managed or accommodated, while bad manners and selfishness are secondary behavior problems to be eliminated by disciplinary measures. His new book, *The Emotional Problems of Normal Children* (Turecki & Wernick, 1994), attempts to advance further the competence of parents in dealing with behavioral problems. However, his current explanation of temperament is blurred by the multiplication of the nine temperament characteristics into 18, with no research evidence to support the expansion.

A COMPREHENSIVE PROFESSIONAL PLAN FOR HANDLING BEHAVIOR PROBLEMS

Now we can pull together what various clinicians have learned about dealing with behavior problems in a way that recognizes the critical role of temperamental predispositions. Turecki has shown that it is possible to construct an algorithm that serves as a valuable guide for parents, but we need a separate one for professionals, because of our different perspective on the same terrain. The following plan (Carey, 1989, 1992b), developed originally for the primary care pediatrician, is offered with the understanding that child health and educational professionals will need to adapt and modify this approach to their particular settings. We offer first the algorithm for sorting through the presenting concerns, and then a set of principles for management of the clinical problem identified (see figure 8.1).

The initial presentation of the problem varies, depending on the setting—primary medical, educational, or consultation. If the problem has reached a consultant, it is already somewhat identified and plans for resolution have been undertaken. On the other hand, in the primary health care or educational setting, the concerns and treatment strategies may not be well formulated. The clinician must first work through these preliminary stages.

1. *Define the concern.* The first step is to discover the behavior areas that arouse concern, either from the caretakers or the clinician. If such concern is expressed as the reason for the visit or comes up in the course of an initial inquiry, the interviewer should find out who has the concerns, what the concerns involve, why they exist, and why they are emerging at this time. Charlie's mother was upset by the recent onset of his aggressive behavior, brought on by the birth of his younger brother. If, by contrast, the caretaker reports complete satisfaction with the child's status and progress in all areas, the routine evaluation process can be greatly abbreviated.

2. *Establish an agreement.* Once the area of concern has been discovered, the next step is to determine whether the family wishes to have the clinician help them with it. The primary care physician cannot simply take charge of the diagnostic and therapeutic procedure, as he or she does with physical illnesses such as ear infections or pneumonia. For behavioral issues, the process of evaluation and management is shared with the family, and an agreement must be established as to what the

Figure 8.1

Algorithm for Pediatric Management of Concerns about Behavior

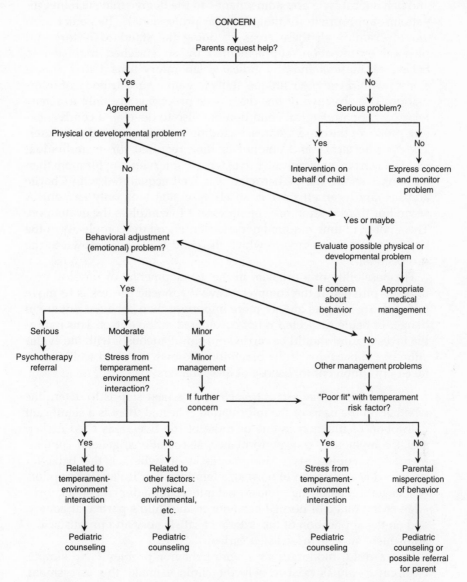

family expects and what the professional will provide. If the family does not want help, the clinician can only express appropriate concern and monitor the problem, unless it is so severe that intervention on behalf of the child is mandatory. Encopresis is annoying but does not require an obligatory intervention; a child showing signs of parental neglect cannot be ignored. When this agreement is reached, the process of diagnosis can continue.

3. *General evaluation.* At this point, the professional makes a comprehensive assessment of the child's physical status, developmental level, and behavioral style and adjustment—to the degree that such investigation is appropriate for the particular professional. The pediatrician would examine all these areas by doing the standard history and physical examination, supplemented by an enriched inquiry into behavioral matters and any indicated laboratory tests. Other professionals would use their unique skills to gain a similar body of information. The objective of this diagnostic process is not only to screen for a psychopathological condition but also to develop a comprehensive profile of the child's status, including successes as well as failures. The specific tactics and amount of time required for an individual child vary from a few minutes to extensive interviewing for more than an hour. Because the pediatrician was well acquainted with Charlie and his family, an effective counseling session took only an hour. A second or third session may be necessary to complete the evaluation. The amount of time required depends largely on the complexity of the situation and the degree to which the child is already known to the professional.

The possibility of a problem in the developmental or physical area must be pursued if the comprehensive diagnostic process is to move forward. These areas are not more important than behavior but are in danger of being neglected if not considered at the outset. This part of the investigation should be carried out simultaneously with the evaluation of the behavior. If the practitioner knows the child well, it may take only a moment to dispose of these matters.

4. *Is there a behavioral adjustment problem?* The next step is to determine whether on the basis of the information collected there is a significant disruption of function in one or more of the five areas cited earlier: social competence, task performance, self-relations, general contentment, and coping style. Judgments as to whether the behavior described is a variation of normal, a temporary or isolated disruption, or a deviation requiring professional intervention depend on a knowledge of the range of normal behavior in the child's particular context and on the application of the criteria of satisfactory and unsatisfactory adjustment such as those listed earlier.

Is it a mild, moderate, or severe behavior problem? No simple, clear-cut formulas exist to help the clinician make this assessment. Determination of the magnitude of the problem is a clinical decision that depends on the type and degree of the dysfunction and the duration and intensity of the stress. Minor problems, such as nail biting and nose picking, require only minor professional attention. Severe conditions, such as major depression or anorexia nervosa, call for psychiatric referral. Between minor and severe degrees are many moderately severe behavioral conditions that can benefit from professional help, including aggressiveness toward siblings or peers, deficient school adjustment or performance, poor self-esteem, reactive depressions following parental separation or death in the family, and physiological disruptions such as recurrent pains and sleep disorders.

5. *When a child presents a moderately severe behavior problem, does it result from the stress of a temperament-environment mismatch or is it predominantly the product of other factors—noxious environmental influences, such as parental discord or inadequate discipline?* Assessing and weighing the possible contribution of environmental elements requires careful evaluation of their strength and salience. Some sort of evaluation of the child's temperament is essential at this point. Available techniques are discussed in chapter 2, but we would not insist that there is only one way to get this information. The senior author can report, however, that in his general pediatrics practice one of our questionnaires has been of great value in quickly providing a highly pertinent body of material about a child before the beginning of the counseling session. These data must, of course, be supplemented by the further details on temperament and other matters derived from interviewing the parents and sometimes the child. Determining the relative importance of the temperamental predisposition and the noxious environmental elements is a matter of clinical judgment.

    The reader will note that in this algorithm, as compared with the parent's decision tree prepared by Turecki, the question of the contribution of a temperamental component is not raised until later in the process. Attention is first paid to determining whether there is an adjustment problem.

6. *When there is no behavioral adjustment problem.* If the investigation of the several areas of adjustment fails to uncover any true dysfunction but caretakers or others remain concerned, there are two principal explanations. As mentioned earlier, there may be a parental misperception of dysfunction, due to unfamiliarity with normal variations or to misinformation, such as the inability of most 12–18-month-old toddlers to cooperate with parental efforts to toilet-train them. Or the problem may lie with the parents' own psychosocial conflicts, as when a mother undergoing the agony of marital separation sees any activity in her child as excessive. On the other hand, there may be stress from the interaction of the child's temperament and the values and expectations of the caretakers, but reactive symptoms have not yet developed. Although the parents may complain about the child's inflexibility and negative mood, they have been reacting to it with sufficient patience and consistency to avoid secondary problems. The management of such temperament risk factors without secondary conditions was discussed in chapter 3.

Handling Behavioral Problems Related to
Temperament-Environment Interaction

By now it should be quite clear that several simple principles govern the clinical care of behavioral problems in which temperament appears to be an active participant:

1. *Help parents improve the fit to decrease the interactional stress.* For the fit to improve, the areas of friction must be clearly defined and the extent of the unnecessary conflict determined. Then the clinician tries to help the parents discover different ways of interacting with the child to reduce the stress and conflict for both parent and child without sacrificing the main objectives of behavioral adjustment, such as social competence and task performance. The idea is to encourage parents to find a more compatible accommodation of the child's reactive style, bearing in mind that doing so does not require them to surrender their authority. Successful changes result in a diminution or removal of the friction and an improvement in or disappearance of the secondary problem.

   Charlie stopped his violent rebellion against his younger sibling and his mother when, among other measures, his mother gained perspective on the situation and changed from overreacting to his flamboyant expressions of normal sibling jealousy to exercising a more restrained and sympathetic tolerance. Gerry's antisocial behavior at school derived from the stress of a rigid teacher expecting her to adapt faster than she was able to. The solution lay in persuading the teacher to be more flexible herself and to let Gerry take a little longer to get used to new experiences. In both cases, neither the parents nor the children had preexisting or subsequent behavioral disorders, but both children displayed temporarily abnormal behavior when they were subjected to discordant interactions. The points of maximum friction were fairly easily identified and the problems overcome by reducing the unnecessary interactional stress.

2. *Help parents to manage their child's temperament with greater understanding and tolerance.* We strive to understand a child's temperament not only to help find a solution to an existing clinical condition but for other reasons as well. There are realistic limits on the intervention effort. We cannot expect by our efforts to make a difficult child change into somebody else or for other temperament risk factors to disappear. An essential part of the therapy in managing behavioral problems is ensuring that the parents acquire sufficient understanding and tolerance of their child's temperament to minimize, perhaps even avoid, later conflicts. Both Charlie's and Gerry's parents, for instance, learned that they had to be prepared for strong reactions to stress and change from their children in the future.

3. *Other measures for other behavioral issues.* When temperament risk factors are only partly or not at all involved in the genesis of the presenting clinical condition, the management strategy becomes somewhat different. Other factors involved may be issues such as physical illness or disability or an unfavorable psychosocial environment, due to parental inexperience, unrealistic expectations, personal problems, or social stresses. When other factors such as these come into play, therapeutic efforts must be directed not only at helping the parents interact differently with the child but primarily at altering the noxious environmental factors themselves, whether they be family dysfunction, neighborhood violence, or frightening television. Other elements of behavioral management may also be necessary: discipline, behavior modification, psychotherapy for the child or parents, or family therapy. For example, if a child's aggressive behavior seems to be due in part to insufficient limit setting by the parents, the remedy lies in helping them to understand the importance of limits and getting them established. The management of Charlie included not only improving the fit and educating his mother about his behavioral style but also reestablishing her repertory of sensible disciplinary measures, which had been neglected and distorted by the confusion of the arrival of the new baby and the absence of her husband.

These environmental manipulations are methods that are sufficiently well covered in books and other sources of advice on child rearing. No further elaboration is needed here. But the problem with standard books of advice on child rearing, as we have maintained throughout, is that they almost universally fail to acknowledge and allow for the temperamental predispositions of children. The standard wisdom on rearing children does not work equally well with all kinds of children.

4. *Other resources.* In chapter 3, we discussed the value of other educational resources besides professional contacts and written materials, such as support groups. These strengthen parental skills and self-esteem and should be used when available and suitable. Referral to mental health specialists should not be necessary for management of abrasive temperament alone. For behavior problems secondary to dissonant temperament-environment interactions, only the most severe should require such referral, provided that the training of the child health or education professional in charge is sufficient to handle mild to moderate ones.

We agree with Chess and Thomas (1986) that the best first line of attack against the common behavior problems at the primary care level is appropriate and effective parental guidance aimed at accommodating the child's individual differences.

CHAPTER 9

Middle Childhood and School Performance

THE CONSEQUENCES of temperament interactions for performance in school are no less important than they are for behavioral adjustment, but they have not been as extensively explored or appreciated. This chapter begins with Vince's story, which shows how a temperamental predisposition can lead to poor scholastic achievement when it is accompanied by other risk factors.

The school complained to his parents that 6-year-old Vince could not sit still and pay attention to his work. The teacher recommended that they take him to see his pediatrician about getting some medication to solve the problem. He was regarded as quite bright but was suffering from low self-esteem because of his ongoing failure at school. The doctor, who had known him most of his life, was certain that there was no physical or neurological problem. He asked the parents to complete the Behavioral Style Questionnaire and confirmed the presence of a temperament pattern that could explain Vince's inattentiveness. He displayed a low task orientation profile with low persistence/attention span, high distractibility, and high activity, and low adaptability. Since the school had not done sufficient psychological testing, the pediatrician also arranged an examination by a psychoeducational specialist. This psychologist revealed that Vince also had some information-processing disabilities, especially in the area of visual-motor and spatial perception. The teacher, the psychologist, and the pediatrician worked out a program of management that did include use of methylphenidate (Ritalin) but also altered handling in school and behavioral management at home. His school performance, family relations, and self-esteem began to improve right away.

Clara's situation was the same as Vince's in some ways, quite different in others, and her temperament profile was almost exactly the same. Her experience, however, illustrates how temperamental predisposition alone, with no other contributing elements, may not yield such an unfavorable result as it did with Vince.

Clara's profile had been assessed at 6 years and again at 10, not because of a clinical problem but because she took part in the standardization samples of the Behavioral Style and Middle Childhood Temperament Questionnaires. On both tests, her mother had rated her with similar amounts of low task orientation characteristics as well as elements of temperamental difficulty. But Clara had no learning disabilities and no evidence of behavioral or emotional problems. Like Vince, she had supportive parents and a good school system. Through elementary and high school, her career was marked by high scores on aptitude tests but only average results on achievement tests. For her abilities, she was underachieving, getting Bs and Cs when she could have earned straight As. Her parents were disappointed but not worried. The school counselor was also mildly dissatisfied with Clara's level of performance but did not urge testing or medication, and she was never taken to the pediatrician for evaluation of her level of school achievement as a problem. No diagnosis of abnormality was entertained to explain her school performance because she was not in academic trouble. She continued with her desultory work habits throughout high school, always managing to get her work done surprisingly well at the last minute because of her high intelligence. Her disorganization could have led to disaster in the less structured college environment, but by then her intellectual curiosity had been activated. Newly motivated, she forced herself to overcome her poor work habits and learned to function at a level that utilized her abilities more fully. She graduated from college with high academic honors.

These two case studies demonstrate that the issues involved in the contributions of temperament to school performance are complex and controversial. This chapter attempts to make sense of what is probably the most confusing area in temperament research at present and to suggest a rational approach to a puzzling situation.

WHAT DO WE KNOW? THE MAJOR ROLE OF TEMPERAMENT IN SCHOOL PERFORMANCE

Middle childhood, the period between ages 6 and 12, is certainly not a time of "latency," as it used to be called. Besides the expanded and more complex social world of this age group, a new set of challenges is presented by the beginning of formal education. The role of temperament in social adjustment remains as important as it was earlier, but the requirements of cognitive development call into prominence elements of behavioral style that mattered less before. A child's temperament has a major impact on various aspects of school adjustment and performance.

Increased Importance of Persistence/Attention Span

Some observers have expressed the opinion that, even though temperament may be real and significant in infancy, it has become largely irrelevant and subordinated to the effects of experience by the time a child is ready for school. As discussed in chapter 2, the research evidence indicates that the opposite is likely to be true: genetic differences are poorly expressed at birth, being overwhelmed by perinatal factors, and become more evident during the next several years. Over the first few years of a child's life, evidence of genetic effects actually increases and temperament stabilizes.

The most important change when a child enters middle childhood, therefore, is not in the expressions of the temperament itself but in the altered salience or significance of the characteristics. During the preschool years, achieving social adjustment and competence is the principal goal. The difficult/easy traits of approach, adaptability, mood, and so on, are most likely to figure in issues of goodness of fit and problems in behavior and function. Achievement and task performance are not unimportant during these early years, but with the beginning of formal education, they assume a paramount position in the child's interaction with the environment. Teachers expect children to sit still, pay attention, and avoid distractions to a degree not demanded previously.

The original New York Longitudinal Study was concerned mainly with social adjustment, as experienced by parents, and it was not until psychologists—Barbara Keogh (1982, 1986, 1989) in particular—began to study temperament as rated by teachers in school that the characteristics most important for schooling were fully appreciated. Revising the 64-item Thomas and Chess (1977) Teacher Temperament Questionnaire to a 23-item short form, she found a different factor structure from what Thomas and Chess had seen in posing similar questions to parents. The most important characteristics for functioning well in school were subsumed under the "task orientation" factor: high persistence, low distractibility, and low activity. Keogh identified a second factor, similar to the difficult/easy one, that she called the "personal social flexibility" factor, consisting of high adaptability and approach and positive mood. She labeled a third cluster of traits "reactivity," made up of high intensity, low threshold, and negative mood. Thus, while the temperament characteristics that were so important for socialization in the first few years remain prominent, they are rivaled in middle childhood, in the view of teachers, by the traits that affect a child's style of handling tasks.

Another complexity that emerges in school is that goodness of fit may be an issue not only in the child's relations with the people present—classmates and teachers—but also in the varying content of the curriculum. A teacher can sometimes alter her handling of a child to achieve a better fit with the child's personal needs, but any changes in the instructional subject matter are accomplished only with great difficulty and may not be possible in most schools as presently constituted.

TEMPERAMENT AND COGNITIVE STYLE

Beside the individual differences in temperament that affect task performance and the psychopathological syndrome of attention deficit hyperactivity disorder, there is a third way of looking at approximately the same set of characteristics. The phenomenon of cognitive style is found in the educational literature, but it seems to have been subjected to limited inquiry and what we know about it has been given little practical application. The dimensions of cognitive style have been described as persistence, flexibility, and reflectivity (Gaskins & Barron, 1985). These characteristics are thought to be styles of thinking, but their possible relationship to and overlap with behavioral style (temperament) characteristics have yet to be explored. Their close resemblance to Keogh's three factors leads to the speculation that cognitive style may be simply a part of behavioral style, or that both are elements of an overall reactive style. This promising area deserves more attention from researchers.

IMPACT OF TEMPERAMENT ON SCHOLASTIC ACHIEVEMENT

The first major presentation of the results of the New York Longitudinal Study by Thomas, Chess, and Birch (1968) was primarily concerned with social adjustment and had relatively little to say about the possible impact of temperament on scholastic achievement. An earlier work by the group (Gordon & Thomas, 1967) had pointed in this direction by reporting that teacher judgments of kindergarten children's intelligence were significantly influenced by the children's traits of approach and adaptability. Another survey from the NYLS population a little later (Chess, Thomas, & Cameron, 1976) suggested that these two characteristics could be related to scores on academic achievement tests.

The major contributions in the area of temperament's role in school achievement have come from the work of psychologists. Barbara Keogh (1982, 1986, 1989, 1994; Keogh, Bernheimer, Haney, & Daley, 1989) and her associates at the University of California at Los Angeles, besides demonstrating the differing clusters of significant temperament characteristics in the school setting, have added to the early work of Thomas and Chess the conclusion that "there are moderate relationships between children's temperament and their educational competence as measured by performance on standardized achievement tests" (Keogh, 1986). They also demonstrated these relationships in a sample of learning disabled children (Keogh, 1986).

Roy Martin and his colleagues (1989a, 1989b, 1994; Martin, Olejnik, & Gaddis, 1994) have explored this relationship more extensively. Five studies in the elementary school years have related teacher ratings of lower activity, lower distractibility, and higher persistence with higher scores on standardized achievement tests performed up to five years later. Correlations were generally in the .20–.50 range between ratings of activity and reading grades, mathematics grades, and standardized test scores. The mean correlations were about .10 less for standardized test scores than for grades.

A similar pattern was observed in the relationship of low distractibility and high persistence to achievement. However, the correlations for these two variables were .10 higher on average than for activity, ranging from about .30 to .60. The validity of teachers' ratings of activity, distractibility, and persistence in predicting achievement over a four-year interval is particularly impressive. In one study, first-grade ratings of activity, distractibility, and persistence predicted standardized achievement scores in fifth grade at .41 on average (with a range of .25–.48). This outcome indicates considerable continuity of these characteristics over the early elementary school years (Martin, 1989a). A further analysis of these findings confirms them and suggests that these task orientation temperament characteristics "had a much stronger impact on reading performance than did scholastic ability" (Martin et al., 1994, p. 66).

Martin (1989a, 1989b) comments further on this association of higher activity level, greater distractibility, and lower persistence with lower achievement, speculating that three factors may be operating. First, the traits may actually be related to scholastic ability. Second, they may alter how efficiently a child learns, regardless of the level of ability. Third, they may affect not only the process of learning but also the completion of homework and skill at handling standardized tests.

The same characteristics are not uniformly pertinent throughout the curriculum and at all ages. Keogh (1986) believes that the contribution of temperament to school achievement is not pervasive, but rather that its influence is more apparent on school tasks that require the characteristics of high task orientation than it is on those that call for the generation of new problem-solving strategies. "In other words, temperament appears to influence a child's ability to use what he knows."

Robin Hegvik (1985), following 58 children through second to fifth grades, found that the significance of temperament shifted for various academic subjects from elementary to middle school. She also made some unique observations about the characteristics that constitute risk factors for individualized music lessons: low approach, high distractibility, both low and high intensity, and both low and high threshold (Hegvik, 1989).

Evidently, the connection between temperament and scholastic achievement does not diminish as children get older. The Quebec group, studying mainly extremes of temperament (greater than the 70th percentile for four of the five difficult characteristics: low adaptability, withdrawal, intensity, negative mood, and "low [sic] distractibility"), confirmed only minimal correlations with mathematics and reading achievement at age seven. But at age 12, all the characteristics except activity and distractibility were related to mathematics scores (range: r = .37–.49), and reading was associated with approach (r = .38), threshold (r = .37), and distractibility (r = .37). They concluded that the original difficult/easy clusters may not be the best way to examine the connections between behavioral style and academic achievement (Maziade, Côté, Boutin, Boudreault, & Thivierge, 1986).

Correlations of ratings of temperament with scholastic performance are not limited to those made by teachers but also can be shown for ratings by independent observers, the parents. For 100 children aged 10 to 13, parental ratings of temperament on the Middle Childhood Temperament Questionnaire accounted for 5–10% of the variance in academic achievement after factoring out IQ. Persistence was the characteristic most prominently involved with achievement, showing moderately high correlations with reading performance (r = .66) and total learning (r = .45). Other correlations in this range were found for approach, intensity, distractibility, and predictability (Guerin, Gottfried, Oliver, & Thomas, 1994).

The relationships described here have been shown to apply to children throughout a broad spectrum of socioeconomic status; their pertinence has been documented even among highly disadvantaged youths in Soweto, South Africa (Skuy, 1989). Also, links are seen not only in average and learning disabled children but even in intellectually gifted children, who must have a positive task orientation if their skills are to result in optimal performance (Schecter & Reis, 1992).

Assuming a random distribution of temperament characteristics, the percentage of children with low task orientation traits in a typical school population must be fairly high, about 10–20%. Some of them (perhaps 5–10% of the population) are presently being given the controversial diagnosis of attention deficit hyperactivity disorder. Quite apart from the strengths and weaknesses of that designation, what about the rest of the children in this group, the more ordinary active and inattentive ones? Like Clara at the beginning of the chapter, their status is poorly defined or recognized.

To summarize, children's temperaments have been confirmed to have an extensive influence on scholastic performance, as measured by grades and standardized achievement tests. The characteristics most involved are in the task orientation cluster: persistence/attention span, distractibility, and activity. All the other traits, however, may play a part in the learning process. These conclusions appear to apply to children at all levels of cognitive ability and from a broad range of socioeconomic situations. Much of the outcome depends on other elements of the fit between the child and the school situation, such as age, subject matter, cognitive skills, motivation, and the flexibility of the teacher.

IMPACT OF TEMPERAMENT ON TEACHER ATTITUDES

Teachers are likely to be more objective than parents in judging the behavior of the children in their care. Another body of evidence, however, identifies a separate effect of children's temperaments on the attitudes of their teachers and on teachers' evaluations of their students and their interactions with them. Experienced teachers may have learned how to accommodate different behavioral styles in children, even if they have not become acquainted with the concept of temperament or thought explicitly in those terms. Others may misinterpret the expressions of aversive temperaments as maladjustment, handle such children inappropriately, and describe them pejoratively to the parents and fellow teachers. Thus, their responses to their students' temperaments may result in a variety of indirect effects on their scholastic performance and behavior.

We have mentioned the early investigation in New Jersey of 93 kindergarten children (Gordon & Thomas, 1967). Their teachers systematically overestimated the intelligence of children who were approaching and adaptable and underestimated it in those who were slow to warm up. The reasons are not hard to imagine: quick acceptance of novelty can easily be confused with intelligence.

Teachers have different ideas about how "teachable" individual children may be (Keogh, 1982, 1989). When teachers were asked to identify the characteristics they would like to see in the ideal student, they listed cognitive and motivational characteristics and some socioeconomic considerations, but certain temperamental traits were valued equally. They described teachable children as high in task orientation (high persistence, low distractibility, and low activity), high in flexibility (adaptable, approaching, and positive in mood), and low in reactivity (high threshold and low intensity). The practical importance of these findings is that "pupils' temperamental variations may influence teachers' attributions about the causes of behavior, these attributions in turn affecting teachers' instructional and management decisions" (Keogh, 1989, p. 446).

Confirmation of these findings can be found in the investigations of Roy Martin (1989a):

> These studies indicate that teachers find less active, less distractible, and more persistent children more enjoyable to work with, and would like to remove children who are more active and more distractible from their classrooms. Assuming these attitudes relate to teacher behavior in some way, it might be hypothesized that teachers respond to more active, more distractible, and less persistent children in a less

warm and helpful manner (perhaps being more critical), which would further add to the burden these children face in the classroom. (p. 455)

In summarizing the limited research and current thinking in this area, Keogh concluded that children's temperament is an important variable in interactions between teachers and pupils, being associated with the frequency of pupils' interactions with teachers, with teachers' decisions about management within the classroom, and with teachers' instructional strategies (1989, p. 441).

ROLE OF TEMPERAMENT IN SCHOOL BEHAVIORAL PROBLEMS

Gerry's story at the beginning of chapter 8 should remind us that the issues involved in behavioral adjustment in school are much the same as those that are important in the home. When temperament is involved, it is a matter of poor fit with a temperament risk factor. However, moving out into an environment of increased demands produces some greater complexities.

In beginning formal education, a child encounters the challenges of changes in location, new adults and peers, greater expectations and rules, and higher levels of cognitive activity. Some achieve these transitions more easily than others, depending on a variety of factors that include not only the character of the school and the child's abilities and background but also the child's temperament (Chess & Thomas, 1986).

The child's initial entry into school is particularly stressful for the slow-to-warm-up child. The tendency of these children to hold back and delay assimilation into the school community is one of their defining traits. Unfortunately, their teachers sometimes mislabel them "anxious" or "insecure," and parents are occasionally misinformed that such children are in need of psychological counseling, as with Harry at the beginning of chapter 6. These children typically adjust gradually to the new situation in the early days or weeks of school, eventually becoming indistinguishable from the rest of the student body. However, further challenges of novelty, either later in the year or at the beginnings of the next few school years, may reevoke their shyness.

Temperamentally difficult children may similarly arouse the concern of their teachers, who may regard them as "immature" because they are quick and explosive in their complaints. Owing to the stressful interactions teachers often have with children of such temperament, they may actually adjust socially less well. In a group of 51 kindergarten and first-grade children, mothers' ratings of adaptability were significantly correlated with the teacher's judgments of behavioral adjustment ($r = .35$) (Carey, Fox, & McDevitt, 1977).

The characteristics of low persistence/attention span, high distractibility, and high activity also cause teachers to make unfavorable judgments about the classroom behavior of their students (Martin, 1989a, 1989b).

Some other investigations have attested to the view that teachers find most bothersome those who display the combination of low persistence, low approach, and low adaptability (Guerin et al., 1994) or those traits combined with high activity (Klein & Ballantine, 1988).

With entry into school, a new area of stress may emerge. A child may experience a good fit between her temperament characteristics and her parents at home, but the teacher's different values and expectations may call for different behavior from her in order to attain a similarly harmonious relationship at school. For example, the high degree of intensity that is encouraged at home may be criticized by the teacher as too disruptive at school. On the other hand, the degree of fit may be better at school than at home. Such discrepancies can be confusing and distressing for the child and the parents.

Thus, the characteristics that predispose a child to social behavioral problems at school are more or less the same as those that constitute a risk at home and as those that influence the occurrence of scholastic problems.

Influence of Temperament on Health Problems at School

We have no data to suggest that health problems related to temperament differences are substantially dissimilar in school from those noted in the home (see chapter 7). Going to school introduces new stressors and increases exposure to contagious diseases, but it appears that the same mechanisms of symptom production are likely to be operating.

Relationship of Temperament and Cognitive Ability

In view of the established connection between temperament and scholastic achievement, it is reasonable to speculate whether temperament and intelligence or other cognitive skills are related. Although theoretically these two domains are conceptually distinct (see chapter 2), temperament does seem to have an effect on development in the preschool years (see chapter 8). What does the evidence have to say about this influence in the middle childhood period?

Keogh (1986) concluded that, "with a few exceptions, most studies suggest that there are at best only modest and often no significant relationships between temperament and cognitive ability as expressed in IQ's." With additional data from several more recent studies, Martin (1989a) arrived at a different view. He found that the strength of the association is affected by the sample and measure used, the temperament variable studied, and the gender of the child. With correlations running as high as .64 between persistence and IQ on the Stanford-Binet or McCarthy, he wondered "whether or not temperament ratings by teachers are influenced by the teachers' perception of the child's academic ability." Besides this possibility and the likelihood that persistent and nondistractible children work more efficiently, he attributed some part of the high correlations to the probability that such children are more skillful takers of the aptitude tests, and that attention is partly a cognitive function as well as a behavioral one. Matheny (1989) arrived at a similar conclusion: some overlap is inevitable because characteristics such as adaptability have both temperamental and cognitive features.

Although the phenomena of temperament and cognition remain clearly separate human functions, there appears to be some overlap between them. The amount of that overlap and the extent to which they influence each other remain to be defined more clearly.

THE CONFUSION OF TEMPERAMENT WITH ADHD

We come now to the most confusing but perhaps the most important application of the concept of temperament in the school setting: the relationship of normal temperament variations to the pathological syndrome referred to as attention deficit hyperactivity disorder (ADHD). Stated simply, our view is that the term ADHD is commonly used in the United States today to refer to an oversimplified grouping of a complex and variable set of normal but incompatible temperament variations, disabilities in cognition, problems in school function and behavior, and sometimes neurological immaturities. We believe that many different conditions are being called by this one name. We propose that many of the children now being given this diagnosis of brain dysfunction or disorder simply have normal temperament variations that do not fit at school and that nothing at all is wrong with their brains.

We do not wish to minimize the importance of the problems being given this label but rather to point out the inadequacies of the label itself. Let us try to make some sense out of the confusion by reviewing the history of ADHD, defining its current status, pointing out the weaknesses of the present conceptualization, and then suggesting a tentative solution. It is not, however, within our powers to resolve completely the diagnostic bewilderment at this time.

Historical Background

In chapter 2, we described environmentalism, the view popular among theorists in the first half of the twentieth century and up through the 1950s that the environment is almost completely responsible for behavioral outcome in children. As the inadequacies of exclusive environmentalism became clearer, two main theories of intrinsic differences evolved to explain children's contribution to problems in behavior and learning. One view has held that subtle brain malfunction is responsible; the other says that variations of normal temperament traits in neurologically intact individuals could induce the same problems owing to conflict, or "poor fit," between these normal behavioral predispositions and environmental requirements.

The concept of ADHD originated in the 1920s with the notion that brain-injured children exhibit a characteristic syndrome of behavior, first referred to as the brain damage behavior syndrome. In the 1960s a U.S. Public Health Service task force met and published a monograph (Clements, 1966) that attempted to clarify the mounting confusion by standardizing terminology and providing a definition of minimal brain *dysfunction* (as opposed to *damage*). The definition specified the presence of "certain learning or behavioral disabilities ranging from mild to severe, which are associated with deviations of function of the central nervous system." It embraced a considerable variety of behavioral, cognitive, and neurological findings but neglected to mention the minimum criteria for a firm diagnosis of minimal brain dysfunction. Nor did it specify the nature of the nervous system dysfunction or how to detect it.

Little help came from the second edition of the American Psychiatric Association's *Diagnostic and Statistical Manual of Mental Disorders* (*DSM-II*, 1968). The APA redefinition of this phenomenon as the "hyperkinetic reaction of childhood" was, in its entirety, a "disorder . . . characterized by overactivity, restlessness, distractibility, and short attention span, especially in young children; the behavior usually diminishes in adolescence." No delineation of these characteristics was offered, and no criteria were set for the diagnosis.

With the *DSM-III* (APA, 1980) and the *DSM-III-R* (APA, 1987), the focus of the diagnosis shifted and the name was changed, first to attention deficit disorder and then to attention deficit hyperactivity disorder. The *DSM-III-R* lists 14 behavioral descriptions, eight of which must be present to qualify for the diagnosis, and they must have been evident for at least six months, with onset before seven years of age. Items are stated in terms of general impressions, such as, "often talks excessively," and, "has difficulty playing quietly." No clarification of these items is presented, and no mention is made of a requirement that a child so diagnosed be having problems in socialization or school performance.

The history of ideas about temperament was already described in chapter 2 and elsewhere. We shall not repeat it here except to mention that theories of temperament variation and theories based in brain dysfunction—the two principal streams of thought about innate contributions to individual behavior differences—have existed separately in the last several decades, with very little communication between their proponents. This gap, mainly between developmental psychologists and psychiatrists, shows no signs of narrowing at present.

Current Status of ADHD

With the new definition of ADHD in the recently published *DSM-IV* (APA, 1994), some of the problems in earlier editions have been ameliorated. Now the diagnosis rests on the fulfillment of six of nine inattention criteria or six of nine hyperactivity-impulsivity items. The behavioral descriptions continue to be phrased in general terms ("is often easily distracted by extraneous stimuli," or, "often has difficulty organizing tasks

and activities"). The advance lies in the inclusion of two new requirements: "There must be clear evidence of clinically significant impairment
in social, academic, or occupational functioning." And the impairment
must be present in two or more settings, including social, academic, and
occupational functioning.

ADHD has been characterized as the most common significant behavior disorder in childhood, involving perhaps 5% of children, especially
males (E. H. Wender, 1990). The cause is thought to be a brain malfunction, one either genetically determined or resulting from some sort of
insult to the brain. Generally, little or no contribution from the environment is described as necessary for the expression of the typical clinical
picture; the problem is in the child. The diagnosis is almost always based
on reports given to the clinician by either the parents or the teacher, and
virtually never on findings from a neurological examination or any other
objective measurement of the intactness of the central nervous system.
The *DSM-IV* perpetuates the vague standards for defining the behaviors
by stating that they are "more frequent and severe than is typically
observed in individuals at a comparable level of development."
Logically, then, the diagnosis could be applied to much of the population:
a child would qualify as abnormal if, for example, he or she was above
average in activity or below average in attentiveness.

Some of the leading spokespersons for ADHD have offered opinions
on the relationship between that disorder and temperament. Paul
Wender (1987) suggests that "the two major causes of ADD seem to be:
(1) an exaggeration or an excess of traits that normally vary from person
to person; (2) a genetically determined disorder" (p. 28). He neither dis-
closes how one might discriminate between the two forms nor acknowl-
edges sufficiently that it may be the environment rather than the magnitude of the characteristics that makes the temperament "excessive."

Russell Barkley (1990), one of the most widely read authorities on the
subject, believes that "behavioral disinhibition, or the inability to adequately regulate behavior by rules and consequences, is the sine qua non
of this disorder . . . rather than an attention deficit" (p. 73). Could he be
talking about low adaptability? He also describes a family history of the
problem and signs of difficult temperament in the preschool years as
early predictors of ADHD, but he does not take the logical further step of
proposing that what is being called ADHD may in fact be at least in part
a continuation of that difficult temperament into the school years. He tells
us that "one of our major objectives is to teach parents that ADHD is in
large part an inborn biological temperamental predisposition, which parents and children must learn to cope with over time, rather than cure."
But in the same paragraph, he adds that it is "primarily a motivational
disorder" (p. 431), a conclusion that seems inconsistent with our understanding of the nonmotivational nature of temperament.

Goldstein and Goldstein (1992) assert that "as many as 70% of difficult
infants develop school-age problems" (p. 50). We are unaware of the evi-

dence to support this statement; moreover, we must wonder why this high figure did not lead them to consider the possibility that at least part of what is getting diagnosed as ADHD in school is actually a continuation of difficult temperament. All of these observers seem to be saying that the difficult temperament in a preschooler changes into, or is replaced by, ADHD at some point before school starts.

Critique of the ADHD Terminology

Despite the current popularity of the ADHD concept and the benefits it has conferred by taking blame away from parents and offering management strategies that are often very helpful, it is encumbered with some major problems (Carey, 1992c; Carey & McDevitt, 1980; Carey, McDevitt, & Baker, 1979):

1. Even some of its most ardent adherents (e.g., Sleator & Pelham, 1986) agree that ADHD is not a coherent syndrome. There is neither sufficient concurrence of the supposed elements nor sufficient differentiation between them and other phenomena to justify speaking of a syndrome in the usual sense of the word. The behavioral traits said to characterize the syndrome do have a tendency to cluster, but they occur in a variety of other groupings as well. Low or high activity can be found with low or high attention span and low or high distractibility or impulsivity. There is little interrater and cross-situational reliability. For example, two teachers in the same school may form different impressions of a particular child. Clinicians vary too: between 15% and 90% of a population referred to a pediatric neurologist for problems in school function or behavior could be given such a diagnosis, depending on how the criteria were applied (Carey & McDevitt, 1980; Carey, McDevitt, & Baker, 1979).

2. The behavioral components of ADHD are not clearly distinguishable from what is normal, and they can arise from various causes. No proponent of the ADHD syndrome has yet satisfactorily clarified at what point high activity becomes hyperactivity or normal inattentiveness turns into a pathological attention deficit. Some have suggested that it is when the behavior is at the extreme, or when it leads to dysfunction in the child. But as we have maintained throughout this book, extremes of these behavioral style characteristics are not abnormal by themselves, nor do they result in behavioral problems without the contribution of other elements, such as family dysfunction. The same degree of a characteristic might be dysfunctional for one child but not for another, depending on the accompanying features of the temperament-environment interaction. Furthermore, the inattentiveness ascribed to ADHD not only can be a temperament variation but may arise from depression, anxiety, physical illness, or other causes. A learning disability can make a child inattentive because of the difficulty in learning,

and that inattentiveness can lead to the other behavioral symptoms associated with ADHD.

3. Many children who are inattentive, distractible, and active do not develop clinical problems but perform acceptably, or even well, in school. These behaviors have no invariable outcome; as we saw earlier, Clara expressed these temperament traits in school without being diagnosed with ADHD. The *DSM-IV* criteria state that the child must have not only the designated behaviors but dysfunction in two or more settings. How would that system label those with the behaviors but not the dysfunction? Strict application of the *DSM-IV* terminology does not allow us to call them normal. Those with "prominent symptoms of inattention or hyperactivity-impulsivity that do not meet criteria for Attention-Deficit/Hyperactivity Disorder" are to be designated "ADHD Not Otherwise Specified"—still a pathological diagnosis.

   Common sense, however, urges us to avoid using a pathological diagnosis to describe children who are not having clinical problems. Clinical research data validate our position that the inattentive, distractible, and active behaviors are not the disorder itself but signs of a *predisposition* to develop difficulty in school. A review of the temperament ratings of the 305 children from the senior author's private practice component of the standardization sample of the Middle Childhood Temperament Questionnaire (Hegvik, McDevitt, & Carey, 1982) revealed 15 children who were greater than one standard deviation in high activity, low persistence, and high distractibility. In all but one of these cases, adequate data on school performance were available. It was no surprise that half of the 14 were reported by their parents to be having school function problems. What is of greater interest, however, is that the other half of these children were performing either adequately or better than average. Similarly a questionnaire survey of the parents of 1,022 four- to twelve-year-old children in Japan found that 7.7% of the children met the *DSM-III-R* criteria for ADHD, but less than half (41.5%) of those children were cited by their teachers as having hyperactive or inattentive behaviors (Kanbayashi et al., 1994).

   These findings and clinical experience compel the recognition that many children with these behavioral traits never come to clinical attention because they are not attracting the concern of their teachers. It is reasonable to suppose that they have sufficient compensatory traits, such as intelligence, motivation, and adaptability, or a family and school that can supportively handle their needs. It appears that the behaviors described as constituting the "disorder" of ADHD are instead the risk factor or predisposition rather than the clinical problem itself.

4. Low adaptability or inflexibility may be more prevalent among children given the ADHD label than the group of behaviors usually mentioned. In a sample of 61 children referred to a pediatric neurologist for problems in behavior and learning and tested with parental ratings on

the Behavioral Style Questionnaire, the commonest temperament characteristic, regardless of the ultimate diagnosis, was low adaptability. They were also high in activity and low in persistence, but their low adaptability was the strongest association (Carey, McDevitt, & Baker, 1979). Low adaptability may be at the heart of Barkley's (1990) comment that children with ADHD have an "inability to adequately regulate behavior by rules and consequences" as their fundamental problem. What is most likely to lead to dysfunction may not be a child's inattentiveness as much as his or her inability or disinclination to moderate this predisposition when circumstances call for it.

5. The thinking on ADHD lacks evolutionary perspective. The current practice is to say that children who are insufficiently attentive in modern classrooms have something wrong with their brains. Would it not be fairer to acknowledge that our bodies and minds, which presumably evolved over many millennia of hunting and gathering on the savannas of Africa, may not yet have evolved beyond the requirements of the Stone Age and become adapted to the highly artificial environment of the modern school? Short attention spans and high activity may have been highly adaptive and served our ancestors well, promoting survival in a world full of predators.

A Solution to the ADHD-Temperament Confusion

The confusion over ADHD has resulted in much inconclusive or uninterpretable research, much perplexity in clinicians, parents, and children, and much care of children and their parents that is inaccurate, unhelpful, and even harmful. We cannot finish this description of the problem without suggesting a way out. We have, in fact, already done so on several occasions (Carey & McDevitt, 1980; Carey, 1986; Carey, 1988). What follows is a summary of the clarification we have offered.

1. *Attention deficits exist.* Many children do have trouble paying sufficient attention to meet environmental requirements. There is no reason why we cannot say that those with this symptom have an "attention deficit," as long as we resist the temptation to assume that the presence of a symptom means that a standard syndrome is present. Not every child with a rash has the rash syndrome; not everyone with a fever is diagnosed with fever disorder. The causes of inattention are various and include a primary cognitive disability, a temperament variation in persistence, and other problems such as anxiety, depression, and some physical illnesses. Preliminary study shows that attention has several components: planning and reflection, selection and vigilance, inhibition and resistance to distraction, continuity and persistence, and monitoring and self-correction (Levine, 1992a). Of these elements, the standard *DSM* criteria consider primarily only the ones related to persistence. Attention deficits can also vary in pervasiveness, intensity,

accompanying strengths (such as adaptability) and liabilities (such as learning disabilities), and interactions and outcomes.

The main contribution of temperament research to our understanding of the problems in the ADHD system is the point that the low task orientation characteristics (inattention, distractibility, and high activity) probably predispose a child to poor performance but are not the "disorder" itself. The mixture of other factors determines whether the child has trouble or not. Vince's story illustrates how clinical problems can arise when the low task orientation characteristics are accompanied by a learning disability and limited flexibility. Yet Clara, with the same behavioral pattern but otherwise free of liabilities, was not having trouble in school.

Another important point to remember is Martin's (1989b) demonstration that low task orientation is not a categorical disorder that some children have and other children do not. The relationship between the characteristics and scholastic performance is linear: Those students with low task orientation do less well than students with average amounts of these characteristics, but the average students, about whom nobody is concerned, do less well than those with high task orientation.

2. *More comprehensive diagnostic formulation should be used.* What is the confused teacher or health care worker to do in the present situation? The ADHD terminology is embedded in our present culture, and ADHD has become almost a household word. It does have some advantages, such as providing a clear-cut diagnosis that relieves parents of unwarranted guilt about their child's problem, and it also can be a helpful label to obtain needed services from the school system. Yet although we may be obliged to use the term in official communications and as a diagnosis on insurance forms, whether we like it or not, our thinking and practice need not be cramped and thwarted by the diagnostic limitations of our times. We would urge an avoidance of unsubstantiated diagnostic labels whenever possible. These suggestions apply to both educators and health care personnel.

In place of the pathology-oriented diagnostic system currently in use in health care settings, we urge that educators and health care workers at least think in terms that are more consistent with the research findings. Simply telling a child and the family that he or she does or does not have ADHD is not a sufficiently detailed diagnostic description. We have suggested the use of a biopsychosocial or neurobehavioral profile, which organizes objective findings under six headings:

1) General physical status, including growth

2) Neurological status, based on examination findings as to motor function, reflexes, coordination, "soft signs," and sensory status of vision and hearing

3) Information-processing abilities

4) Maturation, both psychomotor (including speech) and cognitive abilities

5) Temperament or behavioral style, in particular adaptability, persistence/attention span, and activity

6) Psychosocial adjustment, encompassing evidence of social competence, task performance, self-assurance, and other mental and physical functions.

The profile could describe the child's living situation, including mention of the environmental input and interaction. If the child is seen by parents or teachers as abnormal in any respect, the person complaining should be identified and the nature of the interactional difficulty fully described. The profile would be incomplete if it did not mention the child's strengths as well as disabilities or other concerns. The advantage of using such a profile is more accurate and individualized educational and clinical diagnosis and practice. In research, a more precise definition of the subjects examined could result in studies that can be understood better, accelerating a reduction of the present confusion.

3. *The "goodness of fit" concept is useful but has limitations in the school setting.* Interactions do matter for the functioning of schoolchildren, whatever their behavioral styles may be. Schoolteachers can to some extent modify their handling of individual children to accommodate their temperament patterns in the social area, and curricula can sometimes be tailored to the learning styles of particular students. Yet we must recognize that in school there are limits to the application of the goodness-of-fit concept. Some behavioral characteristics and some environmental properties make a healthy consonance between child and school extremely difficult to achieve. When the child's abilities and behavioral characteristics fit poorly with the requirements of the curriculum content, the inanimate course materials (such as the number of tasks to be completed in one hour) cannot be flexible with the child the way the teacher can. In this case, the poor fit itself becomes a clinical problem, whether or not it generates excessive stress and secondary behavioral symptoms.

4. *New terminology is needed.* The terminology changes in *DSM-IV* have been a move in the right direction, but even greater changes must be made before *DSM-V* is published. The question of separating normal temperament variations from pathological brain function has not even been mentioned. In the meanwhile, the American Academy of Pediatrics will soon publish the *Diagnostic and Statistical Manual for Primary Care (DSM-PC)*, which will offer diagnostic terms for less

severe behavioral concerns, but the details of that manual are still undergoing changes at the time of writing. At least brief mention of temperament is expected.

How should ADHD be redefined? As Michael Rutter (1983) proposed a dozen years ago: "There may be a less common, valid syndrome, definable in terms of overactivity and inattention, that is manifest across a range of situations and circumstances. So far the evidence in support of this hypothesis is too slender to consider it validated, but it remains a possibility well worth further investigation." Little progress toward that goal has been achieved. To his criterion of pervasiveness of symptoms we would add the requirements: (1) that such a valid syndrome contain behavioral characteristics that are qualitatively rather than just quantitatively different from the norm; and (2) that there be, in fact, objective evidence of disordered function of the central nervous system, not just the assumption of its presence based on parental or teacher reports.

If the underlying cause is a deficiency of norepinephrine in the ascending reticular activating system of the brain, as some have suggested, then more substantial proof should be offered and some reliable measure of that status devised. A response to stimulant medications cannot be accepted as a diagnostic criterion since completely normal children have been shown to improve their performance with them (Bernstein et al., 1994; Rapoport et al., 1978). The fact that 25 adults considered to be "hyperactive" since youth showed an average of 8.1% less glucose utilization in parts of their brains than controls on a positron emission tomograph does not provide us with a suitable diagnostic technique (Zametkin et al., 1990).

When the true "disorder" is identified, it may be useful to look to the example of how Jones (1944) brought order out of diagnostic confusion over rheumatic fever. After his report, it was no longer possible to say that any child with fever and joint pains had rheumatic fever. The physician was required to demonstrate two major or one major and two minor signs of the disease supported by evidence of a streptococcal infection. All of these manifestations are objective findings (with the exception of the arthralgia or joint pain, one of the minor ones), and none is based on hearsay evidence. Most observers do not doubt that what is now called ADHD will be similarly defined someday, but we judge that it will have a prevalence rate of less than 1% of the child population.

WHAT CAN WE DO? PRACTICAL PRINCIPLES FOR ENHANCING SCHOOL PERFORMANCE

In this chapter, we have covered a wide range of topics about the impact of children's temperaments on schooling. We must now try to distill from that information and from experience a set of practical principles for use by teachers, clinicians, and parents of school-age children. Our knowledge about these matters is far from complete. But at the same time, far too much valid information is available now to justify sitting on our hands and waiting for greater certainty.

EDUCATING TEACHERS, CLINICIANS, PARENTS, AND CHILDREN

Professional Education of Teachers and Clinicians

It is likely that a majority of educators at all levels and clinicians of various disciplines are largely unaware of the research results contained in the first part of this chapter. Although our understanding of this field is in its early stages, there can be little doubt that children's temperaments have a significant influence on their scholastic performance, their behavior at school, and on teachers' attitudes toward them. This information should be included in the curriculum of both the graduate and continuing education of the health and education professions.

The concept of temperament should not be foreign to most educators. They may not know the technical terminology, but most experienced teachers have witnessed a variety of behavioral styles and learned that different children require different strategies for optimal management and performance. With a little specific instruction, these educators could enhance their skills rapidly. Keogh (1982) noted that

> it is interesting that the teachers who have participated in our research have reported that consideration of pupils' temperament has made them more sensitive to their own perceptions of individual children. The temperament dimensions apparently provide a differentiated framework for viewing children. Recognition of temperament patterns is particularly helpful in anticipating problem situations and allows teachers to modify their own behavior in order to get a better approximation of the "goodness of fit" suggested by Thomas & Chess (1977) in their work with clinical populations.

Michael Pullis (1989) has carried Keogh's research further, suggesting three types of situations in which teachers might utilize temperament information and a goodness-of-fit perspective in their decision making:

1. Managing negative teacher feelings about problem students: If teachers can correctly identify a child's annoying behavior as temperamental rather than intentional, they can deal more dispassionately and effectively with the negative feelings that the behavior may generate in them.

2. Accommodative strategies to improve classroom fit: Teachers can do as parents do—modify their beliefs or behavior to diminish the stress for a child in those situations where his or her behavioral style

is clashing with classroom expectations. Teachers can examine systematically the demands of each of the activities in their classroom, noting those students who consistently present problems and analyzing the components of the problems.

3. Skill development to deal with children's strengths and weaknesses: A teacher can use a variety of supportive approaches to help students take advantage of their strengths and compensate for areas of weakness.

Pullis concludes with a plea that training procedures be established to ensure that teachers acquire the necessary knowledge and skills and that evaluative studies in the classroom be undertaken to monitor the progress of this development.

Education of Parents by Teachers and Clinicians
Once informed about temperament and its importance for experiences at school, teachers and clinicians should pass these insights on in general terms to the parents of their students and patients and, when pertinent, discuss the individual features of the particular child that may make him or her likely either to perform well or to be at risk for problems. The teacher or clinician can instruct parents directly or refer them to some of the available written materials (see chapter 1 and appendix 4). Material on ADHD should be recommended with caution because virtually all of it fails to recognize the existence of normal temperament variations that have been confused with more abnormal conditions. We specifically discourage alternative therapies of unproven value for activity and attention problems, such as diets, vitamin therapy, patterning, optometric visual training, sensory integration therapy, and tinted lenses.

Parents, of course, have access to other sources of this information, as well as their own opinions about their children. Teachers, however, have more experience with a variety of children and have had opportunities to compare the particular child with others in a setting that is quite different from the home. Besides the usual issues, the discussion in parent-teacher conferences can also include exchanges of information about the child's behavioral style.

Parents and Others Helping Children Understand Their Own Styles
One of the more valuable kinds of understanding that parents can help a child acquire in the early years of life and later is some perspective on the distinctive qualities and the normality of the child's own temperament. If a child is so persistent that he has trouble changing appropriately from one activity to another, how much healthier it is for parent and child to recognize that his persistence is a generally laudable, if sometimes bothersome trait, not oppositional behavior needing discipline. By the same token, is it not better for all to acknowledge that a child's shyness is a

bearable variant of normal, not a sign of parental inadequacy or emotional insecurity in the child?

Melvin D. Levine has written two excellent books for children to help them get some understanding of and perspective on their learning abilities and disorders, *Keeping a Head in School* (1990) and *All Kinds of Minds* (1993). We are not aware, however, of any similar written materials designed for children to help them get a broad view of behavioral style patterns and find themselves within the normal spectrum.

As children grow older, adults, particularly parents and teachers, can help them not only to understand their own temperaments better but also to modify the expression of them to enhance a reasonable adjustment to the realities of the environment. As discussed earlier, children can learn to moderate tantrums, to suppress shyness, and to facilitate transitions in order to get along better with people who are important in their lives. Particularly helpful for the school-age child are suggestions on how to sustain attention for longer periods and how to block the disruptive effects of distractions.

IDENTIFICATION OF STUDENTS' TEMPERAMENTS

When teachers become aware of the dimensions of temperament and understand their importance for children's school experiences, they will easily be able to form an impression of each student's individual patterns. This new perspective should greatly augment the skill with which they interact with students and make management decisions.

We do not propose that at this time there is any established rationale for routine, formal temperament assessment of students, such as would be obtained from a standardized questionnaire, a structured interview, or a period of organized observations. Some have proposed routine evaluations of all students at the point of school entry and perhaps later. Parents would probably cooperate in completing questionnaires, but we cannot recommend such a procedure: the dangers of misinterpretation or misuse of the data are too great at present (Carey & McDevitt, 1989).

Furthermore, we must disagree with the advice of Goldstein and Goldstein (1992), who propose that pediatricians and family practitioners routinely screen all infants for temperamental difficulty; they believe that "we can identify a group of children who appear to be at greater risk of being diagnosed as hyperactive in childhood" (p. 55). There is no firm research basis for assuming that measurements of temperamental difficulty in infancy have such powers of prediction. In fact, our own work (Carey, Fox, & McDevitt, 1977) confirmed only a nonlinear and probably inconsequential relationship between infant temperamental difficulty and school adjustment at five and a half to seven years. Contemporary temperament, especially adaptability, was more closely related to behavioral adjustment. Screening for temperamental difficulty alone, without also assessing its interactions with and effect on the environment, will, we believe, inevitably produce weak predictions at best. Pediatricians and other health care workers would do better to inquire routinely about the quality of parent-child interactions and to be sensitive and responsive to parental expressions of concern that things are less than satisfying and pleasant.

INTERVENTIONS IN THE SCHOOL SETTING

Although the routine measurement of temperament in all schoolchildren would probably introduce more risks than benefits, the situation is different when a particular child is having behavioral or scholastic problems in school. Then it becomes essential to determine as well as possible the nature and extent of the child's contribution to the situation. Traditionally, however, assessments have been limited to the child's cognitive and motivational status. These areas are essential, of course, to an educational evaluation, but they do not cover the assets and liabilities of the child's behavioral style, which may make a critical difference in his or her academic performance. "Thus, it is reasonable that temperament be included in psychologists' evaluations" (Keogh, 1989, p. 444). At the beginning of chapter 8, the pediatrician's evaluation of Gerry's school adjustment problem would have been incomplete and probably inaccurate without a determination of her temperament profile.

Keogh adds several cautions about the use of temperament measurements in the resolution of school problems. Anyone using this information must be aware that there are several different conceptualizations of temperament and should also understand the limitations of assessment instruments. The user should be fully informed on the subject of temperament and must not issue oversimplified or erroneous interpretations of the results. Appropriate application of the findings also requires considerable clinical skill. In other words, competent use of temperament data can be enormously helpful, but attempts by unqualified persons may be more harmful than helpful.

When inattention at school is the chief complaint, an unusual degree of proficiency is required of the person doing the assessment. It is far too simple an attempt at evaluation just to have a teacher fill out a brief, impressionistic questionnaire with as few as 10 items, such as those devised by Keith Conners for parents and teachers (see Barkley, 1990, appendix), and then send the child off to the physician with a request for medication. Furthermore, it is not appropriate for teachers to make the diagnosis of ADHD in discussing students' problems with their parents. An ADHD diagnosis should be made by appropriate persons in the medical or mental health fields. To stem the current overuse of this confusing terminology, teachers should limit themselves to descriptions of the problem, rather than offering diagnoses in their conferences with parents and in formal reports to them.

A thorough assessment of a child's attention deficits includes a comprehensive evaluation consisting of:

- documentation from multiple sources of the degree and pervasiveness of the symptoms, as well as an analysis of the complicating factors and strengths;

- a physical and neurodevelopmental examination;

- evaluation by a psychoeducational specialist to elicit the child's general and specific learning abilities and weaknesses;

- a psychosocial evaluation of the child's behavioral and emotional status and interactions with significant people;

- a comprehensive diagnostic profile that lists assets as well as deficits and avoids the use of labels; and

- a determination of the individual service needs of the child, not just a standard list of remedies. (Levine, 1992a)

We hope that the *DSM* diagnostic scheme will soon evolve beyond the present oversimplification of allowing practically any inattentive child to be referred to as having ADHD. In the meanwhile, we urge teachers and clinicians to remain skeptical about the current ADHD terminology. It is improving gradually, but we have a long way to go before our use of this terminology includes an acknowledgment that most children's problems with inattention in school are probably not due to a disorder in brain function but result from a poor fit between a difficult or low task orientation temperament and the many other factors we have mentioned in this chapter.

Physicians and psychologists who become familiar with the findings reported in this chapter will probably find themselves using the ADHD diagnosis more hesitantly and less frequently and looking forward eagerly to a clarification of the terminology. Given what we know about temperament, we would do well to interpret adjustment and performance problems in school as much as possible in terms of temperament and goodness of fit and to reserve the more serious ADHD diagnosis for the few who meet stricter criteria of pervasiveness and qualitative differences of the behaviors and, ideally, who show some objective evidence of cerebral malfunction.

Is it necessary to diagnose a brain malfunction, as one does with the label of ADHD, to justify the use of cerebral stimulants such as methylphenidate (Ritalin)? Since we know that normal individuals can enjoy enhanced performance with such drugs, no pathological diagnosis is needed to support the use of such medication. If all other means have been tried without success in an effort to bring a student's ability to concentrate up to an acceptable level, could such medication be justified without recourse to an excessive diagnosis?

An extensive discussion of the problem of inattention in school lies beyond the scope of this book. The interested reader is referred to a more detailed and highly competent treatment of the subject by Melvin Levine, a well-qualified person who is determined to evaluate accurately the true complexity of children and to avoid the dangerous business of thinking that simply affixing a label on a child is of much value to anyone. Two of his works, a book (1987) and a shorter treatment of only 22 pages (1992a, chaps. 53 and 54), are highly sophisticated introductions to the handling of problems in this area.

SUPPORT RESEARCH

Our understanding of temperament and its impact on school performance has made an exciting beginning, but it must advance much further before we can feel confident that we grasp the matter fully. Temperament researchers seem to be less confident than ADHD spokespersons that we have arrived at an adequate comprehension of the subject. Progress will entail studies of large numbers of children, sometimes with detailed evaluation of them. Although these research efforts may sometimes inconvenience teachers, we encourage full cooperation with and support of any well-designed projects that promise to increase our knowledge of these issues. Our professional effectiveness and the welfare of our children depend on these endeavors.

CHAPTER 10

Adolescence

THE ROLE OF TEMPERAMENT in various aspects of life has been studied and evaluated less for adolescence than for any other period of childhood. Available research data and clinical impressions, however, leave no doubt of its continuing existence and practical significance. The two case studies below should remind the reader of some of the ways in which temperament matters for teenagers. Fred's mild, adaptable nature delayed his utilization of medical care and adversely affected his health.

Fred had always been an easygoing, agreeable boy who got along well with just about everybody. When ill, he typically complained so little that his parents had to be careful that they were giving him sufficient attention. This generally desirable trait usually served him well, but it got him into trouble when he was 14 years old. One evening after supper he began to have some pain in his right lower abdomen extending down into his groin. Nevertheless, he did his homework, watched some television as usual, and then went to bed. By midnight some tenderness had become noticeable in his right testicle, but he did not believe it necessary to bother his parents at that point. By morning the pain had become severe, and he had started vomiting. His parents immediately called the pediatrician, fearing that he might have appendicitis. The doctor quickly recognized that Fred had a torsion (twisting) of the testicle and referred him at once to a urologist. Unfortunately, the blood supply to the testicle had been cut off for too long, and it was too badly damaged to be saved. His typically mild and uncomplaining response to illness, which over the years had made his care so easy for his parents, had cost him a testicle. His mother later remarked to the pediatrician that this sort of behavior was typical of Fred, but that with his younger brother it would have been a different story. She was certain that his younger brother would have yelled and demanded attention at the first twinge of pain, thus making possible a successful surgical intervention.

George's temperamental difficulty, which seemed to have disappeared earlier in childhood, resurfaced in adolescence during challenges to his adjustment.

George had been a very difficult infant who cried a lot and adjusted very slowly despite the skill and patience of his devoted parents. With some help from their pediatrician, they were able to understand the nature of the problem and to handle him in such a way that no secondary behavior problems emerged as the result of a poor fit. In fact, he was soon regarded as a well-adjusted child by those who met him. He was slower than average in making the necessary adaptations to the routines in kindergarten, but his teacher soon overcame his resistance by using the same strategies his parents had found helpful in earlier years.

George became an outstanding student because of his abilities and the years of understanding management by his parents. He achieved a successful adaptation between his temperament, his abilities, and the requirements of his environment. For the most part, he suppressed his tendency to resist change with negative explosions by using learned behavioral controls. However, from time to time, when faced with major challenges to his flexibility, the old traits temporarily reemerged.

When George had to start wearing glasses in order to see the board at school, he refused to wear them for weeks and became angry when reminded by his parents or teacher. Finally, he recognized that his schoolwork was suffering from his inability to obtain important information from the board, and he started to use them. One of the more dramatic reemergences of his old temperamental traits occurred when his parents took him to college at the beginning of his freshman year. He had done well academically, socially, and athletically in high school, but now he was going away from home for the first time. After a sullen trip in the family car, he loudly ordered his parents not to stop at his dormitory but to keep on driving and leave the campus for a while. Two hours later, holding back tears, George walked into the dormitory with a load of belongings. Within an hour he was all moved in, and he sent his parents off, insisting that things would be all right. He did adjust well in the next few weeks and eventually had as distinguished a career at college as he had had in high school.

To these two stories could be added many others that would further elucidate how temperament differences continue to exist and to matter into adolescence. This chapter reviews what has been documented so far and describes the shifting management plan as the teenager becomes more responsible for his or her own affairs.

WHAT DO WE KNOW?
THE CONTINUED IMPORTANCE OF TEMPERAMENT INTERACTIONS IN ADOLESCENCE

The life of the adolescent has much in common with that of the younger child, but some major changes have occurred. The adolescent's social life requires more elaborate social skills for the steps of separating from parents, moving closer to peers, and forming more complicated relationships with the opposite sex. High school work calls for greater levels of cognitive function and better work habits. Other important challenges are the physical and sexual changes of puberty, the need to achieve a sense of identity, and possibly the pursuit of employment outside the home (Carey & Earls, 1988).

Chess and Thomas (1984) concluded from their New York Longitudinal Study that adolescence is not a uniquely stressful part of childhood. They suggest that the period's reputation as a time of unusual problems in parent-child relationships and child behavior is based for most families on the ambivalence parents feel about the changes in their children and on their loss of absolute parental control. To this view we might add the fact that adolescents are more articulate and outspoken than younger children and more likely to let their grievances be known. By contrast, how often does one hear toddlers describing in detail their conflicting feelings about toilet training, or preschool children proclaiming on television talk shows how angry they are about going off to day care when they feel ill? (Carey & Earls, 1988). Subsequent research is likely to inform us that, as with toddlerhood, a child's temperament makes the normal passage through adolescence rougher or smoother (Lerner & Lerner, 1994).

THE SAME DEFINITION OF TEMPERAMENT

The definition of temperament as behavioral style used for earlier ages is still appropriate in adolescence. We should continue to observe the principle that the child's temperament is the behavioral style prevalent at the time and not attempt the impossible task of trying to separate out the genetic components from those arising from other sources.

Although behavioral style and behavioral adjustment can and should be distinguished in adolescence, the process of differentiation may have become more complex by this time. After over a decade of interaction with other factors, especially psychosocial ones, a child's temperament is likely to have produced a strong imprint on his adjustment and also to have induced substantial changes in his environment.

The shift in the clinical significance of the temperament characteristics, described in chapter 9, endures during adolescence. Persistence/attention span and distractibility remain vital factors in school performance. Sensory threshold is not unimportant but has declined from its salience in infancy. The traits that would best identify "difficulty," or a risk of social conflict and behavior problems, have not been specifically identified for this period, but there seems little doubt that low adaptability and negative mood would still be at the heart of such a cluster (Carey & Earls, 1988).

ORIGINS: SOME NEW FACTORS

We emphasized in chapter 2 that temperament cannot be explained only in terms of genetic processes and the psychosocial environment, as is usually the case in the investigations of developmental behavioral geneticists, but must also be subject to considerations of a child's physical status and the nonhuman environment. As the child moves into adolescence, the need to recognize the greater complexity of temperament factors is reinforced. The hormonal changes of puberty that bring about structural and functional physical changes are well documented, but the possibility that adolescents experience a greater sexual differentiation in temperament has yet to be clearly defined and established. The irritability of premenstrual syndrome is too well known to require elaboration, but we have no information on more enduring differences in temperament that can be related to increased or varying levels of the sex hormones. Folklore and anecdotes abound, but scientific study is still missing except for some early beginnings (Windle, 1992a).

Aspects of the adolescent lifestyle that could be investigated for their effects on temperament include dietary eccentricities, sleep deprivation, rigorous athletic training, and drug use.

The development of the ability to alter reaction style patterns consciously and voluntarily in response to social pressures is another factor in temperament variations, or at least their expression, by adolescence. If a child perceives that free display of her temperament leads to conflict or criticisms from significant persons, she may try to alter those responses to diminish the discomfort. An intense child may discover that demonstrations of explosive emotions are not acceptable to family or friends and may seek to moderate these behaviors. A shy or slow-to-warm-up child may find his inhibition a handicap in social settings and may force himself into new situations despite the uneasiness he feels. The intense child may continue to feel the intensity, and the shy one may still regard himself as shy, but the overt behavior witnessed by others appears otherwise (Carey & Earls, 1988).

STABILITY

The trend in earlier childhood is increasing stability of temperament with advancing years. We may speculate that this trend continues into adolescence, but no research data are available to confirm this opinion. Studies of stability during childhood and from childhood into early adolescence are available, but we could find no studies of stability during adolescence or from then into young adulthood. An important element in the slow progress in this area has been the limitations of the measurement techniques available for this period of childhood. Another obstacle has been the issue of what constitutes change: Is it what the individual feels or what others see?

George is an example of a child who may seem to have changed in temperament—because he has consciously suppressed his predisposition to inflexibility or shyness—only to have it break through and reemerge temporarily at times of extraordinary stress, such as leaving home to go to college.

LIMITED MEASUREMENT TECHNIQUES

Although the earlier Guilford-Zimmerman (1949) and Thurstone (1953) questionnaires have been used with adolescents, the age group is not well served by scales derived from the widely accepted New York Longitudinal Study conceptualization. The Middle Childhood Temperament Questionnaire (Hegvik, McDevitt, & Carey, 1982) covers the beginning of adolescence for some children who have matured by the age of 12, but there is no published scale specifically designed for the ages of 12 to 21 years. The Dimensions of Temperament Survey (DOTS) (Lerner et al., 1982), which was revised as the DOTS-R by Windle and Lerner (1986), and the EAS Scale of Buss and Plomin (1975, 1984) are intended for use in research at any age and have been employed in research with adolescents. However, because they include a relatively small number of generally stated items and have not been tested in clinical situations, these scales should not be substituted for clinical interviewing or for more specifically designed scales for adolescents yet to be devised and published.

An important methodological problem awaits resolution by the developer of such a temperament scale specifically for adolescents. Should the source of data be the parents, the youngster, or both? Parents are more experienced observers and are presumably less subjective than their children, but children are more aware of their own feelings and of the full range of their experience. If the result were widely differing ratings on some items or in some areas, as seems likely, how would the scorer fuse the two views into a single score? Perhaps the best method would be to obtain independent ratings from both and to record them separately on the same summary sheet. This procedure would allow systematic and unbiased comparisons between parents and their children.

It seems likely, however, that parents and adolescents would more often be in agreement than at odds. Supporting the similarity of parents' observations and adolescents' self-evaluations is a recent study of 56 adolescents with a variety of clinical problems, using the DOTS-R. Parents and patients were significantly in agreement on all nine dimensions at correlations between .646 and .795 (median $r = .739$) (Luby & Steiner, 1993).

OLD AND NEW CLINICAL ISSUES

In most areas, such as social adjustment and school function, the relationship of temperament to behavioral outcome remains similar in adolescence. What changes in this period is that new and more typically adolescent areas of interaction appear, such as aggression and drug use.

Social Adjustment and Behavior Problems

In chapter 8 we pointed out that, in the NYLS sample of 133 children, temperament played an important role up until about age nine, and then a lesser role during early adolescence. The 44 behavior problems arising between two and nine years averaged about six new cases a year, with a peak of 10 between ages five and six, followed by a decline in incidence. Between nine and 12, the NYLS group found only one new behavior problem of any kind. By adolescence, over half of the behavior problems of earlier childhood had improved or resolved completely, but a substantial number (16 out of 44) were unchanged or worse. Between 13 and 16 years, new behavior problems increased again, to a total of 12, or about three or four a year. But only two of them were judged to be reactive behavior problems in which the child's temperament participated. The others arose from a variety of major conditions, including depression and conduct disorders.

In other words, temperament appeared to play an important role in generating behavior problems in early and middle childhood, some of which continued into adolescence, but it was much less involved in the production of new problems in adolescence. From these data one could conclude that, if temperament-environment interactions are going to produce a behavioral problem in childhood, they have probably already done so before adolescence.

A subsequent analysis (Tubman, Lerner, Lerner, & von Eye, 1992) of the same NYLS population performed determinations of temperament at 16–17 years, 18–21 years, and 25–31 years and found that "extremely difficult temperament" (high scores on a numerical total of the five difficult dimensions) in a subgroup of six children was associated with lower levels of social adjustment throughout this period. The study did not, however, separate out the new problems from the old ones that had originated earlier in childhood.

More longitudinal investigations are needed before we can come to firmer conclusions as to whether, and to what extent, temperament is a predisposing factor in the major problems, such as depression, conduct disorder, substance abuse, and anorexia nervosa, that occur during the teen years. (Longitudinal studies are preferable to cross-sectional ones because they allow the researcher to trace the evolution of the clinical problems from the antecedent factors. In a cross-sectional study, which can only note the simultaneous occurrence of the various elements, it is generally more difficult to separate out cause and effect.) Aside from the issue of how temperament predisposes to the incidence of major problems, we should recognize that it may add to their persistence or severity and that, for that reason, it may need to be considered in planning clinical management. For example, the persistence of an adolescent with a conduct disorder might affect the frequency of her antisocial acts and her intensity might affect their magnitude.

Several cross-sectional studies are available to offer some suggestions as to what the longitudinal ones may demonstrate. For example, Kolvin, Nicol, Garside, Day, and Tweddle (1982) found several significant adverse temperament differences—that is, more of the "difficult" characteristics—in a randomly selected group of 38 excessively aggressive secondary school boys.

In a cohort of 975 high school students, Michael Windle (1992b) demonstrated a relationship between several temperament characteristics and depressive symptoms and delinquent behavior. Low to moderate correlations were revealed between depressive symptoms and arrhythmicity, withdrawal, inflexibility (the highest at $r = .48$), negative mood, high distractibility, and low persistence. The several significant correlations with delinquency were fewer and weaker.

Another investigation reported that major depression was associated only with "high emotionality," but the study assessed only the EAS dimensions of Buss and Plomin (1984) (Goodyer, Ashby, Altham, Vize, & Cooper, 1993).

Finally, among 297 high school students, more difficult temperament factors were associated with a higher percentage of use of cigarettes, alcohol, and "hard drugs" (Windle, 1991). In another sample of 99 ten- to twelve-year-old boys, a temperament-induced conflictual relationship between father and son in substance-abusing families was "apt to spark the premature disengagement of the son from the parental sphere of influence to a deviant peer network or toward social withdrawal that is antecedent to early-age onset of substance abuse" (Blackson, Tarter, Martin, & Moss, 1994).

It is tempting to say that difficult temperament leads to all these problems, but it is also possible that the adjustment problem somehow influences the temperament, or that they are both the consequences of some other unidentified antecedent factor. These cross-sectional studies have established only that there is some sort of relationship.

School Performance

The great majority of investigations of the interrelationship between temperament, identified as such, and school performance have involved only children in elementary school. One longitudinal study of about 100 children (mentioned in chapter 9) has so far followed its subjects up to age 13. "Results showed that parent ratings of temperament accounted for approximately 25 to 30 percent of the variance in teacher ratings of classroom behavior, 5 to 10 percent of the variance in academic achievement when entered after IQ, and 10 percent of the variance in self-concept and pupil-teacher relationships" (Guerin, Gottfried, Oliver, & Thomas, 1994). Persistence/attention span was the dimension most consistently associated with successful functioning at school.

We offered the view in chapter 9 that much of what is today being identified as attention deficit hyperactivity disorder, a supposed abnormality of brain function, is probably misinterpreted normal variations of temperament. If our estimate is correct, many of the multitude of studies of the origins, evolution, diagnosis, comorbidity, and management of ADHD are, in fact, investigations of temperament. Unfortunately, one cannot simply reinterpret these studies in terms of temperament because the conceptualizations, diagnostic techniques, and clinical interpretations are too discordant with temperament thinking to allow an easy translation. Our best hope lies in the possibility that some of the researchers in the field of ADHD will soon realize that there are normal temperament variations that resemble the supposed symptoms of ADHD and that they must take care to differentiate between normal and abnormal. An appropriate use of the pathological diagnosis of ADHD would clearly differentiate between normal variations of temperament that sometimes lead to problems in certain circumstances and a true cerebral dysfunction that invariably produces dysfunctional behavior. Efforts along these lines will also have to be made by temperament researchers, many of whom seem more interested in building theories about temperament than in solving pressing clinical problems such as this one.

Other Interactions

It is reasonable to assume that, when research efforts are extended into adolescence, evidence will be found not only for the impact of temperament on social behavioral adjustment and school performance but also for an extensive interactive influence on parental care, physical health care, and responses to stressors and other crises.

There seems little doubt that the parental care issues are just as important in adolescence as during the first decade. A substantial portion of the friction between parent and adolescent may stem more from the child's preexisting temperament and the interactions it has generated than from the altered conditions of the teen years. The obstacle to our understanding is simply the lack of documentation of this connection in the professional literature.

As Fred's story illustrates vividly, a teenager's temperament can have a strong influence on the outcome of a physical problem. We could add countless similar but less dramatic examples. But we need more data on where, when, and how much this influence is felt.

As the reader will learn in chapter 11, some of the studies that evaluate the impact of various stressors on children, such as parental divorce and natural disasters, have extended their investigations up into the period of adolescence. We have looked in vain, however, for investigations of the interactions of temperament with uniquely adolescent issues, such as rapid physical growth and maturation, the development of a sense of personal and sexual identity, and the achievement of independence and emancipation from the family. Surely an individual's temperament, and the coping style he or she has developed incorporating the temperament, will be shown to color these experiences deeply.

WHAT CAN WE DO? INVOLVING ADOLESCENTS DIRECTLY IN EDUCATION, IDENTIFICATION, AND INTERVENTION

Throughout childhood and at the beginning of adolescence, children's professional contacts are almost always initiated and maintained by their parents or guardians. By the end of this period, at 18 or 21 years of age, young people are, or should be, independent individuals who manage these affairs on their own. The activities of professionals like pediatricians and teachers during this time of transition must therefore be adjusted to the teenager's level of functioning, but always fostering greater responsibility and autonomy.

EDUCATING THE ADOLESCENT

By the time their son or daughter has reached adolescence, the parents know the young person quite well. That understanding should include a familiarity with their child's temperament pattern: what it consists of, where it comes from, how it affects life in the family and elsewhere, and how best to manage it to minimize unnecessary stress and reactive problems. The child care professional in contact with the parents at this time should make certain that they have general information about inborn behavioral style differences. It is not too late to provide parents with a general education even after a decade on the job with their child.

Since adolescents are increasingly taking over the responsibility for their lives, it is fitting that during this period the professional is shifting his or her primary effort at education away from the parents and toward the adolescents. Teenagers may be well read and sophisticated about human nature or may still be burdened with notions of environmentalism or other misinformation. Child care professionals therefore share in the responsibility to ensure that our adolescent patients, students, or clients are aware of the inborn differences in behavioral style.

Deciding when to fulfill this educational obligation and how to do it is up to the individual professional. It may be convenient to refer to the importance of temperament in a discussion about some specific issue, such as a response to an illness, a test at school, or a family crisis. The question of how to do it calls attention to the fact that, although there are now books for parents and professionals about temperament, nothing appropriate has been published for teenagers. Young people, who are taking over control of their lives and are usually interested in learning about themselves and acquiring a clearer sense of identity, cannot find books or other literature that provide background material to augment the information they may obtain from their informed professional or parents. We hope that need will soon be met.

IDENTIFICATION, FOCUSING ON THE
ADOLESCENT'S SELF-UNDERSTANDING

Consistent with what we recommended in chapter 3 and elsewhere, we do not advise routine identification of a child or adolescent's specific temperament profile by physicians, educators, or other professionals. If things are going well, it is not a wise use of limited professional time to test and identify the temperament pattern of everyone with whom we come in contact. However, when a parent or child (or adolescent) expresses concern about relationships or adjustment, then identifying the child's individual reaction pattern is much more likely to be useful by contributing to an understanding of the components of the situation and suggesting an appropriate course of action.

Two sources are available to help the adolescent obtain this insight: parents and professionals. Parents generally have a fairly clear picture of their child's reaction pattern, as the result of being in the relationship for over a decade. Often parents have helped a child understand himself over the years. For example, a parent may have used the tactic of saying, "Johnny, I know you don't like to change suddenly from one thing to another, so I am going to help you by giving you some warnings when you have 10 minutes and then five minutes to go before we have to go out to the store." Another way a parent might teach a child some self-understanding would be to say, "Susie, I know you are the kind of person who has trouble feeling comfortable in big groups (and there is nothing wrong with that), so I'll come with you to Mary's birthday party and will stay around somewhere out of sight for a few minutes until you tell me it is time for me to leave."

On the other hand, parents may have little perspective on their child's temperament, thinking, for example, that a normally active son is "hyperactive." They may be uninformed as to where temperament differences come from, wrongly blaming delivery complications, diet, or their marital problems. Some parents may have distorted their child's formation of an accurate self-image by, for example, repeatedly referring to expression of feeling as being uninhibited. Or the parents may not have shared with the child their insights as to what sort of child she or he is.

If, for whatever reason, the adolescent lacks insight into his behavioral style, and there are clinical indications for obtaining such information, then it falls to the professional to facilitate the educational process. The objective, as at other times when identification is undertaken, is to help the adolescent get a more organized and accurate picture of his own behavioral style, as well as a better perspective on how much that style is like or unlike that of other persons he knows.

The technique for helping the teenager obtain such insights and perspective must depend on the ingenuity of the professional. We have noted that there is no questionnaire from our series designed for use by adolescents or their parents. Some might suggest using the DOTS-R or the EAS scales, but they are highly impressionistic and have not been adequately applied clinically to test their effectiveness and usefulness in counseling situations. Opportunities for observation are generally very limited, except perhaps when a teacher, physician, or nurse has known the adolescent for many years and has enough background information for the process of identification. Lacking questionnaire answers or observational data, the professional must rely on information derived from talking to both the parents and the adolescent. The length of such an interview depends on why it is being pursued. For most purposes, such as getting a better picture of an adolescent's inflexibility, shyness, disorganization, or inattentiveness, an adequate body of examples should be obtainable within 5–15 minutes. The process does not require hours of investigation.

INTERVENTION, WITH THE ADOLESCENT'S ACTIVE PARTICIPATION

We have suggested that when a clinical problem arises earlier in childhood from a poor fit between the temperament and the environment, the solution lies in altering parental handling so that the excessive stress and conflict diminish and the problem disappears. This solution remains relevant in the adolescent years, except that increasingly during this period the adolescent takes over providing the diagnostic information and developing and carrying out the management plan. By the end of adolescence, the responsibility has shifted entirely to the young person.

An example would be the shy boy who, under the stress of unfamiliar situations or challenges, develops recurring abdominal pain. In the early years of life, the parents' primary management plan would probably be to shield the child from unnecessary stresses and to reassure him when the pain occurs. In the elementary school years, the parents could help the child see more clearly the association between the stressors and the symptoms and might help him develop some coping strategies, such as persuading himself that the dangers are simply not as big as his insides tell him they are, and not letting himself be overwhelmed by the symptoms, which he knows from experience will be gone within an hour or so.

The adolescent not only can be helped to understand the relationship between the situation and the symptoms but can learn to plan his life so as to avoid the stresses when possible, to control his feelings of anxiety about challenges more effectively, to be ready for the symptoms when they come, and to find ways to minimize the disturbance they cause. All of this is best achieved by direct contact between the physician or nurse and the teenager, although the parents should not be excluded from the planning.

The teacher can also be helpful by working with the student to develop ways of persuading himself that for a person of his abilities the anxiety is an excessive reaction and by practicing test-taking skills that carry him through despite the feelings of stress and discomfort.

But the responsibility for implementation of these techniques lies increasingly with the adolescent, while the role of the parent diminishes.

CHAPTER 11

Environmental Stressors and Crises

CHILDREN REACT in various ways to environmental stressors and crises in their lives, and temperament is one of the factors that determines the quality and quantity of those reactions. Our first case study in this chapter describes a shy girl confronting the stress of leaving home for college.

Sixteen-year-old Betty was a shy person. Her parents and her pediatrician were aware of it. Her slow-to-warm-up traits had been confirmed on a Middle Childhood Temperament Questionnaire, done four years before as part of the standardization sample rather than for clinical reasons. In her junior year in high school, she expressed distress and doubts about her abilities and great indecision about her future plans, despite her good school record and her satisfactory social relations. Betty's parents asked their pediatrician for some advice on dealing with this perplexing situation. With only brief counseling, they were able to recognize that their daughter was just a shy person who was feeling temporarily overwhelmed by the impending separation from her family for the first time. They helped her with her self-esteem and gave her opportunities to discuss uncomfortable feelings. She made the necessary decisions for herself and eventually left for college timidly but confidently. Consultation with a mental health specialist was not needed.

The second story depicts the differing behavioral styles with which two siblings responded to the distressing crisis of their parents' divorce.

After seven years of deteriorating marital relations and considerable fighting in the home, Joe and Cindy started divorce proceedings.

They both were concerned about the effect of their dysfunctional family life on their six-year-old twins, Barbara and Bobby. However, they were unable even with marital counseling to overcome their differences and reunite the family. The children had been unhappy at the friction in the home but showed no outward signs of disturbance until Joe left the house angrily one night and moved to his lover's apartment. Barbara, the one with the easier temperament, frequently asked her mother about what would become of them but did not seem to her mother to be very disturbed. Actually, she was troubled by grief and fears but refrained from expressing them because of concern about upsetting her parents. Bobby, on the other hand, who always responded intensely and negatively when challenged by a requirement to adjust, was more openly distressed by his parents' separation. He sobbed frequently and wanted to sleep in his mother's bed. He had trouble concentrating in school, with the result that his work suffered. Both parents congratulated Barbara for her apparently rapid adjustment to the divorce, but both grew angry at Bobby for his annoying behavior and were punitive and unsupportive with him. As Bobby's behavior worsened, however, the parents agreed that he needed psychological counseling. The psychologist, by involving the whole family in the therapy sessions, clarified for the parents that both children needed help in coping with the divorce and that Bobby was just reacting more visibly and in a way that was more bothersome to his preoccupied parents.

Professionals can help children confront stressors and crises, ranging from school entry and sibling births to disasters and parental divorce or death. A review of the part played by the child's temperament in adjustments to stress, and appraisal and management of such adjustments, is the substance of this chapter.

WHAT DO WE KNOW? THE VARIABLE IMPACT OF TEMPERAMENT IN REACTIONS TO STRESSORS AND CRISES

Chapter 5 was concerned with the interactions of a child's temperament with general parental care. This chapter examines its relationship to other environmental influences, particularly the various major stressors and crises. We know that a child's style of reacting to the multitude of life challenges makes an important difference in the experience and outcome for the child. The degree to which events are perceived as stressful depends to some extent on that goodness of fit between the child and the circumstances. Some children welcome the demands presented by novelty, while others are disturbed and threatened by it.

Varied Stressors and Crises

In chapter 2, we defined a child's "developmental niche" as divided into three components: (1) the immediate physical and social structure in which the child lives, such as the family configuration and housing arrangements; (2) the larger culture or customs of child care and child rearing provided and promoted by the community; and (3) the individual beliefs, values, and practices of the parents. In chapter 5, we elaborated upon the interactions of children with their parents and with the broader culture.

Our attention here shifts to the challenges presented by physical and social structural changes. Family structure can be altered by the addition of a new sibling, the departure or death of a family member, parental separation or divorce, the illness or hospitalization of a parent, or foster placement. Children must adjust to physical structure changes as well, such as the challenges presented by geographical residential moves or natural or civil disasters. When the physical structure presents chronic demands for adjustment, such as noisy neighbors or inadequate household heating, we think of those demands as "daily hassles," or chronic stressors. By contrast, a death in the family or an earthquake would be an acute crisis.

Range and Frequency of Children's Responses

Children are almost invariably affected adversely by disruptive physical and social changes in their environments (Shannon, Lonigan, Finch, & Taylor, 1994; Sugar, 1992; Udwin, 1993). Their responses vary considerably. Some children may seem to have little or no resulting psychopathology and may not need psychotherapy. Wide-ranging nonspecific reactions include anxiety, depression, disturbances of physical functions such as sleep or sphincter control, social withdrawal, and poor schoolwork.

Other children develop post-traumatic stress disorder (PTSD). PTSD refers to the syndrome of the behavioral consequences of an unusually psychologically traumatic event. According to the *DSM-IV* (APA, 1994), a person can develop PTSD after being exposed to a traumatic event that involved actual or threatened death or serious injury to self or others and a personal response of intense fear, helplessness, or horror. The resulting symptoms consist of persistent reexperiencing of the event in various ways, persistent avoidance of associated stimuli, and a variety of symptoms of increased arousal, such as sleep disturbance and difficulty concentrating.

The percentage of children diagnosed with PTSD after disasters varies. In the region of Charleston, South Carolina, after Hurricane Hugo in 1989, "more than 5% of the sample reported sufficient symptoms to be classified as exhibiting this post-traumatic stress syndrome" (Shannon et al., 1994). But a recent literature review (Udwin, 1993) put the figure higher: "A significant proportion of child survivors of disasters (possibly 30–50%) are likely to develop PTSD symptoms." These percentages differ depending on how the definition of PTSD is applied and on diverse factors operating in the sample selected for study.

FACTORS AFFECTING CHILDREN'S RESPONSES

Several factors affect a child's response to stressors or crises. Some of them increase vulnerability; others afford protection. Only by recognizing these moderating influences can we understand the variable reactions displayed by children to the same traumatic experience.

- The nature, intensity, duration, and disruptiveness of the trauma itself: The death of a grandparent is of greater consequence for a child when there has been a close friendship between them than when they have never met. Being on the periphery of a hurricane is quite a different matter from being in the middle of it and seeing the family's house and possessions lost or destroyed.

- Emotional support: The availability and supportiveness of the parents and other trusted adult figures count heavily toward stabilizing the child's life and buffering him or her from the harshness of the trauma (Wertlieb, Weigel, & Feldstein, 1989). Parents are of little value to their children if they themselves become incapacitated physically or psychologically.

- Age and gender: Girls and younger children have been more likely to report PTSD symptoms (Udwin, 1993).

- Temperament: The role of temperament has not been widely studied yet, but there are definite indications from the available literature that it is an important determinant of the nature and magnitude of the reaction.

More specifically, in a study of the impact of stressors on the behavior of 155 normal six- to nine-year-old children enrolled in a large health maintenance organization (Wertlieb, Weigel, Springer, & Feldstein, 1987), higher levels of stress were clearly associated with higher levels of behavioral symptoms. Eight of the nine NYLS dimensions were found to be significantly related to the development of behavioral symptoms associated with either "undesirable life events or daily hassles." The dimensions connected with behavioral symptoms were "high activity level, low adaptability, withdrawal from new stimuli, distractibility, high intensity, unpleasant or unhappy mood, a lack of persistence, and an irregular or unpredictable behavioral style." These were, of course, presumably predisposing characteristics rather than outcomes of the stress. The amount of social support the children received was also highly influential in mitigating the outcomes.

The Hurricane Hugo study (Shannon et al., 1994) reported that "children's level of trait anxiety and their reported emotional reactivity during the hurricane were more strongly related to the presence of PTSD symptoms than were the exposure factors." "Trait anxiety" was determined by the children's responses to the Revised Children's Manifest Anxiety Scale after the hurricane but was thought to reflect levels of anxiety unrelated to the disaster, that is, "their tendency to experience anxiety or negative emotionality." Emotional experience during the hurricane was measured by a simple eight-item adjective checklist during the evaluation after the event. The investigators did not assess temperament as such and did not even mention the word, but they seem to have been thinking along those lines. They concluded that a child's immediate emotional reactions to the trauma may have been the most important for the development of subsequent post-traumatic sequelae because they reflected the severity of the trauma, the dispositional characteristics of the child, and the interaction between them (Lonigan, Shannon, Taylor, Finch, & Sallee, 1994).

As in other temperament studies, support for a genetic contribution to this reactivity to environmental stressors comes largely from the comparison of twins. A study of more than 4,000 monozygotic and dizygotic male twin pairs, all of whom had served on active military duty during the Vietnam War, found evidence for a genetic influence in the development of PTSD symptoms even after adjustments were made for differences in combat exposure. Genetic factors accounted for 13–34% of the variation in the presence of the typical symptom clusters. Childhood and adolescent environmental factors shared by the twin siblings did not contribute to the susceptibility to development of these symptoms (True et al., 1993). Thus, in a specific highly traumatic environment, genetic similarity predisposed to greater similarity of outcome, while greater genetic difference promoted divergence.

Children's Responses in Various Situations

Let us review some of the specific stressful situations, beginning with the more common ones.

School Entry

The universal childhood experience of starting school has been mentioned in earlier anecdotes that illustrated how differently children react to this event, depending on their temperament characteristics. Initiation into the educational system is one of a child's greatest challenges.

Sibling Births

The importance of temperament characteristics for general sibling interactions was mentioned in chapter 5. Despite the tradition of attributing the quality of sibling relationships entirely to parental care and blaming the parents for the ambivalence, rivalry, or aggression siblings express, there is a growing body of evidence that children react to their siblings as much with their inborn temperaments as with behavior learned from their parents (Stoneman & Brody, 1993).

Of particular interest for this chapter is the research of Judith Dunn (1994; Dunn & Kendrick, 1982; Munn & Dunn, 1989) on children's responses to the birth of a younger sibling, considered by some to be one of life's greatest crises. Their reactions were highly varied and did not conform to the stereotypical pattern of inevitable upheaval. The differences in how children reacted were related to their temperament characteristics before the birth. According to Dunn's findings, "children who readily adapted to new situations, and whose responses were typically positive, mild, and regular before the birth of a sibling, showed this same pattern of responses when their sibling was born." Children who exhibited various components of temperamental difficulty (the opposite characteristics) were more likely to display sleep problems, clinging behavior, and lack of positive interest in the baby.

These temperament differences continued to affect how the firstborn infants interacted with their mothers and their baby siblings as the months went by. Children of low malleability (adaptability) and high intensity were especially likely to protest when their mothers were engaged with the baby while performing caretaking tasks, and they were less likely to ignore such exchanges. The intense older brothers or sisters more often watched the interactions while sucking their thumbs or holding comfort objects.

Parental Separation, Divorce, and Remarriage

With almost 50% of marriages in the United States ending in divorce, a great many children are experiencing the stresses of these disruptions. The significance of marital disruption for children's behavior depends on its interplay with vulnerability factors, which increase the effects of stressors, and protective factors, which diminish them. Such influences include the child's characteristics, the family milieu, and the availability of extrafamilial supportive persons or agencies (Hetherington, 1989).

Many individual characteristics in children affect their responses to marital transitions. Intelligent children are more resilient. Older children are more disturbed. In E. Mavis Hetherington's (1989) study of children in 180 families described as "well-educated, middle-class white," boys were "more adversely affected than girls by divorce and life in a mother-custody one-parent household, and girls had more long-term difficulty than boys in adjusting to the introduction of a stepfather." In her six-year follow-up study, Hetherington also considered the influence of the children's temperaments. The temperament ratings were made by nurses based on pediatric records of well-baby visits during the first two years of life, including such common variables as irritability, soothability, activity, sociability, and regularity. Hetherington concluded that these individual differences played an important role in protecting children from, or making them more vulnerable to, the negative consequences associated with their parents' marital problems. Rather than concentrate on the long-term adjustment of the children, she examined how the children's temperaments affected the interactions at the time. When mothers were particularly stressed, difficult children were more likely to evoke aversive behavior from their mothers and become the target for it. These children were less able to cope with the situation in general or with abusive behavior from the parents when it occurred.

Knowing that difficult temperament makes children in this situation more likely to become clinical cases, we must wonder how often the characteristics of that predisposition are misinterpreted clinically as part of the reactive symptoms. For example, how often is preexisting difficult temperament mistakenly ascribed to the impact of the divorce?

We can find no reports of investigations specifically of the role of children's temperaments on their long-term behavioral adjustment. Judith Wallerstein (1992), in her longitudinal study of the impact of divorce in California, lists seven components, one being "the individual assets, capacities, and deficits that the child brings to the divorce," but she made no temperament measurements. Given the interactive and pervasive qualities of temperament, one can imagine that closer inspection would reveal a network of relationships. Considering how often our children are experiencing this disruption of family life, further investigation of these issues should receive the highest priority.

Complicated Births

Abnormalities of the pregnancy and delivery generate critical situations with a variety of possible physical consequences and parental responses. As the Kauai longitudinal study demonstrated (see chapter 8), some children with multiple physical and psychosocial risk factors are "vulnerable but invincible" and do not develop the expected learning or behavioral problems because certain factors, including their temperamental traits, seem to protect them. Since then, however, concern has been raised that some of these seemingly competent individuals may have less conspicuous emotional problems (Luthar & Zigler, 1991).

Foster and Adoptive Placement

With about 2% of the child population in the United States being adopted at present, and over half a million children in foster care at any time, many young people are experiencing this major shift in family life. One early study found that a group of 66 foster and adopted children placed with a county agency displayed no more difficult temperament than controls (Carey, Lipton, & Myers, 1974). If that survey were to be replicated with larger numbers and a more diverse population, we might be able to conclude that children being adopted and going into foster care are not much different temperamentally from the general population. However, we hesitate to draw that conclusion with certainty at this time. With the greatly expanded and more lenient criteria for acceptable adoptive placement in the last 20 years, the pool of available infants and children now includes many more who have experienced unfavorable physical and psychosocial risks prenatally or after birth.

Nevertheless, the role of temperament in adjustment to the changes of foster and adoption placement seems certain to prove to be of consequence when it becomes more fully recognized in the professional literature. One report is available to support the importance of the goodness of fit in these relationships. In a sample of 51 foster children ranging from five to 10 years of age (Doelling & Johnson, 1990), the temperament of foster parents and children was assessed with the DOTS-R. "The combination of an inflexible mother and a child with negative mood was shown to predict relative placement failure in terms of greater conflict, lower maternal satisfaction, and [lower] case workers' ratings of placement success. The present findings, in fact, suggest that this is the most troublesome combination in terms of placement outcome." Some other relationships predicting lower maternal satisfaction with the placement were also noted, such as the combination of an inflexible mother and a child low in rhythmicity.

Disasters

The lives of children are frequently challenged by disasters, both circumscribed ones such as car crashes, shootings, and fires, and more widespread ones such as hurricanes, earthquakes, floods, and warfare. The pervasive impact of these events on children is well documented; not so well examined are the ways children's temperaments make them more or less vulnerable to the accompanying stress. We mentioned earlier the finding of the Hurricane Hugo study that post-traumatic stress symptoms were strongly related to children's level of trait anxiety and their reported emotional reactivity during the hurricane. A review of studies of children war victims suggests that "children's cognitive immaturity, plasticity, and innate adaptive capacities may mitigate war's effects in low to moderately intense wartime settings" (Jensen & Shaw, 1993). This is an area that requires further study.

In fact, in some areas the state of our knowledge is deplorably inadequate, to the point of being harmful. Since the nuclear power plant accident at Chernobyl in the Soviet Union in April 1986, one response of Ukrainian physicians to the understandable concern about radiation exposure has been to diagnose extensively a phenomenon they call "vegetative dystonia." This supposed disorder, thought by some to be an imbalance of the vascular tone of the circulatory system with diverse consequences, appears in neither our textbooks nor theirs. But Ukrainian physicians unanimously believe in it and have convinced worried parents that their children's vague complaints are caused by it, are serious, and require extensive diagnostic tests and prolonged hospitalizations. The excessive diagnosing and treatment of nondisease must have been massive. In this case, the medical profession appears to have done poorly at separating out the true effects of the radiation, the emotional consequences of worrying about it, and the normal problems of childhood (Stiehm, 1992).

Other Critical Life Events

The life of the growing child can be affected by a great variety of other crises. Parents may become acutely sick, be hospitalized, become chronically ill, or even die. They may have to be away from home for long periods of time for a number of reasons, such as business trips, imprisonment, or calls to military duty, including combat. The average American family makes a geographical move every few years, challenging each time the adaptive capacities of each member of the family. Surveys of the impact of these events on the feelings and thinking of children have been limited to the general kinds of reactions likely to be exhibited. Inquiries so far have seldom, if ever, recognized and investigated the individual differences that make these changes more difficult for some than for others.

WHAT CAN WE DO? INCLUDING TEMPERAMENT IN EVALUATIONS AND MANAGEMENT OF CHILDREN'S RESPONSES TO STRESSORS AND CRISES

Although the last five chapters may seem to have dealt with issues primarily associated with the day care, medical care, mental health, and educational professions, they have also been addressed to any professional group charged with the care of children. Psychosocial and other environmental stressors and crises are of concern to all the disciplines dealing with young people. All of us must be prepared to understand and be helpful to children when they experience any of a broad range of challenges, from sibling births to deaths in the family to disasters. Our professional competence is greatly enhanced when we use our knowledge of individual differences to understand and manage wisely the varied responses children exhibit in these circumstances.

EDUCATING PROFESSIONALS AND PARENTS ABOUT RESPONSES TO STRESSORS AND CRISES

Education about the impact of temperament on reactions to stressors and crises should take place on two levels: in the training of professionals in the child care disciplines, and in their education of the parents and children in their care.

Professional Education

Not just physicians, psychologists, and educators but also social workers, nurses, and others should have their professional education modernized to include a thorough understanding of the phenomenon of temperament and a working knowledge of techniques on how to apply it. All of these professionals need to be aware of what kinds of children react in what sorts of ways in which situations. The pediatrician or psychologist, for example, needs to be aware of the typical reactions of a four-year-old child to parental divorce, how far the normal range extends, and what constitutes an abnormal or atypical response. This kind of information should be included in professional training at the graduate level starting immediately; for those who are already launched in their careers, the material should be disseminated by whatever means of continuing education their discipline uses.

Parental Education

Professionals who are equipped with this knowledge and these skills can then pass on to parents what they have learned from formal training and personal professional experience. We have mentioned how parents can be educated as both a prophylactic and a therapeutic measure in a variety of settings. When confronted by the stressors or crises mentioned in this chapter, we can perform the valuable role of helping parents (and sometimes the child as well) to understand not only what the usual reactions are to a specific crisis—whether impending or having already occurred—but also how children's responses are quantitatively and qualitatively different, depending on their behavioral style. For example, the family preparing for a move to a distant city, a sibling birth, or the death of a grandparent can be reminded not only of the typical expected impact of the event on the children but also of how various children adjust in different ways.

IDENTIFYING THE DIFFERENT REACTIONS

We have proposed throughout this book that formal assessment of children's temperament profiles need not be done routinely, but that when a caregiver expresses concerns about a child's behavior, a more detailed identification is likely to be very helpful. The other indication that identification is in order is when the professional becomes aware of a significant discrepancy between the parents' general perceptions of the child's reactions and what they report is actually happening. Helping children who have been exposed to environmental stressors is no different: Identification and general counseling may take place before or during the event, or after the impact has been felt.

Parents may consult with professionals before the child undergoes the forthcoming ordeal because it is one known to have inevitable consequences for children, as in the case of a parental divorce, or because the child is known from prior experience to be temperamentally difficult and to have unusual trouble with adjusting to changes. The counseling in the first case can follow the traditional lines of describing the expected behavioral changes at different ages, but we should not lose this opportunity to mention some variations the parents may expect in view of their own child's reaction pattern. The six-year-old child caught in a parental divorce can be expected to express the usual open grieving and feelings of rejection (Wallerstein, 1992), but the child's response is likely to be colored deeply by his or her temperament. The temperamentally difficult child can be expected to express feelings with greater intensity and negativity than the milder, pleasanter one.

When the parent asks for help in the face of an impending crisis and is already equipped with the knowledge that in the past the child has demonstrated a pattern of slow and difficult adaptation to extraordinary demands, we have an unusual opportunity to practice preventive mental health. The behavioral outcome in the child will be strongly influenced by the level of understanding incorporated into the handling by the parents and other adults.

Many stressors and crises are of sudden and unexpected onset and do not permit a child's family to make such deliberate attempts at preparation. One of the few situations that allows advance planning is foster and adoptive placement of children. To our knowledge, social welfare agencies have not as yet included a matching of child and family for goodness of fit prior to placement. Doelling and Johnson (1990) reported that the fit between foster mother and child often made a big difference in the success of the placement. Does it follow that attempts at such matching should become standard agency policy? If so, what constitutes a satisfactory placement?

Our judgment at this time must be that our acquaintance with temperament and its interactions with the environment is still too incomplete to serve as the basis for foster and adoption placement. The danger of misuse of the concept looms large. Even with complete knowledge of the behavioral styles of the child and the members of the foster or adoptive family and an understanding of how they are likely to interact over the years, it seems unrealistic at present to think that we can routinely plan perfect families. There are too many other uncontrollable factors, some of them unknown, in the overall scheme of interactions. A more practical answer lies in appreciating temperament differences and learning to manage them in both biologically and nonbiologically formed families, not in thinking that we are so clever that we can construct ideal families.

INTERVENTION: MANAGING TEMPERAMENT VARIATIONS AND PATHOLOGICAL REACTIONS DIFFERENTLY

When a child is undergoing a stressful experience, the traditional way to explain her emotional and behavioral symptoms has been to attribute them to the nature and extent of the stressor, her prior experience, and the ability of the parents and others to supply her with the right kind of emotional support. Differing reactions between children of comparable backgrounds and seemingly equal exposure to the stressor have been either left unaccounted for or attributed to subtle differences in the factors just mentioned. Considering the potential contribution of a child's temperament goes a long way toward making these variations comprehensible.

When intervening to help a child cope with a stressor or crisis, the diagnostic process can follow the algorithm proposed in chapter 8 (see figure 8.1). After the preliminary negotiations about defining parental concern and establishing an agreement, the professional performs the general evaluation of the child, the family, and the situation using the tools of his or her discipline. The first major question to answer is whether there is a behavioral adjustment problem. In other words, is there evidence of dysfunction in social relations, task performance, self-relations, or general feeling, thought, or body function? If there is, the professional should attempt to discover whether the child's temperament has played a role in generating the problem. If there is no such problem, then the parent's concern may be derived from a misperception of abnormality, or it may be that the child's normal temperament is what the parents are finding aversive. We maintain that making this distinction is essential, because the management depends on which of these diagnoses is made.

The actual intervention on behalf of the child undergoing a crisis or other stressor has been described elsewhere and does not require extensive discussion here (see Lyons, 1987, for references). The principal elements in most plans are: (1) finding ways to diminish the impact of the stressor (move out of the path of the hurricane if possible); (2) helping the child to develop or strengthen coping techniques (involve the child in the care of the newborn sibling); and (3) identifying and making use of the protection and support available from other members of the family and the community (rally the grandparents or uncles and aunts at the time of parental illness or hospitalization).

The essential point is that we must learn when and how to include recognition and understanding of a child's temperament in the general management plan. We know that children's temperaments influence their reactions to stress, making them appear more severe or milder or qualitatively different. In assessing a child's symptoms during or after a crisis, there is no completely reliable way to separate out the part of the reaction that is typical from the part that is related to the child's behavioral style. The most accurate way of accomplishing this difficult task is probably to make a clinical judgment as to whether the observed reaction seems to be within the range of normal for the child's particular age and sex, and in the particular crisis situation, and if it is not, to make a second clinical judgment, based on an understanding of the child's temperament, as to whether the atypical elements of the reaction are similar to the child's established behavioral style reaction patterns. Astute clinicians must therefore be prepared to deal both with the overt symptoms and with what they judge to be the true content of the distress, as contrasted with the style of expressing that distress. The clinician making this distinction must have a thorough knowledge of temperament differences and a high level of clinical skills.

Sixteen-year-old Betty at the beginning of this chapter was expressing doubts and uncertainty about her future. Her parents thought that these feelings were excessive, and we may agree with them that they probably were. An inventory of her current status revealed that she had no behavioral adjustment problem and that her temperament profile was known to be that of shyness. Management called only for enriching the understanding of these phenomena by both Betty and her parents, thereby enabling her parents to increase their support. The stressor itself, the departure from home and entry into college, could not be altered, although the family could have made an extra trip or two to visit the college campus after acceptance to help her cope with its unfamiliarity. In this common kind of situation, this is as far as the intervention needs to go for most individuals. Since there was no behavioral or emotional adjustment problem, such as depression or inappropriate anxiety, a mental health specialist consultation was not indicated.

The twins Barbara and Bobby illustrate another point. Because of their contrasting temperaments, their reactions to the parental separation and divorce looked quite different at the symptomatic level. Barbara seemed less affected because of her mild, adaptable temperament, while Bobby caused more concern because of his more flamboyant whining and clinging behavior. Yet as it turned out, when the psychologist got them both to talk about their feelings, they were just about equally disturbed by the breakup of the family and were both in need of some counseling help.

We have known cases in which consultant physicians and psychologists unfamiliar with the phenomenon of temperament, and either unaware of or inattentive to a child's history of responding to stressors in distinctive or exaggerated ways, have greatly under- or overestimated the magnitude of the problem in the child and launched into inappropriate courses of treatment. For example, Walter, a temperamentally difficult seven-year-old, reacted much more vigorously to his grandfather's death and his father's surgery than did his slightly older and more adaptable brother; Walter was avoiding going to school and also developed a sleep problem. The consultant psychiatrist, contacted on the recommendation of the school psychologist, did not take advantage of the temperament information available from Walter's pediatrician and suggested that the problem was a panic disorder related to oxygen deprivation at birth. She recommended a psychotropic drug not yet approved for use with children. In fact, neither diagnosis was correct. Walter was a neurologically intact difficult child whose limited capacity to adjust had been temporarily overwhelmed. With an opportunity to talk about the stresses, and as their potency diminished over time, Walter returned rapidly to normal functioning without any medication.

Referral to Mental Health Specialists

In view of the fact that children invariably experience some degree of distress from stressors and crises, the question arises as to when their reaction can be handled by the parents, perhaps with help from the primary medical care physician, the educator, or others not usually identified as having special expertise in the area. When such professionals correctly recognize the child's behavior as a matter of temperamental exaggeration and not a severe disturbance, they should be less quick to make referrals to specialists. Referrals should be made, however, when a child exhibits significant dysfunction, such as aggression, withdrawal, decrease in school performance, diminished self-esteem, depression, or excessive anxiety.

Psychiatrists' recommendations on this issue have not generally made this distinction in the professional literature for physicians, educators, and other child care professionals. Obviously, not all children who display disturbed behavior after a parental divorce or a flood can be referred for psychotherapy; there would not be enough professionals available to handle so many referrals. One of the few clear-cut bits of advice on this matter appears in a textbook chapter about management of children subjected to disasters and showing signs of post-traumatic stress disorder: "Psychiatric consultation is indicated if the youngster's symptoms continue unabated for several weeks after the family has stabilized, despite reassurance, support, and medication. Immediate psychiatric attention is in order when there is risky or dangerous reenactment or post-trauma play" (Sugar, 1992). Reenactment play refers to such post-traumatic behaviors as playing games with a knife after witnessing a murder in which such an instrument was used.

In view of the great frequency of stressors and crises, any enhancement of the skill of professional counseling for children's reactions to them would be welcome. Including a recognition of temperament differences in the evaluation and management of these responses would be a big step in that direction.

CHAPTER 12

Conclusion: An Opportunity to Improve the Care of Our Children

C HAPTER 1 BEGAN WITH two accounts of children whose temperaments were not recognized and handled appropriately by the professionals with whom they came in contact. Let us revisit these case studies to discern how the professional services could have been more effective and the outcomes better.

Two-year-old Johnny was very active and had been so since before birth. His mother wondered about "hyperactivity." The perplexed pediatrician referred the family to a neurologist. None of them had even considered the possibility that his activeness might have been a normal variation; all had been concerned only with the possibility of abnormal behavior. A happier outcome would have entailed several major changes. In the first place, his mother would have been prepared for the normal variations displayed by children in lectures and reading material obtained through childbirth and parenting classes. She would have observed her baby's behavior and formed her own opinion as to what kind of child he was, using the judgments of friends and relatives when helpful. Also, the pediatrician would have been sufficiently trained to be aware of temperament differences, to consider and recognize them in evaluating her patients in well-child visits, and to know how to appraise them in greater detail in the event of a parental expression of concern. Such expertise in Johnny's case would have resulted in a proper diagnosis at the pediatric visit and would have prevented the unnecessary trip to the neurologist. If for some reason the neurologist had been consulted anyway, he would have been able to recognize that Johnny was simply a normal, highly active child with no physical or behavior problems, and he would have said so without equivocation. How different this second outcome would have been from the first, in which the parents, the pediatrician, and the neurologist had all been unable to distinguish normality from abnormality.

Shy Sally had trouble making the transition to nursery school. Her strong wish to withdraw from the unfamiliar place and her crying and begging to be taken home had been misinterpreted by the teacher as "immaturity." With a few changes, the management could have gone much more smoothly for everyone. In the first four years, her mother could have learned more about Sally's shyness through parent education materials and from health care visits. The medical care personnel with whom she came in contact repeatedly could have played an active role in her education. Although Sally's shyness was not yet a problem, her mother could have been made aware that it might become one in case of a major challenge, such as starting nursery school, and Sally could have been taught some coping skills with which to manage such challenges. When Sally entered nursery school, various preparations could have been made. She could have been told all about the place in advance, she could have become acquainted with one or two other children entering at the same time, and she could have made brief preparatory visits to the school to familiarize her with the school personnel, and them with her. The day care workers would have been knowledgeable about tempera-ment differences and would have been trained in the handling of shy children. These simple and reasonable measures would have resulted in a very different experience for Sally, her parents, and the teachers at the beginning of nursery school.

To ensure that children are managed more as just described and less as described in Johnny's and Sally's stories in chapter 1, more research must be done to expand our knowledge of the phenomenon of temperament, and professionals and parents must be better educated in making greater use of what we already know.

EXPANDING OUR KNOWLEDGE OF TEMPERAMENT: THE RESEARCH AGENDA

At the beginning of this volume, we pointed out that much has been learned about temperament differences and about assessing them, but that this information has spread rather slowly to the professionals whose work would benefit the most from it. Throughout the rest of the book, we have attempted to differentiate between what we are fairly certain we know, what we think we understand but with less certainty, and what we need to comprehend much better. We have discussed valid theories and effective practical techniques, as well as some theories and techniques that are not so solidly founded. In this final chapter, we recapitulate the main points of our knowledge and our principal areas of uncertainty in order to summarize the main items on the research agenda for the field.

Chapters 2 and 3 reviewed what we know about the reality of temperament differences, how they matter for the caretaker-child relationship, and how they matter for the caretaker and the child individually, and we provided a general view of the ways this information can be applied. Three main uses of temperament data were described in some detail: general education, identification of the specific child's profile, and intervention when a poor fit has produced a secondary problem. The gaps in our knowledge are not big enough to keep us from implementing what we already understand, but we will do better when we know even more. For example, we acknowledged that measurement techniques for newborns and for adolescents need to be developed and that the existing ones for other ages need to be improved. Much more investigation must be undertaken to find the best intervention techniques in various situations.

Chapter 4 described the existence of individual behavioral differences in newborns, which are not likely to be the pure genetic endowment that some have hoped to find but appear rather to reflect varying pregnancy and delivery conditions. How best to measure them, where they come from, what happens to them and when, are all matters calling for investigation. We need to know which are the significant influences during pregnancy and delivery, such as drugs and obstetrical complications, and what can be done to alter harmful influences.

How more enduring, genetically based temperament characteristics emerge over the months after birth is poorly defined and urgently requires clarification. Furthermore, we are completely at a loss today when it comes to anticipating what to expect genetically from a given set of parents. As outlined in chapter 5, the parents' interactions with the genetically determined elements of their child's behavioral style over these years are extensive and critically important for the developing child. We should know a great deal more about how that happens. What elements of the environment, such as caregiving practices, alter which aspects of the genetic basis of the child's temperament, and when and how does this come about? We know something about what constitutes normal and abnormal behavior, but not enough about how normal variations can sometimes predispose a child to stressful interactions. And what about the nongenetic physical influences, such as nutrition and toxins? Improved understanding of these phenomena would greatly enhance the working knowledge of parents and the professionals trying to help them.

Research-based data on temperament differences in day care settings are, as reviewed in chapter 6, almost nonexistent. With a large and growing proportion of our children participating in these arrangements, we cannot afford to continue this neglect. Education of day care workers about individual differences is urgently needed, as illustrated by the case of shy Sally. Furthermore, day care centers offer a unique opportunity for prolonged, unobtrusive observations of children's reaction styles in a variety of somewhat standardized situations. Research opportunities abound.

The relationship of temperament to physical conditions has proven to be a rich area of investigation, one apparently not anticipated by the original New York Longitudinal Study group. In chapter 7, we surveyed the many situations in which a child's temperament affects the incidence, outcome, or management of certain physical problems. This evidence persuades us to use temperament data to improve the accuracy of diagnosis and the appropriateness of treatment in such cases. But our information on the influence of temperament on many physical conditions, such as failure to thrive and obesity, is admittedly in an early stage; moreover, research attention should be extended to a multitude of other conditions as yet unstudied, such as functional constipation and eating disorders.

The longest and most extensively investigated relationship of temperament is with behavior problems. Ample experience supports the contributions of the child to such disorders, as detailed in chapter 8. Good management techniques have been worked out in this sphere, and yet even here mechanisms of action and therapeutic approaches are not elaborated as specifically as they could be. For example, it has been only about 10 years since the first appearance in the professional and parent literature of any suggestions on the management of the difficult child. The chapter pointed out some of the areas requiring further exploration. Painstaking longitudinal investigations like the New York Longitudinal Study will provide the most convincing conclusions.

Chapter 9 presented important data on the relationship between a child's temperament and various aspects of school performance, especially academic achievement and teacher attitudes. We discussed what we consider to be the most troubling unresolved problem in the temperament field, the perplexing overlap between normal temperament variations and the brain disorder now called attention deficit hyperactivity disorder. Sixteen years after our first paper calling attention to this confusion (Carey, McDevitt, & Baker, 1979), we find it hard to be optimistic about an early resolution. Nevertheless, we press for it at every opportunity. Since the ADHD terminology originates with the publications of the American Psychiatric Association, the ultimate solution will probably have to come from that body, but we can collect the data to persuade the APA of the necessity for a change in the official system.

Adolescents receive a great deal of attention in the general press for their flamboyant behavior, but there has been little professional consideration of the normal evolution of temperament in that period and its consequences, as pointed out in chapter 10. The absence of a published questionnaire for adolescents based on the NYLS system is in part a result of this general neglect and in turn contributes to it. Some of the clinical issues for adolescents are similar to those of earlier childhood; others are new. Some areas peculiar to adolescence await clarification, such as the question of whether boys and girls really do become more different in temperament as the result of the changed hormone levels induced by puberty. Professional management of temperament-related conditions is quite different because we generally deal directly with the adolescent, not indirectly through the parent, as at earlier ages.

Temperament causes unequal reactions to stressors and other crises, such as parental divorce, as discussed in chapter 11. This is the conclusion from the few available inquiries into these common experiences in the lives of children. We must train ourselves and our students to include recognition of temperament in the evaluation and individualized management of children's responses to these events. There is no shortage of crises available for study in order to increase our comprehension of children's different responses to them and to enhance our clinical effectiveness in their handling.

These are but a few of the areas urgently requiring attention from researchers.

EDUCATING PROFESSIONALS AND PARENTS TO MAKE BETTER USE OF WHAT WE KNOW

Chapter 1 described several factors that are likely to be responsible for the inadequate spread of knowledge about temperament differences: (1) resistance to novelty, especially when it runs contrary to presently held beliefs; (2) the "medical model," which does not recognize that clinical problems can come from nonpathological sources; (3) the greater complexity of the bidirectional theory being introduced; and (4) the prevailing North American political bias against acknowledging any sort of inborn differences. Individual practitioners and researchers can do little to change these widespread attitudes. We can, however, train ourselves to recognize forms of resistance for what they are, defend ourselves as best we can against them, try to be free of them ourselves, and continue to pursue our goals of excellence in child health care and education (Carey, 1993).

Even without formal education about individual differences, many careful observers in the child health and education professions recognize that they exist. Their understanding may come from noticing that the variations they encounter cannot all be ascribed simply to the impact of the environment. The birth of one's own second child is one of the most powerful lessons in individual variation; parents can only marvel that they have produced such an obviously different infant.

We must speculate, however, that many people observing these same phenomena seek other explanations for them because of the prevailing climate of opinion against inborn differences. With or without evidence, many professionals are likely to continue thinking in terms of the generalities about behavior they learned during earlier training, based on the assumption that children should respond to certain situations in narrowly defined standard ways and that any other reaction is abnormal.

As long as these formidable obstacles are blocking the dissemination of this valuable information, the only way to speed up its acceptance and use is continued and strengthened efforts to educate professionals and parents. Anyone awakened to the reality and usefulness of the concept of temperament can be counted on not to slip back into the usual ways of thinking. But first must come the exciting experience of discovery.

The professional training of doctors, nurses, psychologists, teachers, and others must be broadened to include material such as we have presented in this volume. Information on temperament and management techniques should be part of the teaching at the various levels of instruction: undergraduate, graduate, postgraduate, and continuing education of practicing professionals. Our children will be best served if professionals are enlightened at the earliest possible time in their careers. But it is not too late for the 40-year-old day care worker or the 60-year-old pediatrician to enrich their knowledge of this vital aspect of the children they deal with every day.

Such education requires that there be a clear, concise, but comprehensive source of the essential information. In chapter 1, we stressed that no single volume has been published that is both sufficiently scholarly to review the latest research literature and adequately specific about what to do with the information in practical situations. It seemed to us critically important that a book of this sort be made available to facilitate the educational process in the different professions and at the various levels. That is why we decided to take the time from our busy lives as a pediatrician and clinical psychologist to prepare this work.

We deliberately wrote this book in such a way that it could also be used by parents who might be interested in obtaining this information. Although parents are not our intended readership, some of them may find it useful to read for themselves the latest thinking on temperament and on how it matters. If the professionals with whom they are dealing have not yet updated their own education to include this dimension of child behavior, the parents must become the experts. But even with an improved standard of professional performance, parents may want to keep in touch with this fascinating and highly practical aspect of child-rearing knowledge. They will also want to read other books specifically designed for parents, such as those by Turecki and Kurcinka, whose many practical suggestions on management they will be able to use.

IMPLEMENTING THE CHANGES IN PRACTICE

It seems to us that the introduction of the concept of temperament differences and its practical application in clinical and educational settings is a major theoretical breakthrough in the advancement of the mental health of children. Understanding that normal children make a substantial contribution to their environments and to their interactions with them is a major shift in the science of child development. No longer is it necessary to find pathology in the environment, in the child, or in both in order to explain behavioral or other functional deviations. Problems may arise from friction between normal behavioral variations in the child and an environment that is simply incompatible rather than deviant (Carey & McDevitt, 1989). Management primarily through the shorter and less complex intervention of parent counseling, rather than prolonged psychotherapy, should suffice.

A revolution in our thinking stimulates the intellect but serves no practical purpose until it is put to use in managing the lives of our children. A full implementation of our current knowledge has yet to occur. We are hoping that incorporation will be furthered by this book, which is intended not just to increase the knowledge of child health and educational professionals but to persuade them to use this information in their daily work. Until that happens, we have witnessed a reformation only on paper.

VALEDICTION FROM EMERSON AND DANTE

Some of the best literary minds in Western civilization have thought in terms of temperament. For example, Ralph Waldo Emerson (1803–82), the eminent sage of Concord, Massachusetts, had something insightful to say about many of life's mysteries. His essay "Experience" (1844) contains some pertinent observations:

> Life is a train of moods like a string of beads, and as we pass through them they prove to be many-colored lenses which paint the world their own hue, and each shows only what lies in focus. From the mountain you see the mountain. We animate what we can, and see only what we animate. Nature and books belong to the eyes that see them. It depends on the mood of the man whether he shall see the sunset or the fine poem. There are always sunsets, and there is always genius; but only a few hours so serene that we can relish nature or criticism. The more or less depends on structure or temperament. *Temperament is the iron wire on which the beads are strung* [our emphasis].

Expressed more prosaically, temperament is the continuing core of the personality that shapes an individual's experiences of life. Emerson goes on to question the usefulness of fortune, talent, genius, or good intentions if the temperament is not disposed to utilize them.

In a previous volume (Carey & McDevitt, 1989), we cited some elegantly discerning lines by the great medieval poet Dante Alighieri (1265–1321). These words from the *Paradiso* of *The Divine Comedy* bear repeating here, at the conclusion, to stress the importance of adjusting the care of the child to accommodate his or her inborn predispositions.

> *That ever-revolving nature, whose seal is pressed*
> *into our mortal wax, does its work well*
> *but takes no heed of where it comes to rest.*
> . . . .
> *What nature gives a man Fortune must nourish*
> *concordantly, or Nature, like any seed*
> *out of its proper climate, cannot flourish.*
> *If the world below would learn to heed the plan*
> *of Nature's firm foundation, and build on that,*
> *it then would have the best of every man. (1970, ll. 127–29,*
>   *139–44)*

Awareness of inborn, individual behavioral differences has been a part of our culture for a long while. Only in the first part of the twentieth century did we start trying to minimize them. By the end of the century, the climate of opinion has shifted and the biological value of some inborn individual differences and the social acceptability of some others are being increasingly recognized. The time has come for those of us concerned with the professional care of children to free our knowledge and practice of the excessively environmentalist view and bring our work into touch with the wisdom of the great thinkers of the past and with the findings of modern behavioral science. Our hope is that this book will be helpful toward that end.

APPENDIX 1

Questionnaires for Measuring Temperament: Principal Questionnaires in English Using New York Longitudinal Study Categories

Age Span	Name of Test	Authors
1–4 months	Early Infancy Temperament Questionnaire	Medoff-Cooper, Carey, & McDevitt (1993)
4–8 months	Infant Temperament Questionnaire	Carey (1970)
	Infant Temperament Questionnaire–Revised	Carey & McDevitt (1978)
1–3 years	Toddler Temperament Scale	Fullard, McDevitt, & Carey (1984)
3–7 years	Parent Temperament Questionnaire	Thomas, Chess, & Korn (1977)
	Teacher Temperament Questionnaire	Thomas, Chess, & Korn (1977)
	Teacher Temperament Questionnaire–Short Form	Keogh, Pullis, & Cadwell (1982)
	Behavioral Style Questionnaire	McDevitt & Carey (1978)
	Temperament Assessment Battery for Children	Martin (1988)
8–12 years	Middle Childhood Temperament Questionnaire	Hegvik, McDevitt, & Carey (1982)
12–18 years	*none*	
18–21 years	Early Adult Temperament Questionnaire	Thomas, Mittelman, Chess, Korn, & Cohen (1982)

Other Research Questionnaires: Buss & Plomin (1975, 1984); Garside et al. (1975); Bates, Freeland, & Lounsbury (1979); Rothbart (1981); Lerner, Palermo, Spiro, & Nesselroade (1982); Goldsmith, Elliott, & Jaco (1986).

Note: This list does not include: (1) scales that use only observations, such as those by Brazelton (1984 [1973]) and Riese (1983); (2) techniques that may assess temperament but ostensibly measure something else, such as ADHD; (3) scales in foreign languages; (4) unpublished scales; and (5) earlier scales intended primarily for adults, such as those of Eysenck in 1956, Guilford and Zimmerman in 1956, Thorndike in 1963, and Strelau in 1972.

APPENDIX 2

Information on Obtaining Our Five Questionnaires

Listed below are the addresses from which the five temperament questionnaires constructed by the team headed by Drs. Carey and McDevitt can be obtained. These instruments were developed with minimal financial support; please send a contribution of $15.00 for each scale to help cover expenses. You may make as many photocopies as you wish, but any changes in wording or format must be approved by the authors.

1) Early Infancy Temperament Questionnaire (EITQ) (for one- to four-month-old infants): Barbara Medoff-Cooper, Ph.D., F.A.A.N., University of Pennsylvania School of Nursing, Philadelphia, PA 19104–6096.

2) Infant Temperament Questionnaire–Revised (ITQ-R) (for four- to eight-month-old infants): William B. Carey, M.D., Division of General Pediatrics, Children's Hospital of Philadelphia, Philadelphia, PA 19104–4399.

3) Toddler Temperament Scale (TTS) (for one- to three-year-old children): William Fullard, Ph.D., Department of Educational Psychology, Temple University, Philadelphia, PA 19122.

4) Behavioral Style Questionnaire (BSQ) (for three- to seven-year-old children): Sean C. McDevitt, Ph.D., 11225 N. 28th Dr., Suite C103, Phoenix, AZ 85029.

5) Middle Childhood Temperament Questionnaire (MCTQ) (for eight- to twelve-year-old children): Robin L. Hegvik, Ph.D., Suite 210, Falcon Bldg., 1240 West Chester Pike, West Chester, PA 19382.

Note: All five scales assess the New York Longitudinal Study temperament characteristics by eliciting parent responses to 76 specific behavioral descriptions for the EITQ and about 97 (95, 97, 100, and 99, respectively) for the other four scales. For the EITQ, the median category internal consistency was .62 for the whole group; median two- to three-week retest reliability was .68 for one- to two-month-old infants and .79 for three- to four-month-old infants. Total internal consistencies for the ITQ-R, TTS, and BSQ were .83, .85, and .84, respectively; one-month retest reliabilities were .86, .88, and .89. For the MCTQ, the median category internal consistency was .82, and the 2.5-month retest reliability was .87. Some external validity data are available.

APPENDIX 3

Guidelines on Translating the Temperament Questionnaires

We welcome translations of our questionnaires into other languages as long as they are done according to the following principles:

The translation: We have found that the best way to get an exact translation is to have one bilingual person convert the items into the new language. Then a different bilingual person translates them back into English. When the back-translation does not match the original, locate the error. We urge that the original structure of the items be retained, with the main behavioral description first, followed by the clause or phrase that defines the circumstances of the behavior.

Restandardization: Once the scale is translated, it must be restandardized for the new setting. We suggest a standardization population of no less than 200. Experience has shown that the resulting means and standard deviations usually differ from the original ones, and the reason for this is not always clear. Mean differences of less than half of a standard deviation from ours, although possibly statistically significant, are probably not very meaningful.

We have no experience with reading questionnaire items to illiterate parents and would urge caution in doing so unless the results can be shown to be accurate.

Statistical analysis: Appropriate statistical analysis of the translated questionnaire includes determinations of internal consistency and retest reliability. We advise strongly against item factor analysis to try to reduce the number of items or to find simpler groupings of them. Since the items were chosen to measure certain clinically observable and meaningful behaviors, such a process would be quite inappropriate. A better strategy is to examine the item-category (e.g., running-activity) correlations and to eliminate those items for which there is no empirical evidence of intercorrelation.

Changes: We require all users of our scales to obtain our permission before making any changes whatsoever in the wording or format. Our scales are copyrighted.

Final product: Please send a copy of your final restandardized translation to the first author and to Dr. Carey, who is attempting to maintain a complete catalog of existing translations. Please tell us also whether you are willing to share your work with others, either directly or indirectly via us.

Publication: Our general policy on publication has been to recommend announcing the existence of the translation in a professional journal article and distributing the scale itself via personal requests sent to the translator. If the distribution process results in royalties, an equitable division should be negotiated with the first author of the original scale. Only rarely have we approved publication of the entire translated scale. Under no circumstances have we agreed to the publication of any version of our scales in mass-circulation popular magazines.

APPENDIX 4

Educational Materials for Parents

The following materials are good presentations on temperament and related subjects, but we do not stand by every word written or spoken in them. The reader is urged to review these materials before endorsing any of them.

BOOKS

Brazelton, T. B. *Infants and Mothers: Differences in Development*. New York: Delacorte, 1969.

Budd, L. S. *Living with the Active Alert Child: Groundbreaking Strategies for Parents*, revised and enlarged. Seattle: Parenting Press, 1993.

Chess, S., & Thomas, A. *Know Your Child*. New York: Basic Books, 1987.

Chess, S., Thomas, A., & Birch, H. G. *Your Child Is a Person*. New York: Viking, 1965.

Kurcinka, M. S. *Raising Your Spirited Child*. New York: HarperCollins, 1991.

Sammons, W. A. H. *The Self-Calmed Baby*. Boston: Little, Brown, 1989.

Sears, W. *The Fussy Baby: How to Bring Out the Best in Your High-Need Child*. New York: New American Library/Signet, 1987.

Turecki, S., & Tonner, L. *The Difficult Child*, revised. New York: Bantam Books, 1989.

Weissbluth, M. *Healthy Sleep Habits, Happy Child*. New York: Fawcett Columbine, 1987.

Zimbardo, P. G., & Radl, S. L. *The Shy Child: A Parent's Guide to Overcoming and Preventing Shyness from Infancy to Adulthood*. New York: Dolphin, 1981.

NEWSLETTER

Individuals. Publication of the Temperament Project, a nonprofit organization offering support and education to families and caregivers of children with temperament risk factors. Address: 9460 140th St., Surrey, BC, Canada, V3V 5Z4. Subscription: $15/year for families, $25/year for professionals.

VIDEOTAPES

For health care providers: Kaiser Permanente Health Plan in California has developed a series of four tapes:

1) Using temperament concepts to prevent behavior problems
2) Understanding the high-intensity, slow-adapting child
3) Understanding the high-activity, slow-adapting child with low rhythmicity
4) Understanding the withdrawing child with high sensitivity and intensity

These tapes cost $29.95 each, or $100 for all four. If ordering from within California, please add the state tax of $2.47 per tape, or $8.25 for the whole set. Orders should be addressed to: Audio-Visual Department, Kaiser Permanente, 1950 Franklin St., Oakland, CA 94612.

For child care workers: *Flexible, Fearful, or Feisty: The Temperaments of Infants and Toddlers* (1989). Send orders to: California Dept. of Education, PO Box 944272, Sacramento, CA 94244–2720. Inquire about cost.

For early childhood educators and parents: *A Good Fit: An Introduction to Temperament Differences in Children*. Send orders to: Child Study Centre, University of British Columbia, 281 Acadia Rd., Vancouver, BC, V6T 1S1, Canada. Inquire about cost.

References

Als, H., Duffy, F. H., & McAnulty, G. B. (1988). Behavioral differences between preterm and full-term newborns as measured with the APIB system scores. *Infant Behavior and Development, 11,* 305–318.

Als, H., & Gibes, R. (1984). *Neonatal individualized developmental care and assessment program.* Boston: Children's Hospital and Brigham and Women's Hospital.

Als, H., Lawhon, G., Brown, E., Gibes, R., Duffy, F. H., McAnulty, G., & Blickman, J. G. (1986). Individualized behavioral and environmental care for the very low-birth-weight preterm infant at high risk for bronchopulmonary dysplasia: Neonatal intensive care unit and developmental outcome. *Pediatrics, 78,* 1123–1132.

Als, H., Lawhon, G., Duffy, F., McAnulty, G. B., Gibes-Grossman, R., & Blickman, J. G. (1994). Individualized developmental care for the very low-birth-weight preterm infant: Medical and neurofunctional effects. *Journal of the American Medical Association, 272,* 853–858.

Als, H., Lester, B. M., Tronick, E., & Brazelton, T. B. (1982). Towards a research instrument for the assessment of preterm infants' behavior (APIB). In H. E. Fitzgerald, B. M. Lester, & M. W. Yogman (Eds.), *Theory and research in behavioral pediatrics* (Vol. 1, pp. 35–132). New York: Plenum.

American Academy of Pediatrics. (1987). *Health in day care: A manual for health professionals.* Elk Grove Village, IL: AAP.

American Academy of Pediatrics, Committee on Substance Abuse. (1993). Fetal alcohol syndrome and fetal alcohol effects. *Pediatrics, 91,* 1004–1006.

American Academy of Pediatrics. (1994a). Proceedings of the International Conference on Child Day Care: Science, prevention, and practice. *Pediatrics, 94,* 987–1121.

American Academy of Pediatrics, Committee on Drugs. (1994b). The transfer of drugs and other chemicals into human milk. *Pediatrics, 93,* 137–150.

American Academy of Pediatrics. (in press). *Diagnostic and statistical manual for primary care—Child and adolescent version.* Elk Grove Village, IL: AAP.

American Academy of Pediatrics and American Public Health Association. (1992). *Caring for our children: National health and safety performance standards: Guidelines for out-of-home child care programs.* Elk Grove Village, IL: AAP.

American Psychiatric Association. (1968). *Diagnostic and statistical manual of mental disorders.* 2nd ed. Washington, DC: APA.

American Psychiatric Association. (1980). *Diagnostic and statistical manual of mental disorders.* 3rd ed. Washington, DC: APA.

American Psychiatric Association. (1987). *Diagnostic and statistical manual of mental disorders.* 3rd ed., revised. Washington, DC: APA.

American Psychiatric Association. (1994). *Diagnostic and statistical manual of mental disorders.* 4th ed. Washington, DC: APA.

Andersen, C. J. (1994a). Parent support groups. In W. B. Carey & S. C. McDevitt (Eds.), *Prevention and early intervention: Individual differences as risk factors for the mental health of children* (pp. 267–275). New York: Brunner/Mazel.

Andersen, C. J. (1994b). Temperament differences and the child in family daycare. *Individuals* [publication of the Temperament Project, Vancouver, BC], *6* (Spring), 7–8.

Anderson-Goetz, D., & Worobey, J. (1984). The young child's temperament: Implications for child care. *Childhood Education, 61,* 134–140.

Arcia, E., & Roberts, J. E. (1993). Otitis media in early childhood and its association with sustained attention in structured situations. *Journal of Developmental and Behavioral Pediatrics, 14,* 181–183.

Asendorpf, J. B. (1993). Abnormal shyness in children. *Journal of Child Psychology and Psychiatry, 34,* 1069–1081.

Barkley, R. A. (1990). *Attention deficit hyperactivity disorder.* New York: Guilford.

Barr, R. G., Kramer, M. S., Pless, I. B., Boisjoly, C., & Leduc, D. (1989). Feeding and temperament as determinants of early infant crying/fussing behavior. *Pediatrics, 84,* 514–521.

Bates, J. E. (1980). The concept of difficult temperament. *Merrill-Palmer Quarterly, 26,* 299–319.

Bates, J. E. (1989). Applications of temperament concepts. In G. A. Kohnstamm, J. E. Bates, & M. K. Rothbart (Eds.), *Temperament in childhood* (pp. 321–355). New York: Wiley.

Bates, J. E., Freeland, C., & Lounsbury, M. (1979). Measurement of infant difficultness. *Child Development, 50,* 794–803.

Bates, J. E., & Wachs, T. D. (Eds.). (1994). *Temperament: Individual differences at the interface of biology and behavior.* Washington, DC: American Psychological Association.

Bell, R. Q., Weller, G. M., & Waldrop, M. F. (1971). Newborn and preschooler: Organization of behavior and relations between periods. *Monographs of the Society for Research in Child Development, 36* (1, 2), 132.

Bellinger, D. C., Stiles, K. M., & Needleman, H. L. (1992). Low-level lead exposure, intelligence and academic achievement: A long-term follow-up study. *Pediatrics, 90,* 855–861.

Bernbaum, J. C., & Hoffman-Williamson, M. (1991). *Primary care of the preterm infant.* St. Louis: Mosby Year Book.

Bernstein, G. A., Carroll, M. E., Crosby, R. D., Perwein, A. R., Go, F. S., & Benowitz, N. L. (1994). Caffeine effects on learning, performance, and anxiety in normal school-age children. *Journal of the American Academy of Child and Adolescent Psychiatry, 33,* 407–415.

Biederman, J., Rosenbaum, J. F., Bolduc-Murphy, E. A., Faraone, S. V., Chaloff, J., Hirshfeld, D. R., & Kagan, J. (1993). A three-year follow-up of children with and without behavioral inhibition. *Journal of the American Academy of Child and Adolescent Psychiatry, 32,* 814–821.

Billman, J., & McDevitt, S. C. (1980). Convergence of parent and observer ratings of temperament with observations of peer interaction in nursery school. *Child Development, 51,* 395–400.

Birns, B., Barten, S., & Bridger, W. H. (1969). Individual differences in temperamental characteristics of infants. *Transactions of the New York Academy of Sciences, 31,* 1071–1082.

Blackson, T. C., Tarter, R. E., Martin, C. S., & Moss, H. B. (1994). Temperament-induced father-son family dysfunction: Etiological implications for child behavior problems and substance abuse. *American Journal of Orthopsychiatry, 64,* 280–292.

Block, J., & Robins, R. W. (1993). A longitudinal study of consistency and change in self-esteem from early adolescence to early adulthood. *Child Development, 64,* 909–923.

Boyce, W. T., Barr, R. G., & Zeltzer, L. K. (1992). Temperament and the psychobiology of childhood stress. *Pediatrics, 90,* 483–486.

Brayden, R. M., Altmeier, W. A., Tucker, D. D., Dietrich, M. S., & Vietze, P. (1992). Antecedents of child neglect in the first two years of life. *Journal of Pediatrics, 120,* 426–429.

Brazelton, T. B. (1969). *Infants and Mothers: Differences in Development.* New York: Delacorte.

Brazelton, T. B. (1984). *Neonatal Behavioral Assessment Scale.* 2nd ed. London: Blackwell Scientific. (Originally published 1973)

Brazelton, T. B. (1994). Behavioral competence. In G. B. Avery, M. A. Fletcher, & M. G. MacDonald (Eds.), *Neonatology: Pathophysiology and management of the newborn* (pp. 289–300). 4th ed. Philadelphia: Lippincott.

Breitmayer, B. J., & Ricciuti, H. N. (1988). The effect of neonatal temperament on caregiver behavior in the newborn nursery. *Infant Mental Health Journal, 9,* 158–172.

Britt, G. C., & Myers, B. J. (1994). The effects of Brazelton intervention. *Infant Mental Health Journal, 15,* 278–292.

Budd, L. S. (1993). *Living with the active alert child: Groundbreaking strategies for parents*. Revised and enlarged. Seattle: Parenting Press.

Buss, A. H., & Plomin, R. (1975). *A temperament theory of personality development*. New York: Wiley.

Buss, A. H., & Plomin, R. (1984). *Temperament: Early developing personality traits*. Hillsdale, NJ: Erlbaum.

Caldwell, B. M. (1992). Day care. In M. D. Levine, W. B. Carey, & A. C. Crocker (Eds.), *Developmental-behavioral pediatrics* (pp. 187–192). 2nd ed. Philadelphia: Saunders.

Cameron, J. R., Rice, D., Hansen, R., & Rosen, D. (1994). Developing temperament guidance programs within pediatric practice. In W. B. Carey & S. C. McDevitt (Eds.), *Prevention and early intervention: Individual differences as risk factors for the mental health of children* (pp. 226–234). New York: Brunner/Mazel.

Carek, D. J. (1992). [Book review of W. B. Carey & S. C. McDevitt (Eds.), *Clinical and educational applications of temperament research*]. *Journal of the American Academy of Child and Adolescent Psychiatry, 31*, 375–376.

Carey, W. B. (1970). A simplified method for measuring infant temperament. *Journal of Pediatrics, 77*, 188–194.

Carey, W. B. (1972). Clinical applications of infant temperament measurements. *Journal of Pediatrics, 81*, 823–828.

Carey, W. B. (1974). Night waking and temperament in infancy. *Journal of Pediatrics, 84*, 756–758.

Carey, W. B. (1982). Clinical use of temperament data in paediatrics. In R. Porter & G. M. Collins (Eds.), *Temperamental differences in infants and young children* (pp. 191–205). London: Pitman.

Carey, W. B. (1983). Some pitfalls in infant temperament research. *Infant Behavior and Development, 6*, 247–254.

Carey, W. B. (1985a). Clinical use of temperament data in pediatrics. *Journal of Developmental and Behavioral Pediatrics, 6*, 137–142.

Carey, W. B. (1985b). Interactions of temperament and clinical conditions. In M. Wolraich & D. K. Routh (Eds.), *Advances in developmental and behavioral pediatrics* (Vol. 6, pp. 83–115). Greenwich, CT: JAI Press.

Carey, W. B. (1985c). Temperament and increased weight gain in infants. *Journal of Developmental and Behavioral Pediatrics, 6*, 128–131.

Carey, W. B. (1986). The difficult child. *Pediatrics in Review, 8*, 39–45.

Carey, W. B. (1988). A suggested solution to the confusion in attention deficit diagnoses. *Clinical Pediatrics, 27*, 348–349.

Carey, W. B. (1989). Temperament and its role in developmental-behavioral diagnosis. In M. I. Gottlieb & J. E. Williams (Eds.), *Developmental-behavioral disorders* (Vol. 2, pp. 49–65). New York: Plenum.

Carey, W. B. (1990). Temperament risk factors in children: A conference report. *Journal of Developmental and Behavioral Pediatrics, 11*, 28–34.

Carey, W. B. (1992a). "Colic" or primary excessive crying in young infants. In M. D. Levine, W. B. Carey, & A. C. Crocker (Eds.), *Developmental-behavioral pediatrics* (pp. 350–353). 2nd ed. Philadelphia: Saunders.

Carey, W. B. (1992b). Pediatric assessment of behavioral adjustment and behavioral style. In M. D. Levine, W. B. Carey, & A. C. Crocker (Eds.), *Developmental-behavioral pediatrics* (pp. 609–616). 2nd ed. Philadelphia: Saunders.

Carey, W. B. (1992c). Temperament issues in the school-aged child. *Pediatric Clinics of North America, 39,* 569–584.

Carey, W. B. (1993). Dante's three beasts and progress in behavioral science. *Journal of Developmental and Behavioral Pediatrics, 14,* 53–56.

Carey, W. B. (1994). Specific uses of temperament data in pediatric behavioral interventions. In W. B. Carey & S. C. McDevitt (Eds.), *Prevention and early intervention: Individual differences as risk factors for the mental health of children* (pp. 215–225). New York: Brunner/Mazel.

Carey, W. B., & Earls F. (1988). Temperament in early adolescence: Continuities and transitions. In M. D. Levine & E. R. McAnarney (Eds.), *Early adolescent transitions* (pp. 23–36). Lexington, MA: Lexington Books/D. C. Heath.

Carey, W. B., Fox, M., & McDevitt, S. C. (1977). Temperament as a factor in early school adjustment. *Pediatrics, 60,* 621–624.

Carey, W. B., Hegvik, R. L., & McDevitt, S. C. (1988). Temperamental factors associated with rapid weight gain and obesity in middle childhood. *Journal of Developmental and Behavioral Pediatrics, 9,* 194–198.

Carey, W. B., & Levine, M. D. (1992). Comprehensive diagnostic formulation. In M. D. Levine, W. B. Carey, & A. C. Crocker (Eds.), *Developmental-behavioral pediatrics* (pp. 672–675). 2nd ed. Philadelphia: Saunders.

Carey, W. B., Lipton, W. L., & Myers, R. A. (1974). Temperament in adopted and foster babies. *Child Welfare, 53,* 352–359.

Carey, W. B., & McDevitt, S. C. (1978). Revision of the Infant Temperament Questionnaire. *Pediatrics, 61,* 735–739.

Carey, W. B. & McDevitt, S. C. (1980). Minimal brain dysfunction and hyperkinesis: A clinical viewpoint. *American Journal of Diseases of Children, 134,* 926–929.

Carey, W. B., & McDevitt, S. C. (Eds.). (1989). *Clinical and educational applications of temperament research.* Amsterdam/Lisse: Swets & Zeitlinger.

Carey, W. B., & McDevitt, S. C. (Eds.). (1994). *Prevention and early intervention: Individual differences as risk factors for the mental health of children: A Festschrift for Stella Chess and Alexander Thomas.* New York: Brunner/Mazel.

Carey, W. B., McDevitt, S. C., & Baker, D. (1979). Differentiating minimal brain dysfunction and temperament. *Developmental Medicine and Child Neurology, 21,* 765–772.

Carskadon, M. A., & Acebo, C. (1993). Parental reports of seasonal mood and behavior changes in children. *Journal of the American Academy of Child and Adolescent Psychiatry, 32,* 264–269.

Carson, D. K., & Bittner, M. T. (1994). Temperament and school-aged children's coping abilities and responses to stress. *Journal of Genetic Psychology, 155,* 289–302. The longer version presented at the biennial meeting of the Society for Research in Child Development in New Orleans (1993) had more material on creative thinking and coping.

Carson, D. K., Council, J. R., & Gravley, J. E. (1991). Temperament and family characteristics as predictors of children's reactions to hospitalization. *Journal of Developmental and Behavioral Pediatrics, 12,* 141–147.

Carson, D. K., Skarpness, L. R., Schultz, N. W., & McGhee, P. E. (1986). Temperament and communicative competence as predictors of young children's humor. *Merrill-Palmer Quarterly, 32,* 415–426.

Casey, P. H. (1992). Failure to thrive. In M. D. Levine, W. B. Carey, & A. C. Crocker (Eds.), *Developmental-behavioral pediatrics* (pp. 375–383). 2nd ed. Philadelphia: Saunders.

Caspi, A., Elder, G. H., Jr., & Bem, D. J. (1987). Moving against the world: Life-course patterns of explosive children. *Developmental Psychology, 23,* 308–313.

Caspi, A., Elder, G. H., Jr., & Bem, D. J. (1988). Moving away from the world: Life-course patterns of shy children. *Developmental Psychology, 24,* 824–831.

Chehrazi, S. S. (Ed.). (1990). *Psychosocial issues in day care.* Washington, DC: American Psychiatric Press.

Chess, S. (1977). Evolution of behavior disorder in a group of mentally retarded children. *Journal of the American Academy of Child Psychiatry, 16,* 4–18.

Chess, S., & Korn, S. (1970). Temperament and behavior disorders in mentally retarded children. *Archives of General Psychiatry, 23,* 122–130.

Chess, S., & Thomas, A. (1984). *Origins and evolution of behavior disorders from infancy to early adult life.* New York: Brunner/Mazel.

Chess, S., & Thomas, A. (1986). *Temperament in clinical practice.* New York: Guilford.

Chess, S., & Thomas, A. (1987). *Know your child.* New York: Basic Books.

Chess, S., & Thomas, A. (1992). Dynamics of individual behavioral development. In M. D. Levine, W. B. Carey, & A. C. Crocker (Eds.), *Developmental-behavioral pediatrics* (pp. 84–94). 2nd ed. Philadelphia: Saunders.

Chess, S., Thomas, A., & Birch, H. G. (1965). *Your child is a person.* New York: Viking.

Chess, S., Thomas, A., & Cameron, M. (1976). Temperament: Its significance for school adjustment and academic achievement. *New York University Educational Review, 7,* 24–29.

Clements, S. D. (1966). *Minimal brain dysfunction in children: Terminology and identification: Phase 1 of a three-phase project.* Washington, DC: U.S. Department of Health, Education, and Welfare.

Cyphers, L. H., Phillips, K., Fulker, D. W., & Mrazek, D. A. (1990). Twin temperament during the transition from infancy to early childhood. *Journal of the American Academy of Child and Adolescent Psychiatry, 29,* 392–397.

Dante Alighieri. (1970). *The divine comedy.* Vol. 3. Translated by John Ciardi. New York: American Library. (Originally published circa 1320)

Davison, I. S., Faull, C., & Nicol, A. R. (1986). Research note: Temperament and behaviour in six-year-olds with recurrent abdominal pain: A follow-up. *Journal of Child Psychology and Psychiatry, 27,* 539–544.

deVries, M. W. (1984). Temperament and infant mortality among the Masai of East Africa. *American Journal of Psychiatry, 141,* 1189–1194.

DiMario, F. J., Jr., & Burleson, J. A. (1993). Behavior profile of children with severe breath holding spells. *Journal of Pediatrics, 122,* 488–491.

DiPietro, J. (1993, March). *Ontogeny of fetal neurobehavioral development.* Paper presented at the biennial meeting of the Society for Research in Child Development, New Orleans.

Dixon, S. D., & Stein, M. T. (1992). *Encounters with children.* 2nd ed. St. Louis: Mosby Year Book.

Dobson, J. (1978). *The strong-willed child.* Wheaton, IL: Tyndale House.

Doelling, J. L., & Johnson, J. H. (1990). Predicting success in foster placement: The contribution of parent-child temperament characteristics. *American Journal of Orthopsychiatry, 60,* 585–593.

Dunn, J. (1994). Temperament, siblings, and the development of relationships. In W. B. Carey & S. C. McDevitt (Eds.), *Prevention and early intervention: Individual differences as risk factors for the mental health of children* (pp. 50–58). New York: Brunner/Mazel.

Dunn, J., & Kendrick, C. (1982). Temperamental differences, family relationships, and young children's response to change within the family. In R. Porter & G. M. Collins (Eds.), *Temperamental differences in infants and young children* (pp. 87–101). London: Pitman.

Earls, F., & Jung, K. G. (1987). Temperament and home environment characteristics as causal factors in the early development of childhood psychopathology. *Journal of the American Academy of Child and Adolescent Psychiatry, 26,* 491–498.

Emerson, R. W. (1844). *Essays: Second series.* Vol. 3.

Emory, E. K., & Toomey, K. (1991). Fetal responsivity during labor. In J. H. Johnson & S. B. Johnson (Eds.), *Advances in child health psychology* (pp. 331–344). Gainesville: University of Florida Press.

Engfer, A. (1992). Difficult temperament and child abuse: Notes on the validity of the child-effect model. *Analise Psicologica, 1* (no. 10), 51–61.

Escalona, S. (1968). *The roots of individuality.* Chicago: Aldine.

Eysenck, H. J. (1982). *Personality, genetics, and behavior.* New York: Praeger.

Fagen, J. W., Singer, J. M., Ohr, P. S., & Fleckenstein, L. K. (1987). Infant temperament and performance on the Bayley Scales of Infant Development at 4, 8, and 12 months of age. *Infant Behavior and Development, 10,* 505–512.

Feingold, B. F. (1975). *Why your child is hyperactive.* New York: Random House.

Fergusson, D. M., Horwood, L. J., & Lynskey, M. T. (1993a). Early dentine lead levels and subsequent cognitive and behavioural development. *Journal of Child Psychology and Psychiatry, 34,* 215–227.

Fergusson, D. M., Horwood, L. J., & Lynskey, M. T. (1993b). Maternal smoking before and after pregnancy: Effects on behavioral outcomes in middle childhood. *Pediatrics, 92,* 815–822.

Fullard, W., McDevitt, S. C., & Carey, W. B. (1984). Assessing temperament in one- to three-year-old children. *Journal of Pediatric Psychology, 9,* 205–217.

Galambos, N. L., & Lerner, J. V. (1987). Child characteristics and the employment of mothers with young children: A longitudinal study. *Journal of Child Psychology and Psychiatry, 28,* 87–98.

Garcia-Coll, C. T., Emmons, L., Vohr, B. R., Ward, A. M., Brann, B. S., Shaul, P. W., Mayfield, S. R., & Oh, W. (1988). Behavioral responsiveness in preterm infants with intraventricular hemorrhage. *Pediatrics, 81,* 412–418.

Garcia-Coll, C. T., Halpern, L. F., Vohr, B. R., Seifer, R., & Oh, W. (1992). Stability and correlates of change of early temperament in preterm and full-term infants. *Infant Behavior Development, 15,* 137–153.

Garmezy, N. (1985). Stress-resistant children: The search for protective factors. In J. E. Stevenson (Ed.), *Recent research in developmental psychopathology* (pp. 213–233). Oxford: Pergamon.

Garrison, W. T., Biggs, D., & Williams, K. (1990). Temperament characteristics and clinical outcomes in young children with diabetes mellitus. *Journal of Child Psychology and Psychiatry, 31,* 1079–1088.

Garside, R. F., Birch, H., Scott, D. M., Chambers, S., Kolvin, I., Tweddle, E. G., & Barber, L. M. (1975). Dimensions of temperament in infant school children. *Journal of Child Psychology and Psychiatry, 16,* 219–231.

Gaskins, I. W., & Barron, J. (1985). Teaching poor readers to cope with maladaptive cognitive styles: A training program. *Journal of Learning Disabilities, 18,* 390–394.

George, C., & Main, M. (1979). Social interactions of young abused children: Approach, avoidance, and aggression. *Child Development, 50,* 306–318.

Goldberg, S. (1991). Recent developments in attachment theory and research. *Canadian Journal of Psychiatry, 36,* 393–400.

Goldberg, S., Corter, C., Lojkasek, M., & Minde, K. (1990). Prediction of behavior problems in four-year-olds born prematurely. *Development and Psychopathology, 2,* 15–30.

Goldberg, S., & Marcovitch, S. (1989). Temperament in developmentally disabled children. In G. A. Kohnstamm, J. E. Bates, & M. K. Rothbart (Eds.), *Temperament in childhood* (pp. 387–403). New York: Wiley.

Goldbloom, R. B. (1992). Behavior and allergy: Myth or reality? *Pediatrics in Review, 13,* 312–313.

Goldsmith, H. H., & Campos, J. J. (1986). Toward a theory of infant temperament. In R. N. Emde & R. J. Harmon (Eds.), *The development of attachment and affiliative systems* (pp. 161–193). New York: Plenum.

Goldsmith, H. H., Elliott, T. K., & Jaco, K. L. (1986). Construction and initial validation of a new temperament questionnaire. *Infant Behavior and Development, 9,* 144 (abstract).

Goldstein, S., & Goldstein, M. (1992). *Hyperactivity: Why won't my child pay attention?* New York: Wiley.

Gonzales, N. M., & Campbell, M. (1994). Cocaine babies: Does prenatal exposure to cocaine affect development? *Journal of the American Academy of Child and Adolescent Psychiatry, 33,* 16–19.

Goodyer, I. M., Ashby, L., Altham, P. M. E., Vize, C., & Cooper, P. J. (1993). Temperament and major depression in 11- to 16-year-olds. *Journal of Child Psychology and Psychiatry, 34,* 1409–1423.

Gordon, E. M., & Thomas, A. (1967). Children's behavioral style and the teacher's appraisal of their intelligence. *Journal of School Psychology, 5,* 292–300.

Gorski, P. A. (1992). Behavioral assessment of the newborn. In H. W. Taeusch, R. A. Ballard, & M. E. Avery (Eds.), *Schaffer and Avery's diseases of the newborn* (pp. 225–235). 6th ed. Philadelphia: Saunders.

Graham, P., Rutter, M., & George, S. (1973). Temperamental characteristics as predictors of behavior disorders in children. *American Journal of Orthopsychiatry, 43,* 328–339.

Green, M., & Solnit, A. J. (1964). Reactions to the threatened loss of a child: A vulnerable child syndrome. *Pediatrics, 34,* 58–66.

Guerin, D. W., & Gottfried, A. W. (1994). Developmental stability and change in parent reports of temperament: A 10-year longitudinal investigation from infancy through preadolescence. *Merrill-Palmer Quarterly, 40,* 334–355.

Guerin, D. W., & Gottfried, A. W. (in press). Parent reports of infant difficultness: Convergent validity and temperamental consequences during childhood. *Infant Behavior and Development.*

Guerin, D. W., Gottfried, A. W., Oliver, P. H., & Thomas, C. W. (1994). Temperament and school functioning during early adolescence. *Journal of Early Adolescence, 14,* 200–225.

Guilford, J. P., & Zimmerman, W. S. (1949). *The Guilford-Zimmerman Temperament Survey.* Beverly Hills, Calif.: Sheraton Supply.

Hack, M. (1992). The sensorimotor development of the preterm infant. In A. A. Fanaroff & R. J. Martin (Eds.), *Neonatal-perinatal medicine: Diseases of the fetus and infant* (pp. 759–782). 5th ed. St. Louis: Mosby.

Halpern, L. F., & MacLean, W. E., Jr. (1993, March). *The role of infant temperament in postpartum psychological distress and behavior of mothers of full-term and preterm infants.* Poster presented at the biennial meeting of the Society for Research in Child Development, New Orleans.

Hawdon, J. M., Hey, F., Kolvin, I., & Fundudis, T. (1990). Born too small— Is outcome still affected? *Developmental Medicine and Child Neurology, 32,* 943–953.

Hawley, T. L., & Disney, E. R. (1992). Crack's children: The consequences of maternal cocaine abuse. *Social Policy Report* [Society for Research in Child Development, Ann Arbor, MI], *6,* (Winter), 1–23.

Hegvik, R. L. (1985). *Three-year longitudinal study of temperament variables, academic achievement and sex differences in the upper elementary and middle school years.* Doctoral dissertation, Temple University.

Hegvik, R. L. (1989). Application of temperament theory to an individualized educational environment. In W. B. Carey & S. C. McDevitt (Eds.), *Clinical and educational applications of temperament research* (pp. 121–124). Amsterdam/Lisse: Swets & Zeitlinger.

Hegvik, R. L., McDevitt, S. C., & Carey, W. B. (1982). The Middle Childhood Temperament Questionnaire. *Journal of Developmental and Behavioral Pediatrics, 3,* 197–200.

Henretig, F. (1992). Toxins. In M. D. Levine, W. B. Carey, & A. C. Crocker (Eds.), *Developmental-behavioral pediatrics* (pp. 285–291). 2nd ed. Philadelphia: Saunders.

Hertzig, M. E. (1983). Temperament and neurological status. In M. Rutter (Ed.), *Developmental neuropsychiatry* (pp. 164–180). New York: Guilford.

Hetherington, E. M. (1989). Coping with family transitions: Winners, losers, and survivors. *Child Development, 60,* 1–14.

Hubert, N. C., Wachs, T. D., Peters-Martin, P., & Gandour, M. J. (1982). The study of early temperament: Measurement and conceptual issues. *Child Development, 53,* 571–600.

Huntington, G. S., & Simeonsson, R. J. (1993). Temperament and adaptation in infants and young children with disabilities. *Infant Mental Health Journal, 14,* 49–60.

Huttunen, M., & Nyman, G. (1982). On the continuity, change and clinical value of infant temperament in a prospective epidemiological study. In R. Porter & G. M. Collins (Eds.), *Temperamental differences in infants and young children* (pp. 240–251). London: Pitman.

Irwin, C. E., Cataldo, M. F., Matheny, A. P., Jr., & Peterson, L. (1992). Health consequences of behaviors: Injury as a model. *Pediatrics, 90,* 798–807.

Jensen, P. S., & Shaw, J. (1993). Children as victims of war: Current knowledge and future research needs. *Journal of the American Academy of Child and Adolescent Psychiatry, 32,* 697–708.

Johnson, J. (1992). The tendency for temperament to be "temperamental": Conceptual and methodological considerations. *Journal of Pediatric Nursing, 7,* 347–353.

Jones, T. D. (1944). The diagnosis of rheumatic fever. *Journal of the American Medical Association, 126,* 481.

Kagan, J. (1994a). *Galen's prophecy: Temperament in human nature.* New York: Basic Books.

Kagan, J. (1994b). Inhibited and uninhibited temperaments. In W. B. Carey & S. C. McDevitt (Eds.), *Prevention and early intervention: Individual differences as risk factors for the mental health of children* (pp. 35–41). New York: Brunner/Mazel.

Kagan, J., & Snidman, N. (1991). Temperamental factors in human development. *American Psychologist, 46,* 856–862.

Kanbayashi, Y., Nakata, Y., Fujii, K., Kita, M., & Wada, K. (1994). ADHD-related behavior among non-referred children: Parents' ratings of

DSM-III-R symptoms. *Child Psychiatry and Human Development, 25,* 13–29.

Keogh, B. K. (1982). Children's temperament and teachers' decisions. In R. Porter & G. M. Collins (Eds.), *Temperamental differences in infants and young children* (pp. 269–279). London: Pitman.

Keogh, B. K. (1986). Temperament and schooling: Meaning of "goodness of fit"? In J. V. Lerner & R. M. Lerner (Eds.), *Temperament and social interaction in infants and children* (pp. 89–108). San Francisco: Jossey Bass.

Keogh, B. K. (1989). Applying temperament research to school. In G. A. Kohnstamm, J. E. Bates, & M. K. Rothbart (Eds.), *Temperament in childhood* (pp. 437–450). New York: Wiley.

Keogh, B. K. (1994). Temperament and teachers' views of teachability. In W. B. Carey & S. C. McDevitt (Eds.), *Prevention and early intervention: Individual differences as risk factors for the mental health of children* (pp. 246–254). New York: Brunner/Mazel.

Keogh, B. K., Bernheimer, L. P., Haney, M., & Daley, S. (1989). Behavior and adjustment problems of young developmentally delayed children. *European Journal of Special Needs Children, 4,* 79–90.

Keogh, B. K., Pullis, M., & Cadwell, J. (1982). Teacher Temperament Questionnaire–Short Form. *Journal of Educational Measurement, 29,* 323–329.

Klein, H. A. (1992). Temperament and self-esteem in late adolescence. *Adolescence, 27,* 689–694.

Klein, H. A., & Ballantine, J. H. (1988). The relationship of temperament to adjustment in British infant schools. *Journal of Social Psychology, 128,* 585–595.

Klein, P. S. (1984). Behavior of Israeli mothers toward infants in relation to infants' perceived temperament. *Child Development, 55,* 1212–1218.

Kochanska, G. (1993). Toward a synthesis of parental socialization and child temperament in early development of conscience. *Child Development, 64,* 325–347.

Kochanska, G. (1995). Children's temperament, mothers' discipline, and security of attachment: Multiple pathways to emerging internalization. *Child Development, 66,* 597–615.

Kochanska, G., DeVet, K., Goldman, M., Murray, K., & Putnam, S. P. (1994). Maternal reports of conscience development and temperament in young children. *Child Development, 65,* 852–868.

Kohnstamm, G. A. (1989). Historical and international perspectives. In G. A. Kohnstamm, J. E. Bates, & M. K. Rothbart (Eds.), *Temperament in childhood* (pp. 557–566). New York: Wiley.

Kohnstamm, G. A., Bates, J. E., & Rothbart, M. K. (Eds.). (1989). *Temperament in childhood.* New York: Wiley.

Kolvin, I., Nicol, A. R., Garside, R. F., Day, K. A., & Tweddle, E. G. (1982). Temperamental patterns in aggressive boys. In R. Porter & G. M. Collins (Eds.), *Temperamental differences in infants and young children* (pp. 252–268). London: Pitman.

Kowal, A., & Pritchard, D. (1990). Psychological characteristics of children who suffer from headache: A research note. *Journal of Child Psychology and Psychiatry, 31,* 637–649.

Kramer, P. D. (1993). *Listening to Prozac.* New York: Viking.

Kurcinka, M. S. (1991). *Raising your spirited child.* New York: HarperCollins.

Lavigne, J. V., & Faier-Routman, J. (1993). Correlates of psychological adjustment to pediatric physical disorders: A meta-analytic review and comparison with existing models. *Journal of Developmental and Behavioral Pediatrics, 14,* 117–123.

Lavigne, J. V., Nolan, D., & McLone, D. G. (1988). Temperament, coping, and psychological adjustment in young children with myelomeningocele. *Journal of Pediatric Psychology, 13,* 363–378.

Lee, L. W. (1993). *The role of temperament in pediatric pain response.* Doctoral dissertation, University of Illinois at Chicago.

Lerner, J. V., Castellino, D. R., & Perkins, D. (in press). The influence of adolescent behavior and psychosocial characteristics on maternal behaviors and satisfaction. *Journal of Early Adolescence.*

Lerner, J. V., & Lerner, R. M. (1994). Explorations of the goodness-of-fit model in early adolescence. In W. B. Carey & S. C. McDevitt (Eds.), *Prevention and early intervention: Individual differences as risk factors for the mental health of children* (pp. 161–169). New York: Brunner/Mazel.

Lerner, R., Palermo, M., Spiro, A., III, & Nesselroade, J. R. (1982). Assessing the dimensions of temperamental individuality across the life span: The Dimensions of Temperament Survey (DOTS). *Child Development, 53,* 149–159. Revised 1986.

Lester, B. M., Garcia-Coll, C., Valcarcel, M., Hoffman, J., & Brazelton, T. B. (1986). Effects of atypical patterns of fetal growth on newborn (NBAS) behavior. *Child Development, 57,* 11–19.

Levine, M. D. (1987). *Developmental variation and learning disorders.* Cambridge, MA: Educators Publishing Service.

Levine, M. D. (1990). *Keeping a head in school.* Cambridge, MA: Educators Publishing Service.

Levine, M. D. (1992a). Attentional variation and dysfunction. In Levine, M. D., Carey, W. B., & Crocker, A. C. (Eds.) *Developmental-behavioral pediatrics.* Second Edition. Philadelphia: Saunders, pp. 468–476.

Levine, M. D. (1992b). Encopresis. In Levine, M. D., Carey, W. B., & Crocker, A. C. (Eds.) *Developmental-behavioral pediatrics.* Second Edition. Philadelphia: Saunders, pp. 389–397.

Levine, M. D. (1993). *All kinds of minds.* Cambridge, MA: Educators Publishing Service.

Levine, M. D., Carey, W. B., & Crocker, A. C. (Eds.) (1992). *Developmental-behavioral pediatrics.* Second Edition. Philadelphia: Saunders.

Lewis, M. (1992). Individual differences in response to stress. *Pediatrics, 90:* 478–490.

Little, D. L. (1985). Written explanation of temperament scores. *Pediatrics, 75,* 275–277.

Lonigan, C. J., Shannon, M. P., Taylor, C. M., Finch, A. J., Jr., & Sallee, F. R. (1994). Children exposed to disaster: II. Risk factors for the development of post-traumatic symptomatology. *Journal of the American Academy of Child and Adolescent Psychiatry, 33,* 94–105.

Luby, J. L., & Steiner, H. (1993). Concordance of parent-child temperament ratings in a clinical sample of adolescent girls. *Child Psychiatry and Human Development, 23,* 297–305.

Ludwig, S., & Rostain, A. (1992). Family function and dysfunction. In M. D. Levine, W. B. Carey, & A. C. Crocker (Eds.), *Developmental-behavioral pediatrics* (pp. 147–159). 2nd ed. Philadelphia: Saunders.

Luthar, S. S., & Zigler, E. (1991). Vulnerability and competence: A review of research on resilience in childhood. *American Journal of Orthopsychiatry, 61,* 6–22.

Lyons, J. A. (1987). Posttraumatic stress disorder in children and adolescents: A review of the literature. *Journal of Developmental and Behavioral Pediatrics, 8,* 349–356.

Lytton, H. (1990). Child and parent effects in boys' conduct disorder: A reinterpretation. *Developmental Psychology, 26,* 683–697.

Malhotra, S. (1989). Varying risk factors and outcomes: An Indian perspective. In W. B. Carey & S. C. McDevitt (Eds.), *Clinical and educational applications of temperament research* (pp. 91–95). Amsterdam/Lisse: Swets & Zeitlinger.

Malhotra, S., Varma, V. K., & Verma, S. K. (1986). Temperament as determinant of phenomenology of childhood psychiatric disorders. *Indian Journal of Psychiatry, 28,* 263–276.

Marino, R. V., Bomze, K., Scholl, T. O., & Anhalt, H. (1989). Nursing bottle caries: Characteristics of children at risk. *Clinical Pediatrics, 28,* 129–131.

Martin, R. P. (1988). *The Temperament Assessment Battery for Children—Manual.* Brandon, VT: Clinical Psychology Publishing.

Martin, R. P. (1989a). Activity level, distractibility, and persistence: Critical characteristics in early schooling. In G. A. Kohnstamm, J. E. Bates, & M. K. Rothbart (Eds.), *Temperament in childhood* (pp. 451–461). New York: Wiley.

Martin, R. P. (1989b). Temperament and education: Implications for underachievement and learning disabilities. In W. B. Carey & S. C. McDevitt (Eds.), *Clinical and educational applications of temperament research* (pp. 37–51). Amsterdam/Lisse: Swets & Zeitlinger.

Martin, R. P. (1994). Special theme section: Impact of temperament on theory, research, and practice in school psychology. *Journal of School Psychology, 32,* 117–166.

Martin, R. P., Olejnik, S., & Gaddis, L. (1994). Is temperament an important contributor to schooling outcomes in elementary school? Modeling effects of temperament and scholastic ability on academic achievement. In W. B. Carey & S. C. McDevitt (Eds.), *Prevention and early intervention: Individual differences as risk factors for the mental health of chil-*

dren (pp. 59–68). New York: Brunner/Mazel.

Matheny, A. P., Jr. (1989). Temperament and cognition: Relations between temperament and mental test scores. In G. A. Kohnstamm, J. E. Bates, & M. K. Rothbart (Eds.), *Temperament in childhood* (pp. 263–282). New York: Wiley.

Matheny, A. P., Jr. (1990). Developmental behavior genetics: Contributions from the Louisville Twin Study. In M. E. Hahn, J. K. Hewitt, N. D. Henderson, & R. H. Benno (Eds.), *Developmental behavior genetics: Neural, biometrical and evolutionary approaches* (pp. 25–39). New York: Oxford University Press.

Matheny, A. P., Jr., Brown, A. M., & Wilson, R. S. (1971). Activity, motor coordination and attention: Individual differences in twins. *Perceptual and Motor Skills, 32,* 151–158.

Matheny, A. P., Jr., Riese, M. L., & Wilson, R. S. (1985). Rudiments of infant temperament: Newborn to nine months. *Developmental Psychology, 21,* 486–494.

Maziade, M. (1994). Temperament research and practical implications for clinicians. In W. B. Carey & S. C. McDevitt (Eds.), *Prevention and early intervention: Individual differences as risk factors for the mental health of children* (pp. 69–80). New York: Brunner/Mazel.

Maziade, M., Boudreault, M., Thivierge, J., Capéraà, P., & Côté, R. (1984). Infant temperament: SES and gender differences and reliability of measurement in a large Quebec sample. *Merrill-Palmer Quarterly, 30,* 213–226.

Maziade, M., Capéraà, P., Laplante, B., Boudreault, M., Thivierge, J., Côté, R., & Boutin, P. (1985). Value of difficult temperament among 7-year-olds in the general population for predicting psychiatric diagnosis at age 12. *American Journal of Psychiatry, 142,* 943–946.

Maziade, M., Caron, C., Côté, R., Boutin, P., & Thivierge, J. (1990). Extreme temperament and diagnosis: A study in a psychiatric sample of consecutive children. *Archives of General Psychiatry, 47,* 477–484.

Maziade, M., Côté, R., Bernier, H., Boutin, P., & Thivierge, J. (1989). Significance of extreme temperament in infancy for clinical status in pre-school years. *British Journal of Psychiatry, 154,* 535–543.

Maziade, M., Côté, R., Boutin, P., Bernier, H., & Thivierge, J. (1987). Temperament and intellectual development: A longitudinal study from infancy to four years. *American Journal of Psychiatry, 144,* 144–150.

Maziade, M., Côté, R., Boutin, P., Boudreault, M., & Thivierge, J. (1986). The effect of temperament on longitudinal academic achievement in primary school. *Journal of the American Academy of Child Psychiatry, 25,* 692–696.

McCall, R. B. (1986). Issues of stability and continuity in temperament research. In R. Plomin & J. Dunn (Eds.), *The study of temperament: Changes, continuities and challenges* (pp. 13–25). Hillsdale, NJ: Erlbaum.

McClowry, S. G. (1990). The relationship of temperament to the pre- and post-behavioral responses of hospitalized school-age children. *Nursing Research, 39,* 30–35.

McClowry, S. G., Hegvik, R. L., & Teglasi, H. (1993). An examination of the construct validity of the Middle Childhood Temperament Questionnaire. *Merrill-Palmer Quarterly, 39,* 279–293.

McDevitt, S. C. (1986). Continuity and discontinuity of temperament in infancy and early childhood: A psychometric perspective. In R. Plomin & J. Dunn (Eds.), *The study of temperament: Changes, continuities and challenges* (pp. 27–38). Hillsdale, NJ: Erlbaum.

McDevitt, S. C., & Carey, W. B. (1978). The measurement of temperament in 3–7 year old children. *Journal of Child Psychology and Psychiatry, 19,* 245–253.

McDevitt, S. C., & Carey, W. B. (1981). Stability of ratings vs. perceptions of temperament from early infancy to 1–3 years. *American Journal of Orthopsychiatry, 51,* 342–345.

McGurk, H., Caplan, M., Hennessy, E., & Moss, P. (1993). Controversy, theory, and social context in contemporary day care research. *Journal of Child Psychology and Psychiatry, 34,* 3–23.

McInerny, T. K., & Chamberlin, R. W. (1978). Is it feasible to identify infants who are at risk for later behavioral problems? *Clinical Pediatrics, 17,* 233–238.

McLeod, S. M., & McClowry, S. G. (1990). Using temperament theory to individualize the psychosocial care of hospitalized children. *Children's Health Care, 19,* 79–85.

McMillan, M. D. (1986). *The influence of infant temperament on marital satisfaction.* Doctoral dissertation, Wayne State University.

McNeil, T. F., Blennow, G., Cantor-Graae, E., Persson-Blennow, I., Harty, B., & Karyd, U. (1993). Minor congenital malformations and mental characteristics during childhood: High-risk and normal-risk groups. *American Journal of Orthopsychiatry, 63,* 472–480.

McNeil, T. F., & Persson-Blennow, I. (1982). Temperament questionnaires in clinical research. In R. Porter & G. M. Collins (Eds.), *Temperamental differences in infants and young children* (pp. 20–35). London: Pitman.

Medoff-Cooper, B. (1986). Temperament in very low-birth-weight infants. *Nursing Research, 35,* 139–143.

Medoff-Cooper, B. (1994). Specific prevention and intervention strategies used to accommodate individual needs of newborn infants. In W. B. Carey & S. C. McDevitt (Eds.), *Prevention and early intervention: Individual differences as risk factors for the mental health of children* (pp. 205–214). New York: Brunner/Mazel.

Medoff-Cooper, B., Carey, W. B., & McDevitt, S. C. (1993). The Early Infancy Temperament Questionnaire. *Journal of Developmental and Behavioral Pediatrics, 14,* 230–235.

Mettetal, G. (1994, October). *The effectiveness of nonclinical interventions for parents of difficult children.* Poster presented at the Tenth Occasional Temperament Conference, Berkeley, CA.

Minde, K., Popiel, K., Leos, N., Falkner, S., Parker, K., & Handley-Derry, M. (1993). The evaluation and treatment of sleep disturbances in young children. *Journal of Child Psychology and Psychiatry, 34,* 521–533.

Moller, J. S. (1983). Relationships between temperament and development in preschool children. *Research in Nursing and Health, 6,* 25–32.

Morgan, G., Azer, S. L., Costley, J. B., Genser, A., Goodman, I. F., Lombardi, J., & McGimsey, B. (1993). *Making a career of it: The state of the states report on career development in early care and education.* Boston: Wheelock College.

Muir, E. E., & Thorlaksdottir, E. (1994). Psychotherapeutic intervention with mothers and children in day care. *American Journal of Orthopsychiatry, 64,* 60–67.

Munn, P., & Dunn, J. (1989). Temperament and the developing relationship between siblings. *International Journal of Behavioral Development, 12,* 433–451.

Naeye, R. L. (1992). Cognitive and behavioral abnormalities in children whose mothers smoked cigarettes during pregnancy. *Journal of Developmental and Behavioral Pediatrics, 13,* 425–428.

Nass, R., & Koch, D. (1987). Temperamental differences in toddlers with early unilateral right- and left-brain damage. *Developmental Neuropsychology, 3,* 93–99.

Nugent, J. K., & Brazelton, T. B. (1989). Preventive intervention with infants and families: The NBAS model. *Infant Mental Health Journal, 10,* 84–99.

Nyman, G. (1987). Infant temperament, childhood accidents, and hospitalization. *Clinical Pediatrics, 26,* 398–404.

Oberklaid, F., Sanson, A., Pedlow, R., & Prior, M. (1993). Predicting preschool behavior problems from temperament and other variables in infancy. *Pediatrics, 91,* 113–120.

Oberklaid, F., Sewell, J., Sanson, A., & Prior, M. (1991). Temperament and behavior in preterm infants: A six-year follow-up. *Pediatrics, 87,* 854–861.

Parker, S. J., & Barrett, D. E. (1992). Maternal Type A behavior during pregnancy, neonatal crying, and early infant temperament: Do Type A women have Type A babies? *Pediatrics, 89,* 474–479.

Pedlow, R., Sanson, A., Prior, M., & Oberklaid, F. (1993). Stability of maternally reported temperament from infancy to eight years. *Developmental Psychology, 29,* 998–1007.

Peters-Martin, P., & Wachs, T. D. (1984). A longitudinal study of temperament and its correlates in the first 12 months. *Infant Behavior and Development, 7,* 285–298.

Plomin, R. (1990). The role of inheritance in behavior. *Science, 248,* 183–188.

Plomin, R. (1994). Interface of nature and nurture in the family. In W. B. Carey & S. C. McDevitt (Eds.), *Prevention and early intervention: Individual differences as risk factors for the mental health of children* (pp. 179–189). New York: Brunner/Mazel.

Plomin, R., Campos, J., Corley, R., Emde, R. N., Fulker, D. W., Kagan, J., Reznick, J. S., Robinson, J., Zahn-Waxler, C., & DeFries, J. C. (1990). Individual differences in the second year of life: The MacArthur Longitudinal Twin Study. In J. Colombo & J. Fagen (Eds.), *Individual differences in infancy: Reliability, stability, prediction* (pp. 431–455). Hillsdale, NJ: Erlbaum.

Plomin, R., Emde, R. N., Braungart, J. M., Campos, J., Corley, R., Fulker, D. W., Kagan, J., Reznick, J. S., Robinson, J., Zahn-Waxler, C., & DeFries, J. C. (1993). Genetic change and continuity from 14 to 20 months: The MacArthur Longitudinal Twin Study. *Child Development, 64,* 1354–1376.

Plomin, R., Owen, M. J., & McGuffin, P. (1994). The genetic basis of complex human behaviors. *Science, 264,* 1733–1739.

Polan, H. J., Leon, A., Kaplan, M. D., Kessler, D. B., Stern, D. N., & Ward, M. J. (1991). Disturbances of affect expression in failure-to-thrive. *Journal of the American Academy of Child and Adolescent Psychiatry, 30,* 897–903.

Portales, A. L., Porges, S. W., & Greenspan, S. I. (1990, April). *Parenthood and the difficult child.* Poster presented at the International Conference on Infant Studies, Montreal.

Prior, M. (1992). Childhood temperament. *Journal of Child Psychology and Psychiatry, 33,* 249–279.

Prior, M., Smart, D., Sanson, A., Pedlow, R., & Oberklaid, F. (1992). Transient versus stable behavior problems in a normative sample: Infancy to school age. *Journal of Pediatric Psychology, 17,* 423–443.

Pullis, M. (1989). Goodness of fit in classroom relationships. In W. B. Carey & S. C. McDevitt (Eds.), *Clinical and educational applications of temperament research* (pp. 117–120). Amsterdam/Lisse: Swets & Zeitlinger.

Rapoport, J. L., Buchsbaum, M. S., Weingartner, H., Zahn, T. P., Ludlow, C., & Mikkelsen, E. (1978). Dextroamphetamine: Cognitive and behavioral effects in normal prepubertal boys. *Science, 199,* 560–563.

Ratekin, C. (1994, October). *Temperament and its role in adjustment to child care.* Paper presented at the Tenth Occasional Temperament Conference, Berkeley, CA.

Reilly, J. S., Stiles, J., Larsen, J., & Trauner, D. (1994). Affective facial expression in infants with focal brain damage. *Neuropsychologia, 33,* 83–99.

Restak, R. (1991). Politics and temperament. In *The brain has a mind of its own* (pp. 104–109). New York: Harmony.

Riese, M. L. (1983). Assessment of behavioral patterns in neonates. *Infant Behavior and Development, 6,* 241–246.

Riese, M. L. (1986). Implications of sex differences in neonatal temperament for early risk and developmental/environmental interactions. *Journal of Genetic Psychology, 147,* 507–513.

Riese, M. L. (1987). Longitudinal assessment of temperament from birth to two years: A comparison of full-term and preterm infants. *Infant Behavior and Development, 10,* 347–363.

Riese, M. L. (1988). Size for gestational age and neonatal temperament in full-term and preterm AGA-SGA twin pairs. *Journal of Pediatric Psychology, 13,* 521–530.

Riese, M. L. (1990). Neonatal temperament in monozygotic and dizygotic twin pairs. *Child Development, 61,* 1230–1237.

Riese, M. L. (1994). Neonatal temperament in full-term twin pairs discordant for birth weight. *Journal of Developmental and Behavioral Pediatrics, 15,* 342–347.

Ross, G. (1987). Temperament of preterm infants: Its relationship to perinatal factors and one-year outcome. *Journal of Developmental and Behavioral Pediatrics, 8,* 106–110.

Rothbart, M. K. (1981). Measurement of temperament in infancy. *Child Development, 52,* 569–578.

Rothbart, M. K., & Derryberry, D. (1981). Development of individual differences in temperament. In M. E. Lamb & A. L. Brown (Eds.), *Advances in developmental psychology* (Vol. 1, pp. 37–86). Hillsdale, NJ: Erlbaum.

Rothbart, M. K., & Mauro, J. A. (1990). Questionnaire approaches to the study of infant temperament. In J. Colombo & J. Fagen (Eds.), *Individual differences in infancy: Reliability, stability, prediction* (pp. 411–429). Hillsdale, NJ: Erlbaum.

Ruddy-Wallace, M. (1989). Temperament: A variable in children's pain management. *Pediatric Nursing, 15,* 118–121.

Rutter, M. (1983). Introduction: Concepts of brain dysfunction syndromes. In M. Rutter (Ed.), *Developmental neuropsychiatry* (pp. 1–11). New York: Guilford.

Rutter, M. (1987). Psychosocial resilience and protective mechanisms. *American Journal of Orthopsychiatry, 57,* 316–331.

Rutter, M. (1989). Temperament: Conceptual issues and clinical implications. In G. A. Kohnstamm, J. E. Bates, & M. K. Rothbart (Eds.), *Temperament in childhood* (pp. 463–479). New York: Wiley.

Rutter, M. L. (1994). Temperament: Changing concepts and implications. In W. B. Carey & S. C. McDevitt (Eds.), *Prevention and early intervention: Individual differences as risk factors for the mental health of children* (pp. 23–34). New York: Brunner/Mazel.

Sameroff, A. J. (1978). Summary and conclusions: The future of newborn assessment. In A. J. Sameroff (Ed.), *Organization and stability of newborn behavior: A commentary on the Brazelton Neonatal Behavioral Assessment Scale.* Monographs of the Society for Research in Child Development (Vol. 43, pp. 102–117).

Sammons, W. A. H. (1989). *The self-calmed baby.* Boston: Little, Brown.

Sanson, A., Smart, D., Prior, M., & Oberklaid, F. (1993). Precursors of hyperactivity and aggression. *Journal of the American Academy of Child and Adolescent Psychiatry, 32,* 1207–1216.

Scarr, S., & McCartney, K. (1983). How people make their own environments: A theory of genotype → environment effects. *Child Development, 54,* 424–435.

Schechter, N. L., Bernstein, B. A., Beck, A., Hart, L., & Scherzer, L. (1991). Individual differences in children's response to pain: Role of temperament and parental characteristics. *Pediatrics, 87*, 171–177.

Schechter, N. L., & Reis, S. M. (1992). The gifted child. In M. D. Levine, W. B. Carey, & A. C. Crocker (Eds.), *Developmental-behavioral pediatrics* (pp. 589–596). 2nd ed. Philadelphia: Saunders.

Schmitt, B. D., & Krugman, R. D. (1992). Abuse and neglect of children. In R. E. Berman & R. M. Kliegman (Eds.), *Nelson textbook of pediatrics* (pp. 78–83). 14th ed. Philadelphia: Saunders.

Sears, W. (1987). *The fussy baby: How to bring out the best in your high-need child*. New York: New American Library/Signet.

Sell, E. J., Hill-Mangan, S., & Holberg, C. J. (1992). Natural course of behavioral organization in premature infants. *Infant Behavior and Development, 15*, 461–478.

Shannon, M. P., Lonigan, C. J., Finch, A. J., Jr., & Taylor, C. M. (1994). Children exposed to disaster: I. Epidemiology of post-traumatic symptoms and symptom profiles. *Journal of the American Academy of Child and Adolescent Psychiatry, 33*, 80–93.

Shaywitz, B. A., Sullivan, C. M., Anderson, G. M., Gillespie, S. M., Sullivan, B., & Shaywitz, S. E. (1994). Aspartame, behavior, and cognitive function in children with attention deficit disorder. *Pediatrics, 93*, 70–75.

Sheeber, L. B., & Johnson, J. H. (1992). Child temperament, maternal adjustment, and changes in family life style. *American Journal of Orthopsychiatry, 62*, 178–185.

Sheeber, L. B., & Johnson, J. H. (1994). Evaluation of a temperament-focused, parent-training program. *Journal of Clinical Child Psychology, 23*, 249–259.

Simpson, A. E., & Stevenson-Hinde, J. (1985). Temperamental characteristics of three- to four-year-old boys and girls and child-family interactions. *Journal of Child Psychology and Psychiatry, 26*, 43–53.

Sirignano, S. W., & Lachman, M. E. (1985). Personality change during the transition to parenthood: The role of perceived infant temperament. *Developmental Psychology, 21*, 558–567.

Skuy, M. (1989). Pertinence of temperament for learning even in highly disadvantaged youths. In W. B. Carey & S. C. McDevitt (Eds.), *Clinical and educational applications of temperament research* (pp. 87–90). Amsterdam/Lisse: Swets & Zeitlinger.

Slabach, E. H., Morrow, J., & Wachs, T. D. (1991). Questionnaire measurement of infant and child temperament. In J. Strelau & A. Angleitner (Eds.), *Explorations in temperament: International perspectives on theory and measurement* (pp. 205–234). New York: Plenum.

Sleator, E. K., & Pelham, W. E., Jr. (1986). *Attention deficit disorder*. Norwalk, CT: Appleton-Century-Crofts. With commentary by W. B. Carey (pp. 191–200).

Smith, B. (1994). The Temperament Program: Community-based prevention of behavior disorders in children. In W. B. Carey & S. C. McDevitt

(Eds.), *Prevention and early intervention: Individual differences as risk factors for the mental health of children* (pp. 257–266). New York: Brunner/Mazel.

Stevenson, J., & Graham, P. (1982). Temperament: a consideration of concepts and methods. In Porter, R., & Collins, G. M. (Eds.), *Temperamental differences in infants and young children.* London: Pitman, pp. 36–50.

Stevenson-Hinde, J., & Hinde, R. A. (1986). Changes in associations between characteristics and interactions. In Plomin, R., & Dunn, J. (Eds.), *The study of temperament: Changes, continuities and challenges.* Hillsdale, NJ: Erlbaum, pp. 115–129.

Stiehm, E. R. (1992). The psychologic fallout from Chernobyl. *American Journal of Diseases of Children, 146,* 761–762.

Stoneman, Z., & Brody, G. H. (1993). Sibling temperaments, conflict, warmth, and role asymmetry. *Child Development, 64,* 1786–1800.

Strelau, J. (1983). *Temperament personality activity.* New York: Academic Press.

Stuy, M. (1994). Tips for working mothers. *Contemporary Pediatrics, 11,* 63–71.

Sugar, M. (1992). Disasters. In M. D. Levine, W. B. Carey, & A. C. Crocker (Eds.), *Developmental-behavioral pediatrics* (pp. 178–181). 2nd ed. Philadelphia: Saunders.

Super, C. M., & Harkness, S. (1994). Temperament and the developmental niche. In W. B. Carey & S. C. McDevitt (Eds.), *Prevention and early intervention: Individual differences as risk factors for the mental health of children* (pp. 115–125). New York: Brunner/Mazel.

Szymanski, L. S. (1992). Emotional problems in children with serious developmental disabilities. In M. D. Levine, W. B. Carey, & A. C. Crocker (Eds.), *Developmental-behavioral pediatrics* (pp. 552–56). 2nd ed. Philadelphia: Saunders.

Terestman, N. (1980). Mood quality and intensity in nursery school children as predictors of behavior disorders. *American Journal of Orthopsychiatry, 50,* 125–138.

Thomas, A. (1981). Current trends in developmental theory. *American Journal of Orthopsychiatry, 51,* 580–609.

Thomas, A., & Chess, (1977). *Temperament and development.* New York: Brunner/Mazel.

Thomas, A., Chess, S., & Birch, H. G. (1968). *Temperament and behavior disorders in children.* New York: New York University Press.

Thomas, A., Chess, S., Birch, H. G., Hertzig, M. E., & Korn, S. (1963). *Behavioral individuality in early childhood.* New York: New York University Press.

Thomas, A., Chess, S., & Korn, S. (1977). Parent and teacher temperament questionnaire for children 3–7 years of age. In A. Thomas & S. Chess, *Temperament and development* (pp. 222–247). New York: Brunner/Mazel.

Thurstone, L. I. (1953). *Examiner manual for the Thurstone Temperament Schedules.* Chicago: Science Research Associates.

Torgersen, A. M. (1981). Genetic factors in temperamental individuality. *Journal of the American Academy of Child Psychiatry, 20,* 702–711.

Torgersen, A. M., & Kringlen, E. (1978). Genetic aspects of temperamental differences in twins. *Journal of the American Academy of Child Psychiatry, 17,* 433–444.

True, W. R., Rice, J., Eisen, S. A., Heath, S. C., Goldberg, J., Lyons, M. J., & Nowak, J. (1993). A twin study of genetic and environmental contributions to liability for post-traumatic stress symptoms. *Archives of General Psychiatry, 50,* 257–264.

Tubman, J. G., Lerner, R. M., Lerner, J. V., & von Eye, A. (1992). Temperament and adjustment in young adulthood: A 15-year longitudinal analysis. *American Journal of Orthopsychiatry, 62,* 564–574.

Turecki, S., & Tonner, L. (1989). *The difficult child.* Revised edition. New York: Bantam Books. (Originally published 1985)

Turecki, S., & Wernick, S. (1994). *The emotional problems of normal children.* New York: Bantam Books.

Udwin, O. (1993). Annotation: Children's reactions to traumatic events. *Journal of Child Psychology and Psychiatry, 34,* 115–127.

Van den Boom, D. (1989). Neonatal irritability and the development of attachment. In G. A. Kohnstamm, J. E. Bates, & M. K. Rothbart (Eds.), *Temperament in childhood* (pp. 299–318). New York: Wiley.

Varni, J. W., Rubenfeld, L. A., Talbot, D., & Setoguchi, Y. (1989). Family functioning, temperament, and psychologic adaptation in children with congenital or acquired limb deficiencies. *Pediatrics, 84,* 323–330.

Volpe, J. J. (1992). Effect of cocaine use on the fetus. *New England Journal of Medicine, 327,* 399–407.

Wachs, T. D. (1988). Relevance of physical environment indices for toddler temperament. *Infant Behavior and Development, 11,* 431–445.

Wachs, T. D., & Gandour, M. J. (1983). Temperament, environment, and six-month cognitive-intellectual development: A test of the organismic specificity hypothesis. *International Journal of Behavioral Development, 6,* 135–152.

Wallerstein, J. (1992). Separation, divorce, and remarriage. In M. D. Levine, W. B. Carey, & A. C. Crocker (Eds.), *Developmental-behavioral pediatrics* (pp. 136–146). 2nd ed. Philadelphia: Saunders.

Weissberg-Benchell, J., Glasgow, A., & Wirtz, P. (1993, March). *Temperament, environmental demands, adjustment, and metabolic control in children with insulin dependent diabetes mellitus.* Paper presented at the biennial meeting of the Society for Research in Child Development, New Orleans.

Weissbluth, M. (1987). *Healthy sleep habits, happy child.* New York: Fawcett Columbine.

Weissbluth, M. (1989a). Sleep-loss stress and temperamental difficultness: Psychobiological processes and practical considerations. In G. A. Kohnstamm, J. E. Bates, & R. K. Rothbart (Eds.), *Temperament in childhood* (pp. 357–375). New York: Wiley.

Weissbluth, M. (1989b). Sleep-temperament interactions. In W. B. Carey & S. C. McDevitt (Eds.), *Clinical and educational applications of temperament research* (pp. 113–116). Amsterdam/Lisse: Swets & Zeitlinger.

Wender, E. H. (1986). The food additive–free diet in the treatment of behavior disorders: A review. *Journal of Developmental and Behavioral Pediatrics, 7*, 35–42.

Wender, E. H. (1990). Attention-deficit hyperactivity disorder. In M. Green & R. J. Haggerty (Eds.), *Ambulatory pediatrics* (pp. 459–463). 4th ed. Philadelphia: Saunders.

Wender, E. H., & Solanto, M. V. (1991). Effects of sugar on aggressive and inattentive behavior in children with attention deficit disorder with hyperactivity and normal children. *Pediatrics, 88*, 960–966.

Wender, P. H. (1987). *The hyperactive child, adolescent, and adult*. New York: Oxford University Press.

Werner, E. E. (1994). Overcoming the odds. *Journal of Developmental and Behavioral Pediatrics, 15*, 131–136.

Werner, E. E., & Smith, R. S. (1982). *Vulnerable but invincible: A longitudinal study of resilient children and youth*. New York: McGraw-Hill.

Wertlieb, D., Weigel, C., & Feldstein, M. (1988). The impact of stress and temperament on medical utilization by school-age children. *Journal of Pediatric Psychology, 13*, 409–421.

Wertlieb, D., Weigel, C., & Feldstein, M. (1989). Stressful experiences, temperament, and social support: Impact on children's behavior symptoms. *Journal of Applied Developmental Psychology, 10*, 487–503.

Wertlieb, D., Weigel, C., Springer, T., & Feldstein, M. (1987). Temperament as a moderator of children's stressful experiences. *American Journal of Orthopsychiatry, 57*, 234–245.

Widmayer, S. M., & Field, T. M. (1981). Effects of Brazelton demonstrations for mothers on the development of preterm infants. *Pediatrics, 67*, 711–714.

Wieder, S. (Ed.). (1994). *Diagnostic classification of mental health and developmental disorders of infancy and early childhood. Diagnostic classification: 0–3*. Arlington, VA: National Center for Clinical Infant Programs.

Wilson, R. S., & Matheny, A. P., Jr. (1986). Behavior-genetics research in infant temperament: The Louisville Twin Study. In R. Plomin & J. Dunn (Eds.), *The study of temperament: Changes, continuities, and challenges* (pp. 81–97). Hillsdale, NJ: Erlbaum.

Windle, M. (1991). The difficult temperament in adolescence: Associations with substance use, family support, and problem behaviors. *Journal of Clinical Psychology, 47*, 310–315.

Windle, M. (1992a). Revised Dimensions of Temperament Survey (DOTS-R): Simultaneous group confirmatory factor analysis for adolescent gender groups. *Psychological Assessment, 4*, 229–234.

Windle. M. (1992b). Temperament and social support in adolescence: Interrelations with depressive symptoms and delinquent behaviors. *Journal of Youth and Adolescence, 21*, 1–21.

Windle, M., & Lerner, R. M. (1986). Reassessing the dimensions of temperamental individuality across the life span: The Revised Dimensions of Temperament Survey (DOTS-R). *Journal of Adolescent Research, 1,* 213–230.

Wolke, D., Skuse, D., & Mathisen, B. (1990). Behavioral style in failure-to-thrive infants: A preliminary communication. *Journal of Pediatric Psychology, 15,* 237–254.

Wolraich, M. L., Lindgren, S. D., Stumbo, P. J., Stegink, L. D., Appelbaum, M. I., & Kiritsy, M. C. (1994). Effects of diets high in sucrose or aspartame on the behavior and cognitive performance of children. *New England Journal of Medicine, 330,* 301–307.

Worobey, J. (1993). Effects of feeding method on infant temperament. *Advances in Child Development and Behavior, 24,* 37–61.

Worobey, J., & Blajda, V. M. (1989). Temperament ratings at two weeks, two months, and one year: Differential stability of activity and emotionality. *Developmental Psychology, 25,* 257–263.

Zametkin, A. J., Nordahl, T. E., Gross, M., King, A. C., Semple, W. E., Rumsey, J., Hamburger, S., & Cohen, R. M. (1990). Cerebral glucose metabolism in adults with hyperactivity of childhood onset. *New England Journal of Medicine, 323,* 1361–1366.

Zeanah, C. H., & Anders, T. F. (1987). Subjectivity in parent-infant relationships: A discussion of internal working models. *Infant Mental Health Journal, 8,* 237–250.

Zigler, E., & Hall, N. W. (1994). Seeing the child in child care: Day care, individual differences, and social policy. In W. B. Carey & S. C. McDevitt (Eds.), *Prevention and early intervention: Individual differences as risk factors for the mental health of children* (pp. 237–245). New York: Brunner/Mazel.

Zimbardo, P. G., & Radl, S. L. (1981). *The shy child: A parent's guide to overcoming and preventing shyness from infancy to adulthood.* New York: Dolphin.

Zuckerman, B., Bauchner, H., Parker, S., & Cabral, H. (1990). Maternal depressive symptoms during pregnancy, and newborn irritability. *Journal of Developmental and Behavioral Pediatrics, 11,* 190–194.

Zuckerman, B., & Frank, D. A. (1994). Prenatal cocaine exposure: Nine years later. *Journal of Pediatrics, 124,* 731–733.

Zuckerman, M. (1979). *Sensation seeking: Beyond the optimal level of arousal.* Hillsdale, NJ: Erlbaum.

Index